SHAKESPEAREAN NEUROPLAY

Cognitive Studies in Literature and Performance

Engaging Audiences
  Bruce McConachie

Literature, Science, and a New Humanities
  Jonathan Gottschall

The Public Intellectualism of Ralph Waldo Emerson and W.E.B. Du Bois
  Ryan Schneider

Shakespearean Neuroplay
  Amy Cook

Shakespearean Neuroplay
Reinvigorating the Study of Dramatic Texts and Performance through Cognitive Science

Amy Cook

SHAKESPEAREAN NEUROPLAY
Copyright © Amy Cook, 2010.
Softcover reprint of the hardcover 1st edition 2010 978-0-230-10547-8
All rights reserved.

The two photographs of Ingmar Bergman's *Hamlet* (1988) are reproduced by permission of photographer Bengt Wanselius and with thanks to Brooklyn Academy of Music. Cover art designed by Sara Taylor.

First published in 2010 by
PALGRAVE MACMILLAN®
in the United States—a division of St. Martin's Press LLC,
175 Fifth Avenue, New York, NY 10010.

Where this book is distributed in the UK, Europe and the rest of the world, this is by Palgrave Macmillan, a division of Macmillan Publishers Limited, registered in England, company number 785998, of Houndmills, Basingstoke, Hampshire RG21 6XS.

Palgrave Macmillan is the global academic imprint of the above companies and has companies and representatives throughout the world.

Palgrave® and Macmillan® are registered trademarks in the United States, the United Kingdom, Europe and other countries.

ISBN 978-1-349-28997-4   ISBN 978-0-230-11305-3 (eBook)
DOI 10.1057/9780230113053
Library of Congress Cataloging-in-Publication Data

Cook, Amy.
   Shakespearean neuroplay : reinvigorating the study of dramatic texts and performance through cognitive science / Amy Cook.
     p. cm.—(Cognitive studies in literature and performance)

   1. Drama—Psychological aspects. 2. Theater—Psychological aspects.
   3. Semantics (Philosophy) 4. Shakespeare, William, 1564–1616. Hamlet.
   5. Shakespeare, William, 1564–1616—Language. I. Title.
PN1631.C65 2010
809.2001'9—dc22   2010009097

A catalogue record of the book is available from the British Library.

Design by Newgen Imaging Systems (P) Ltd., Chennai, India.

First edition: September 2010
10 9 8 7 6 5 4 3 2 1

Transferred to Digital Printing in 2012

To Martha Cook, who took me to Annie *and* Karen Finley *without making a distinction between the two and to John Cook who taught me that one can make bold claims before doing the research to back them up. Without them, I am literally nothing.*

Contents

List of Illustrations   ix

Acknowledgments   xi

1   Who's There?   1
     Stand and Unfold Yourself   3
     Rivals of My Watch   14
     Minutes of This Night   20

2   Linguistic Synaesthesia   23
     Half Cents   27
     Cunning of the Seen   30
     Her Speech Is Nothing   36

3   Mirror | Mirror; Mirror | rorriM   43
     The Critical Mirror   45
     The Rear-View Mirror   48
     The Mirror Blend   57

4   Meaning Superflux—A Cognitive Linguistic Reading of *Hamlet*   65
     Hand and Soul   69
     Enactures   77
     Hamlet's an Old Minnow   84

5   Play's the Thing—A Cognitive Linguistic Performance Analysis   91
     Inexplicable Dumb Shows on an Unworthy Scaffold   92
     Casting—to out-Herod Herod   105
     Gesture and Performance—"tweaks me by th' nose"   112

6　Past/Future, Microscope/Telescope, Performance/Science　123
　　An Eye of You　125
　　Surpassing Show　138
　　The Inmost Part　141

Conclusion: A Dying Voice　149
　　A Rhapsody of Words　150
　　An Eye of View　154

Notes　159

Index　197

Illustrations

Figures

1.1	Conceptual metaphor theory: TO SEE IS TO KNOW	10
2.1	Conceptual mapping of President Bush as gun seller	34
2.2	Compression of cause and effect in Bush/gun sales	35
3.1	Hamlet's mirror blend	58

Photographs

5.1	The duel begins, Ingmar Bergman's *Hamlet*	98
5.2	The duel ends, Ingmar Bergman's *Hamlet*	99

Acknowledgments

I am grateful to the Mellon Foundation for the fellowship at Emory University in Atlanta, for the time and support necessary to take a dissertation and turn it into a book. The Victoria & Albert Museum, the New York Public Library for the Performing Arts, Sara Taylor, Sharon Lehner at BAM, and photographer Bengt Wanselius have all shared their considerable resources. Pieces of this work have appeared in *TDR* and *Theatre Journal* and I thank David Saltz, Mariellen Sandford, and Megan Nicely for their editorial eyes.

My belief that disciplinary walls are figments of the imagination comes from conversations and friendships with smart people across fields and universities: Laurence Barsalou, Michael Booth, Fritz Breithaupt, Linda Charnes, Barbara Dancygier, Michael Evendon, Rob Goldstone, Paula Leverage, Lisa Paulsen, Bradd Shore, Eve Sweetser, Leslie Taylor, Donald Tuten, Mark Turner, and Ron Wainscott.

I owe particular grateful genuflection to Robert McCauley, F. Elizabeth Hart, and Bruce McConachie for their detailed and pivotal comments on various drafts of the project.

To my partners in disciplinary and intellectual crime—the members of the cognitive studies in theater and performance working group at ASTR and Performance Studies Focus Group at ATHE lead by the steady and determined captains Bruce McConachie, Rhonda Blair, and John Lutterbie—I holler: "damn the torpedos!"

I found an incredible wealth of support, wisdom, and guidance at the University of California, San Diego. V. S. Ramachandran, John Rouse, Seana Coulson, and Rafael Núñez (and the members of the Mental Spaces group) all provided key insights and generously explained gaps in my understanding. I am deeply indebted to my generous committee, kind enough to inspire and criticize this work throughout its development: Jim Carmody, Janet Smarr, Louis Montrose, Gilles Fauconnier, and Mary Crane. I cannot give Gilles enough credit for clarifying my understanding of conceptual blending theory and complicating and guiding my working through of the mirror blend. There's a reason he has inspired so many: he sees what to others is invisible. To my friend and mentor, Bryan Reynolds, I owe many drinks, dedications, and humble-bows of thanks. He provided endless insight, cheerleading, and penetrating challenges of the work at every stage. It goes without saying—though it seems most people do in these acknowledgments—that they share what works here but do not deserve responsibility for my omissions or missteps.

In the years I have been feeling around in the dark to research, write, and rewrite this thing, I have had two sons without whom I would be less exhausted but I would not have found the heart and nerve and sinew to go on. For thy sweet love, Ken Weitzman, such wealth brings that then I scorn to change my place with kings.

Chapter 1

Who's There?

To be a spectator or a reader is to be an individual. To be a part of an audience is to be part of a whole. An audience is an organism that laughs, applauds, and comprehends as one. Not always, of course, but sometimes. Why does a spectator become part of an audience and how? Why did the spectators who did not seem to understand the dense Shakespearean poetry in act one suddenly lean forward together as one on the same line in act four? Why, since the horses were painted on the cave walls in Lascaux, has telling, enacting, and depicting stories had such power and importance in the lives of humans? Why do we return to Shakespeare even though there are plays with clearer language, better plots, and less arcane references? How does the complexity of the language enrich our experience?

Thus armed with a series of questions, I began looking for answers within cognitive science. In the last thirty years, a profoundly different view of how we compose and understand language has taken shape: the metaphor of the brain as computer has shifted to an embodied and creative brain. An application of the cognitive sciences to theater and performance studies, then, has much to offer our creative field. The answer to any and all of my questions should do two things: provide new tools for practitioners in the rehearsal room and open new doors of research and conversation within the academy. To understand a production of Shakespeare—or any embodied fictional world—requires an extraordinary cognitive and biological feat. Because the seemingly simple ability to watch, understand, appreciate, and be moved by a theatrical production involves elements of our biology, an investigation into these questions will encounter research in science.[1] While I believe that such interdisciplinary travels require rigor and caution, I do not believe that anyone is served by disciplinary reverence. Scholars in the field of cognitive studies and performance have deployed many different scientific lenses to theater and performance and I will touch on many of them in this chapter. For our purposes here, however, I will focus my analysis on how cognitive linguistics operates to open up new horizons of research questions and answers. The conceptual metaphor theory of George Lakoff (and others) and the conceptual blending theory of Gilles Fauconnier (and others) suggested—demanded—a rereading of Shakespeare. Because any theory about language onstage must apply to the intellectual shibboleth that is *Hamlet*, I began my investigation with Hamlet's "purpose of playing." A cognitive linguistic analysis illuminates Shakespeare's textual theatrics and initiates a valuable academic interplay.

I will begin this interplay with an introduction to the cognitive linguistic theories I have found most applicable in addressing particular questions within Shakespeare and performance studies. I examine readings of Shakespeare that allude to some of the cognitive mechanisms this project addresses without the benefit of any cognitive research. Because this study is not the first to integrate the sciences into literature or theater, I conclude the chapter with an attempt to articulate the shifting state of the field as I see it in order to locate myself within it. Over the course of the book, I hope to provide the reader with a method of inquiry, rather than just the results of my inquiry.

This shift in the understanding of how we think, speak, and compose meaning creates the larger seismic shift away from the "objectivism" of the traditional view of thinking toward the "experiential realism"[2] of embodied, metaphoric thinking. Lakoff's work since 1987 has been an elaboration and entailment of the paradigm shift he articulates in the preface of *Women, Fire, and Dangerous Things*, and literary criticism is based, at least in part, on understanding the way that symbols correspond to things in the "real world" and how reading is about manipulating symbols and meaning. If this is not how we make meaning, then we have an obligation to reinvestigate our old assumptions and readings of classic texts. One of the important consequences of understanding that we create linguistic and conceptual categories—they are not objective reflections of what is "out there"—is seeing how categories can slip, expand, constrict, and change. One of the arguments of this book will be that theater is a way of staging and challenging categories and that therefore theater does, in a substantial way, make up our minds.

Stand and Unfold Yourself

The traditional theory noticed only a few of the modes of metaphor; and limited its application of the term *metaphor* to a few of them only. And thereby it made metaphor seem to be a verbal matter, a shifting and displacement of words, whereas fundamentally it is a borrowing between and intercourse of *thoughts*, a transaction between contexts. *Thought* is metaphoric, and proceeds by comparison and the metaphors of language derive therefrom. (I.A. Richards, *The Philosophy of Rhetoric*, 94)

Lakoff, a cognitive linguist from University of California, Berkeley, and Vittorio Gallese, a neuroscientist from Parma, Italy, have collaborated theoretically based on empirical data from their respective disciplines.[3] Despite the differences between the disciplines' methodologies and definitions of "evidence," they find enough common ground to connect cognitive linguistics and neuroscience in an investigation into the questions each are asking. Similarly, Seana Coulson and Cyma Van Petten recorded Event Related Potentials (ERPs) from people reading different sentences and found that the metaphoric sentences were read no more slowly than the more literal sentences, but called upon more parts of the brain.[4] This suggests that processing is more involved, not more time consuming, countering the assumption within developmental psychology that processing time equals difficulty. In other words, processing the metaphoric sentences required more of the brain to participate, but this increased firing did not increase the time spent to process the sentence. This study integrates empirical methodology from fields of neuroscience and psychology into questions of metaphor-comprehension previously considered not empirically verifiable and even "non-scientific." Theater audiences process extraordinarily complex information without getting lost. Indeed, perhaps the reason *Richard III* is performed more often than *Knight of the Burning Pestle* is because, not despite the fact that, the richness of Shakespeare's language requires more imagination and "work"; perhaps research on how we understand language, story, and performance could encourage those who wish to argue for fewer plays that have the ease of sitcoms and more plays with the complexity of Shakespeare.

I deploy the sciences not because it is more "objective" or true than previous theoretical movements in theater, but because the interests and findings within that field shed light on this field.[5] Cognitive science does not privilege thinking over feeling and does not separate body from mind. This privileging of imagination, creativity, and the body is part of the reason I find the integration of cognitive science into my research so productive.

Cognitive science is the term that gets blanketed over various fields that look at the interaction between the mind, brain, body, language, and environment. It includes research from neurology, psychology, computer science, linguistics, and philosophy. Despite an effort to communicate and unify across the disciplines, there are major rifts within cognitive science stemming from different foundational assumptions as well as methodological differences. Of course the neurosciences are focused at the level of neurons while linguists are focusing on behavior, so a lack of communication between such areas might be unsurprising, but some rifts actually begin within the areas of study. For example, most current cognitive linguists (defined here as those who study language and, through language, cognition) define themselves against the history of generative grammar, which believes that there is a language area of the brain with an inherited grammar structure.[6] According to generative grammar, language is primarily a system of rules that creates "correct" sentence structure around an objective meaning. This works well for sentences like "the cat is on the mat" but breaks down when linguists begin looking at sentences like "the beach is safe" or "there's no there there." Sentences like these cannot be understood by computing the meaning of each word in terms of its location in the sentence, and then making adjustments for context. The beach is safe from what? The beach is safe for whom? How can "there" mean two different things in one sentence? These sentences require a different idea of meaning creation and categorization. In large part, this generative theory of language has been replaced by the cognitive linguistic theories applied here.

The paradigm shift between seeing the brain as a computer, with input undergoing algorithmic processing, and viewing it more as part of an organism, shaping and being shaped by its environment, is beginning to have a profound impact on various fields. Until the debate is settled, any application of cognitive science to the humanities should foreground the paradigm in which it operates. Perhaps the process of applying both paradigms can operate as a kind of natural selection, with "survival" being awarded to the one more fit to explain the aesthetic, emotional, and cognitive experiences that matter the most to us. My goal is not to enter into the debate about language and meaning in its own terms, but rather to present the theory of language and cognition that I have found most helpful in illuminating the plays of Shakespeare. The conceptual blending theory of Gilles

Fauconnier and Mark Turner has provided me with tools to pursue my interest in the formation of meaning in *Hamlet*. While a close attention to text is not new to Shakespeare scholarship, a different conception of how we compose meaning with that text opens up new connections or avenues of research.

In *Women, Fire, and Dangerous Things*, George Lakoff outlines the ways in which a new understanding of categories shapes how cognitive linguists think about the brain and language. The traditional view of categorization argues that we categorize things by virtue of common traits shared by the members; Lakoff traces the development of a new theory of categorization, based primarily on the work of Eleanor Rosch but informed by the work of Ludwig Wittgenstein, J. L. Austin, Paul Ekman, and others, that understands categories in terms of prototypes and basic-level categories. Rosch's experiments with the language of Dani (a New Guinea language) showed that although the Dani speakers did not have words for certain colors, they could see them and have a conceptual category for them; their language did not wholly determine their conceptual system. This is an important distinction in that it speaks to the discourse around language within the humanities: language can constrain thought without controlling it. In *Metaphors We Live By*, Lakoff and Johnson argue that metaphors define what can be viewed as truth, "In a culture where the myth of objectivism is very much alive and truth is always absolute truth, the people who get to impose their metaphors on the culture get to define what we consider to be true—absolutely and objectively true."[7] Nonetheless, we can see a new color without first having to have a name for it.

Lakoff goes to great lengths to explain and elaborate on the paradigm shift that is Rosch's categorization challenge to the traditional "objectivist" view of categories and language. Categories do not exist; nowhere in our brain is there a circle labeled "mammals," containing animals that give birth to live babies, nurse their young, have hair, have three middle ear bones, a neocortex, and are warm blooded. Categories have "cognitive reference points" and "prototypes," which *organize* the category, but do not *define* the category. The category "dog" is not an entity in the world the way "Fido" is. We may have a prototype for "mammal" or "marriage" that includes some animals or some relationships but not others. There are basic-level categories, such as "chair," superordinate categories like "furniture,"[8] and subordinate categories such as "Eames." While basic-level categories have prototypes (quick, think of a single chair), superordinate categories do not (quick, think of a single furniture). Because language exhibits "prototype effects" (ways in which our understanding of a sentence is based on a concept of a prototype of a category referred to within the sentence), Lakoff argues that that is evidence that "linguistic categories have the same character as conceptual categories."[9] This is important because the thrust of his book (and the work of cognitive linguists in general) is based on the fact that through language we can see important elements of the mind/body/brain.

His argument is that we organize our experience through idealized cognitive models (ICMs), compact models of how certain things work when imported to understand a given sentence. For example, because we have an ICM for "seeing" we use this to understand "see," found in a variety of contexts. Within the ICM for seeing is the idea that if you see something you are aware of it and you see things as they are—two ideas that might not necessarily be true, yet are necessary to understand "see" in the sentence: "I see what you mean." Lakoff notes that some words have a cluster of models, with the appropriate model used depending on the context.[10] For example, "she mothered me" relies on the ICM of "mother" as the provider of nurture, not the genetic model, which understands mother as the genetic forbearer. When we speak of a "working mother" we are applying one of the models in the cluster (nurturance model), because we would not call a woman who gave birth to a child but put it up for adoption a "working mother" even though she is one in terms of the genetic model of "mother" and her employment.[11]

The phenomenon of cluster models of a word is unexplained by the classic understanding of categories wherein concepts have "necessary and sufficient conditions."[12] In this view, categories have rules for inclusion; if a word fits all the rules, it belongs in the category. Defenders of the classic, or "objectivist," view see concepts as internal representations of external reality, and cognitive processes as algorithmic.[13] The sentence "the cat is on the mat" is constructed of a noun phrase, a verb, and an object; and its meaning can be computed by assessing the meaning of the parts in conjunction with the syntactic relationship among the parts. What the classic view fails to account for is the way, as Lakoff argues, "the meaning of the whole is often motivated by the meaning of the parts, but not predictable from them."[14] If the meaning of "working mother" were constructed literally, it would lose its efficient ability to specify the *type* of mother and the *type* of work, a meaning motivated by the cluster models accessed to understand the phrase, not by reference to a long list of definitions of "mother." If categories are defined by prototype effects and ICMs, then thinking is primarily metaphoric, creative, and literary, rather than simply capable of such leaps given education, time, and talent.

To test a hypothesis requires a performance of a particular script, a set of assumptions, a cast of characters. In *Making Truth: Metaphor in Science,* Theodore Brown argues that scientific thought is inseparable from the metaphors used to model and talk about the science. He talks about models as metaphors and how they are a mapping of information from a verbal expression of an idea to a 3D representation of that idea. The model is then used in conducting future experiments, motivating thought experiments, and envisioning future elaborations. If atoms are depicted as orbiting balls, it may be difficult to discover that they can be waves. Metaphor theory helps to see that the similarities *exposed* through metaphor can also be similarities *created* by metaphor. Brown gives the example of protein folding:

> Under appropriate conditions most proteins that are active in biological systems coil up and rearrange lengths of the chains so as to assume a characteristic shape. This process was called "folding" because an analogy was seen between the change the protein undergoes and the folding of objects in the macroscopic everyday world, such as napkins or card table chairs.... As a metaphorical expression it invites us to probe the cross-domain mapping between the literal, everyday act of folding and the changes that occur in a protein as it undergoes the transition we call folding. Thus, the act of naming the process "folding" *creates* similarities.[15]

Language itself can be a tool to imagine, learn, and probe. As Lakoff pointed out, "Since we understand the world not only in terms of individual things but also in terms of categories of things, we tend to attribute a real existence to those categories."[16] Whether discussing science, theater, politics, or the weather, the language we use should be probed for its entailments. I believe that we have only just begun to understand its ramifications in other fields.

While the classic view acknowledges the way "dead metaphors" operate in language to color an idea, the opposition created between dead metaphors ("I see your point") and living metaphors ("sicklied o'er with the pale cast of thought") obscures the powerful life of "dead" metaphors and the ubiquity of "living" metaphors. The very metaphor used to understand metaphor tells a story of a metaphor that lives until it dies, at which point its metaphoric origins are no longer visible. This privileges "living" metaphors and obscures the impact of "dead" metaphors. A more complicated view of category and metaphor will shift our reading of *Hamlet.* Lakoff summarizes the value of this conceptual shift as an ideological reformulation of what we are capable of seeing as "true" and "false":

> If we understand reason as being disembodied, then our bodies are only incidental to what we are. If we understand reason as mechanical—the sort of thing a computer can do—then we will devalue human intelligence as computers get more efficient. If we understand rationality as the capacity to mirror the world external to human beings, then we will devalue those aspects of the mind that can do infinitely more than that. If we understand reason as merely literal, we will devalue art.[17]

It is this reunderstanding, as applied to Shakespeare and theatrical performance, which is the subject of this book. Those of us whose life's work is the value and evaluation of art can benefit from the cognitive theories that place art in relationship to the body/mind[18] and its language.

Lakoff's work since the publication of *Women, Fire, and Dangerous Things* has been to articulate the ramifications (both linguistically,[19] cognitively,[20] and politically[21]) of understanding that: 1) categories are based on prototypes and not objectively assessed shared properties; 2) meaning is embodied; 3) metaphors exist in thought and language; 4) meaning is not literal or transcendental. Metaphor structures both language and thought, there is no literal meaning that receives primary attention, and all cognition and language is embodied.[22] In *Philosophy in the Flesh: The Embodied Mind and its Challenge to Western Thought*, Lakoff and Johnson argue that the "very structure of reason itself comes from the details of our embodiment."[23] We project information about our experience in our bodies onto more abstract concepts in order to understand the more abstract in terms of the concrete and physical. Our experience crawling from one side of the room to the other in the first year of life shapes our conception of life as a journey with a beginning, middle, and end—and possible detours, rough patches, et cetera. When pouring water into a glass we notice that it goes up the more we pour so we use that to understand the stock market going up or the crime rate falling.[24]

Understanding that an increase in the value of a particular stock or the decreased occurrence of crime as movement along an up-down axis organizes that information according to a particular image schema. Lakoff defines image schema as "relatively simple structures that constantly recur in our everyday bodily experience: CONTAINERS, PATHS, LINKS, FORCES, BALANCE, and in various orientations and relations: UP-DOWN, FRONT-BACK, PART-WHOLE, CENTER-PERIPHERY, etc."[25] According to Turner, they are the "skeletal patterns that recur in our sensory motor experience."[26] The container image schema is how we see our body as a container, "a schema consisting of a boundary distinguishing an interior from an exterior."[27] This is not to say that this is an inaccurate way of understanding the body—food does go in and then come out—but that it may not be the *only* way of conceiving of our body. Johnson provides a striking list of examples of the number of experiences we understand through using "in" and "out"; the parts of our world we understand as being containers:

> You wake *out* of a deep sleep and peer *out* from beneath the covers *into* your room. You gradually emerge *out* of your stupor, pull your self *out* from under the covers, climb *into* your robe, stretch *out* your limbs, and walk *in* a daze *out* of your bedroom and *into* the bathroom. You look *in* the mirror and see your face staring *out* at you.[28]

It might be difficult to think of one's room as something other than a container, but a mirror does not have an interior and an exterior and a boundary between them; the image schema of the mirror as a container structures—as well as reflects—our relationship with the object and the concept.

If our conceptual and linguistic categories and image schema are not based on transcendent qualities of the things themselves (e.g., "red" or CONTAINER), then, as Lakoff and Johnson argue "it means abandoning the correspondence theory of truth, the idea that truth lies in the relationship between words and the metaphysically and objectively real world external to any perceiver."[29] One of the consequences of understanding language and cognition as coming from an embodied experience of the world is that there is no transcendental truth that thinking and language attempt to capture and represent.

Lakoff insists that both thinking and speaking are metaphoric, such that information from one domain (source) gets mapped onto a second domain (target) to understand the target domain in terms of the source. In this view, it is not that we use metaphor to suggest meaning; metaphor is how we construct meaning. To conceive of intellection, we imagine it in terms of the visual system, wherein light comes in through the eyes and registers as information in the brain; if you want someone to understand your argument, you must get them to see your point (figure 1.1). Life can be understood as having detours and rough patches because we project an embodied experience of moving along a path onto an abstract concept like "life." Along a path linearity and smoothness equal ease, and progress equals

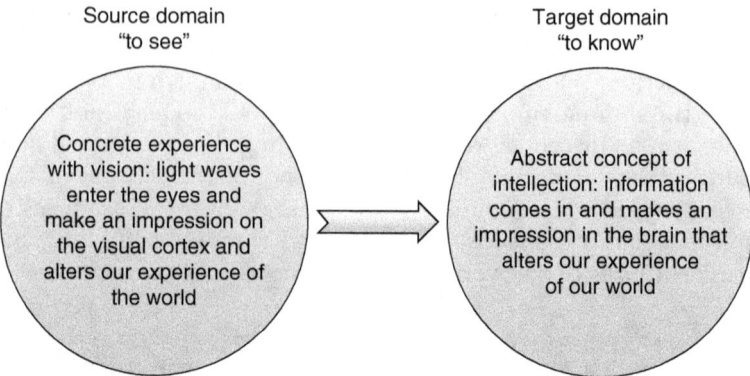

Figure 1.1 Conceptual metaphor theory: TO SEE IS TO KNOW

distance traveled. Abstract concepts such as time and life cannot be talked about nonmetaphorically.

Lakoff and Johnson argue that certain thoughts are contained and defined by the metaphor we use to talk about them.[30] For example, a metaphor like TIME IS MONEY[31] will systematically lead to entailment metaphors (TIME IS A VALUABLE COMMODITY) and our relationship to time becomes defined by this coherent system of thinking of time. This is how, in our society, time can be "spent" or "wasted," and time is seen as something one has for one activity but not another. Metaphors illuminate some elements of the abstract concept and hide others, because a metaphor will only map some information from the source domain (money) to the target domain (time). Lakoff's work has profoundly impacted cognitive linguistics; with his position on the role of metaphor and mapping in mind, I now turn to consider the work of Gilles Fauconnier and Mark Turner on how cognitive blending theory explains language, metaphor, and *The Way We Think*.

Lakoff uses the example of the term "social lie" to explore the category of "lies."[32] He admits that he does not know how the meaning of a social lie comes from the term, because the modifier "social" fails to explain completely the sense of the phrase. If a "social lie" is understood as a deception meant to be helpful to the group, then the modifier "social" does not simply add to our understanding of lie, it also subtracts, because a lie is a deception meant to harm. What Lakoff's metaphor theory fails to account for, blending theory can explain. Here, information from the "social" input space and information from the "lie" input space project into a third blended space. What is important here is not our understanding of "social lie," but rather the way Fauconnier and Turner's conceptual blending theory (CBT) illuminates our understanding and foregrounds the hidden assumptions and beliefs necessary to understand "social lie."

Blending theory builds on Fauconnier's theory of mental spaces. *Mental Spaces* brought awareness to the "hidden, counterintuitive complexities of cognitive construction linked to language."[33] He defines mental spaces as "constructs distinct from linguistic structures but built up in any discourse according to guidelines provided by the linguistic expressions";[34] these are packets of information constructed and framed on the fly in which information is organized. Mental space theory provides a model for meaning construction that is fluid and expandable, capable of explaining many examples in language that the more complicated logical theories cannot, such as (as Lakoff and Sweetser point out in their Forward) "If I were you, I'd hate me," coreference and propositional problems. Some words prompt for meaning, these are "space builders:" such as: "Max believes"[35] or "In that movie."[36] These words set up a space that will inform and/or structure the words/information to come. "Max believes Sarah went to the store" for example, creates an event as understood in relation to what Max believes.

These spaces are not unlike the "domains" referred to by Lakoff or what is implied by the "target" and "source" designations of Richards's understanding of metaphors. In *The Way We Think*, Fauconnier and Turner argue these spaces come together in meaning composition in networks that project and compress into blends. Whereas Lakoff's metaphor theory sees meaning as composed in reference to something else, Fauconnier and Turner argue that there are many things that cannot be explained by an analysis of mapping between two spaces. Blends are constructions of meaning based on projection of information from two or more input spaces to a blended space, such that the blended meaning contains information and structure from more than one space. Thus, the meaning of "social lie" depends upon projecting information regarding lying and information regarding the rules of social etiquette into a blended space. In this way, a "lie" is not understood through mapping information from "social" onto our understanding of "lie," rather, both spaces contribute information to the final understanding. Importantly, though, some information from both spaces is not projected into the third space. It is not a combination or a blurring of two ideas, it is a complicated network evoked and integrated to create a new idea.

There are single-scope blends, where the input spaces share an organizing structure that then projects without obstruction into the blend, and double-scope blends, where the input spaces have different and clashing structures and the final blend must get structural information from elements of both spaces. Single-scope blends are easier to see as metaphors. For example, to describe business competitors as boxers is to understand one domain (business) in terms of another (boxing). The structure of the blended space (the business men[37] "fighting" it out in the boardroom) comes from an "organizing frame," which views both activities as contentious. While boxers use their fists to score points, businessmen may use contracts or money, but both spaces are framed as "fights." The reason Fauconnier and Turner conceive of this as blending rather than as a special case of metaphor is that blending creates a third space where men behave like boxers *and* businessmen. Though Fauconnier and Turner address similar linguistic concerns and make similar arguments to Lakoff and his collaborators, they provide an articulation of meaning construction that is theatrical by its very nature, and thus tremendously powerful in reading theatrical texts and events.

What is so rich about this theory is how it explains so much creative elaboration of metaphoric thought and how taking it apart unveils hidden spaces and assumptions. Once we have blended boxers and businessmen, for example, we can fill out the blend in imaginative ways: we might say of a dispassionate boxer, "just another day at the office," or we might envision a business man stopping a meeting to go to his assistant in a corner for coffee or leaving the meeting with the contract carried triumphantly over his head. The blended space is like a stage set with props and characters, a commedia scenario awaiting enaction and improvisation.

Double-scope blends create emergent meaning by combining structural information from both input spaces. Double-scope integration is not complex, weird, advanced, or literary; as Fauconnier argues, it is everyday and "a mainstay of human thought that shows up throughout human activity, be it artistic, religious, technical, or linguistic" (8).[38] In *The Literary Mind*, Turner explains double-scope blends through the example of a children's story.[39] *The Runaway Bunny*—understood by babies, toddlers, and children for years now—is a story about a baby bunny who wants some space from his mother and so he tells her that he is going to become a fish. His mother bunny responds that she then will become a fisherman. The baby bunny is foiled, because his successful escape depends on her remaining a mother bunny and therefore incapable of catching a baby fish bunny. As a mother fisherman bunny she is able to catch her baby fish bunny. He becomes a boat, she becomes the wind, he becomes a bird, she becomes a tree, etc.

In order to understand this, we first have to project information from our mental space for bunnies with our mental space for humans, because bunnies cannot talk and humans can. We then have to connect these talking bunnies to our understanding of the mother/child dyad, fish, and fisherman, etc. All of this is simultaneously obvious and crazy. When the mother bunny goes into the river to fish for her son, we do not stop the story and object because fishermen use worms to catch fish and doing so usually kills the fish; we understand that the intention of fishing is not projected into the blended space of the talking mother fisherman bunny. In the blended space the talking mother fisherman bunny uses a carrot to catch the talking baby fish bunny and she does so because she loves him, not because she wants to kill him.

The bunnies imagine all these possible worlds and in all of them they remain mother and child. Reading the story is *comprehensible* because we are used to the logical leaps that allow bunnies to talk and it is *powerful* because the author has created a network of spaces (mother, fisher, wind, etc.) that all work together to keep mothers and babies together. Curled up together at the end, the mother and baby bunny become the *network* of ideas—mother/child, fish/fisherman, boat/wind, and so on—not just the final blended one. Conceptual blending theory seeks to understand the way in which language creates emergent structure—novel ideas, creative leaps, and powerful associations.

Reading for the network that makes *The Runaway Bunny* so powerful is not the same as assuming that reading requires uncovering hidden meaning that has been repressed by the text. In a recent introduction to a special issue of *Representations*, Stephen Best and Sharon Marcus call for a movement away from "symptomatic reading," that sees meaning as "hidden, repressed, deep, and in need of detection and disclosure by an interpreter" and that has dominated the literary criticism of Marxism, psychoanalysis, and new historicism, and toward "surface reading" that seeks to "understand the complexity of literary surfaces—surfaces that have been rendered invisible by symptomatic reading."[40] Texts may be thick with meaning and contain layers of historically, culturally, racially, and gendered inflected information, but that need not define the method of analysis. In *Hamlet's Heirs*, Linda Charnes insists on the constant present-ness of the play, "To write from this standpoint is not to be 'unhistoricist' but to wear one's historicism with a difference. Reading Shakespeare for the present is no less valuable than 'historicizing' Shakespeare in his own context. There is room in Shakespeare studies for the contributions of various approaches."[41] It seems to me that any "surface reading" that does not take into consideration research within cognitive linguistics duplicates the same isolated theorizing of the "symptomatic reading" they critique. My reading calls on contemporary theories of cognitive linguistics but also an appreciation for the historical period. This approach respects the context within which the meaning was originally forged, but insists that how the meaning continues to be made, shaped, and used in the present is also important. Whatever it meant or means, the fact that *Hamlet* continues to mean, the fact that we continue to hurl our academic efforts at the play is central to my inquiry.

Rivals of My Watch

Many scholars allude to literature and art as involved in a relationship with the human biology, psychology, or neurology, yet few put pressure on how this might work or what it might mean given historical or contemporary scientific epistemology. The "cognitive turn"[42] in literary and performance studies has already produced new readings of classic texts, new research questions, and challenges to reigning theories. The engagement between the disciplines has already provided exciting work and promises to continue to reshape scholarship in the academy. The movement across disciplines comes from an urge to answer questions unanswered in one's own; the questions being asked at the intersection of literature/theater and cognitive science seem to be: how does a new concept of how language and thinking work alter our understanding of classic plays? What can a study of linguistic processing tell us about a historical period or the brain of the person who wrote the language? Along this interdisciplinary coastline there are different research agendas and questions. I believe that the application of cognitive science to the humanities will work best in a collaborative spirit—creating not a master theorist but a diverse group of scholars asking different questions using a similar (and rigorous) methodology. While nascent, the field is hardly inchoate.

Not inchoate, but not fixed either; interdisciplinary scholars could be defined by their refusal to be defined. The most influential work to date in this area comes from philosophy and literary theory. Mark Johnson shows how the body is pivotal in generating reason and meaning. In *Metaphors We Live By* and *Philosophy in the Flesh*, Lakoff and Johnson argue that the embodied mind uses metaphors and imagination to construct meaning in the world and they address how this understanding fundamentally challenges most of the history of philosophical thought. Johnson explored more of the implications of these theories in his 2007 book, *The Meaning of the Body: Aesthetics of Human Understanding*, insisting that our conception of aesthetics must be the "study of everything that goes into the human capacity to make and experience meaning."[43] For Johnson, percepts, concepts, propositions, and thoughts are not "quasi-objects," they are "patterns of experiential interaction" and,

> The only sense in which they are "inner" is that my thoughts are mine (and not yours), but they are not mental objects locked up in the theater of the mind, trying desperately to make contact with the outside world. As we will see, thoughts are just modes of interaction and action. They are *in* and *of* the world (rather than just being *about* the world) because they are processes of experience.[44]

Art is always already an embodied experience of meaning, "Beneath and within what is said is the vast richness of what is meant, and this meaning pulsates with corporeal significance."[45] Johnson does not apply cognitive science to philosophy, he shows how they have always been inextricably linked.

Mark Turner's early work on how literature creates meaning introduced conceptual metaphor theory into literary studies. An early traveler, Turner moved from a literary department at Berkeley disinterested in his questions and answers, to the cognitive studies program and Lakoff, with whom he collaborated on *More Than Cool Reason*, perhaps the foundational text in cognitive literary studies. Also foundational, Donald Freeman used the idea of image-schemata (ways of organizing perception around a material object) to understand *Macbeth* as being tightly constructed around the image-schemata of PATH and CONTAINER.[46] He then goes on to argue that this metaphoric structure dictates the way critics write and think of the play, as if Shakespeare taught them to speak through reading the play, "The critical tradition—including those who write against the grain of that tradition—understands *Macbeth* in terms of their [PATH and CONTAINER schemata's] entities and structure."[47] Barbara Dancygier, another early collaborator with cognitive studies, pursues how issues of semantics inform literature.[48] Ellen Spolsky applies the current research from the sciences to reimagine a historical moment in light of the minds/bodies that found a particular work of art compelling.[49] In *Satisfying Skepticism,* she argues that the brain creates art as a way of projecting ambiguity outside itself, as a way to manage its lack of complete knowledge (because the embodied brain can never know enough as it is always inseparable from that which it studies).

Some pursue these questions from psychological and/or evolutionary perspectives. Norman N. Holland has connected neuropsychology to our enjoyment of and desire to work with literature. He argues that when we stop paying attention to our bodies or our plans, as we do in a theater or when reading a book, we cut off the connection between our emotions and our prefrontal cortex. We still feel the emotions, but they no longer go to the prefrontal cortex for reality testing and planning. The planning that's done in the prefrontal cortex, requires that we "imagine a future and a past for an object, neither of which is true now…And as long as we do not plan to move while reading a book or watching a play or movie, we do not test the reality of what we are perceiving. Thus, we willingly suspend disbelief. The minute we do plan to move, we, as we say, break the spell. […] In short, we can feel real emotions toward unreal fictions, because two different brain systems are at work."[50] John Tooby and Leda Cosmides place "involvement in fiction" at the center of human evolution and have been influential in the development of an "evolutionary theory of aesthetics."[51]

Within Shakespeare scholarship, Bruce Smith insists on incorporating the physics of sound, the biology of the listener and historical conceptual categories into any study of meaning made in Shakespeare's Globe. Smith insists on an embodied understanding of sound; theater must be heard, "Texts can be read; works must be heard and seen. It is not only the performer's body that distinguishes 'work' from 'text' but the *listener's* bodies."[52] Because of the importance of sound to language, meaning, and community, Smith argues that theater enjoyed a "privileged position" in the "formation of early modern subjects."[53] In her influential book *Shakespeare's Brain*, Mary Crane links Shakespeare's language—and thus conceptual categories—to Shakespeare's brain. Some scholars call what they do cognitive poetics, cognitive aesthetics, cognitive literary studies, or neuroaesthetics, and others do not claim membership in a new field but rather use research in the sciences to focus the object of their study or the method by which they search for answers. This particular meeting between the sciences and the humanities can only be defined, it seems to me, on the basis of the questions it pursues and the new questions it unveils. The difficulty of navigating shifting categories is outweighed, however, by the possibilities of this movement.[54]

Though newer, cognitive performance studies have applied a disparate array of scientific research to a range of questions of historiography, performance analysis, dramaturgy, and practices. Such a broad field begs for some parsing and organizing. Some focus on the actor/performer and others on the audience. The prototypes within the actor/performer category might be Rhonda Blair, who articulates an acting theory informed by current research on memory, empathy, and mirror neurons, and John Lutterbie, who expands the phenomenology of consciousness, intersubjectivity and acting training to include current research in cognitive science.[55] The prototype in the audience category might be Bruce McConachie, who argues that because theater shapes its audience cognitively, the relationship between history and theater must adapt to take this relationship into consideration.[56] Yet my division here occludes the importance of the cognitive lens applied to the object of study—*how* they are looking, not upon *what* they are focusing—and creates distinctions between the two (actor and audience) that are imprecise at best and misleading at worst. If I were to map the field on the basis of the cognitive scientific theories applied, however, it would create similar problems. There is a diverse range of lens and objects. The research that has proved most fruitful does not separate into discreet fields—a study on the depiction of trauma onstage, for example, might include references to mirror neurons, memory, embodiment, or linguistic theories of perspective taking. Bryan Reynolds asks how an understanding of memes might alter a reading of performance; Blakey Vermeule applies cognitive psychology to the question of how we understand fictional characters; Naomi Rokotnitz (and others) explores the relationship between mirror neurons and an embodied understanding of what happens in performance; Pil Hansen uses research from neuroscience to examine the role of and expand the potential for the dramaturg in rehearsal.[57] Such diversity speaks to the multiple ways cognitive science can help scholars in the humanities ask and answer the questions that interest them.

As Rhonda Blair argued in her plenary address at the 2006 American Society of Theater Research (ASTR) conference in Chicago:

> Part of the form and pressure of our time is the ever-changing impact of science on our lives. As we learn more about this and as the science increasingly and inevitably lets us shape and control the biological, we may have to give up parts of comfortable definitions of what it means to be an actor or an audience member, or what a feeling or a memory

or a thought or an action is, or even what theatre is, but this should only free us to be more flexible, powerful, and sensitive in the way that we understand the actor and the audience, and feeling, memory, and action, and in the way that we make and think about theatre.[58]

In his account of Shakespeare's theater, *The Purpose of Playing*, Louis Montrose finds that the "cognitive and ideological dissonance"[59] found in Shakespeare's plays, adjusts cognition. Montrose concludes, "Elizabethan drama-in-performance also had the capacity to work as cognitive and therapeutic instrument."[60] Though a new historicist in methodology, Montrose articulates the organizing idea behind the field of cognitive performance studies. Whatever the object of study or whatever the method of looking, scholars in cognitive performance studies take Montrose's depiction of a theater which operates as an instrument and asks what that instrument looks like and on what is it working. Theater provides a live interaction with language, embodied performance, memory, and the construction and manipulation of imagined mental spaces—subjects that have been radically reconceived by cognitive scientists in the last thirty years.

What does CBT offer the literary/or theater scholar that a traditional close reading does not? This is one of the criticisms of what Raymond Tallis calls neuroaesthetics. Tallis, an Emeritus Professor of Geriatric Medicine at the University of Manchester, whose essay titled "The neuroscience delusion: Neuroaesthetics is wrong about our experience of literature and it is wrong about humanity"[61] points to an essay in *TLS Commentary* by A. S. Byatt in which she turns to neuroscience to explain her love of John Donne's poetry. Tallis's claims that Byatt could have given her reading without the sciences and that may be true, but that assumes that the goal is to create readings of literature and not explanations of humans and their engagement with literature.

In addition to arguing that her reading could have been just as persuasive without turning to the sciences, Tallis also suggests that if Byatt believes the sciences have explanatory power, why not conduct her own empirical research to support her theory? Tallis calls Byatt's essay "neurospeculation" rather than "neuroscience," recapitulating a positivist distinction between science and speculation, wherein if it is not science it is gobbledygook. (Interestingly, it is just this doe-eyed appropriation of science of which he accuses Byatt.) Fauconnier and Turner are working from the other end: explaining the data from an experiment that has already happened. Donne wrote poems long ago. We still read them, love them and learn from them. They survived and thrived while many others did not. Byatt wants to understand why and one of the explanatory methods of cognitive pleasure is cognitive science. Fauconnier and Turner did not predict that, given the language input of the first three acts of *Hamlet* and the historical context, Hamlet will explain theater as a mirror that both editorializes (shows Virtue her feature, for example, and not just Virtue) and also reflects without bias (it is simply held up). The test for me of the application of conceptual blending theory or neuroscience to works of literature is not if it answers with finality some question, but rather whether or not it helps us get to the next question of interest. The cognitive turn is a tool to put pressure on old readings and generate future research questions. The question, then, is not what does Hamlet mean by describing theater as a mirror held up to nature, but rather what further questions can we ask about *Hamlet* once we have used blending theory to explain *how* he makes his meaning?

My work asks what is the cognitive structure of drama and performance? Though elsewhere I pursue some of the questions/intersections/applications discussed above,[62] this work will focus on how conceptual blending theory informs our understanding of the literary, technological, and conceptual structure of Shakespeare's mirror. Specifically: how does an unpacking of the mirror blend help us to see Shakespeare's works differently? How might the staging of the idea of the mirror (and by this I mean the cognitive conception or category, not the material object itself) impact the cognitive conception of what the mirror—both as a tool for seeing and a metaphor of performance—can do? How does our conception of "mirror" impact what we are capable of seeing and how we understand seeing as related to knowing? This book incorporates conceptual blending theory into a theatrical inquiry. How can theater practitioners mobilize this research to make better theater? What makes an audience understand and feel moved by Shakespeare? What's the relationship between language, cognition, and performance? Despite (or because of) this specific focus, I do not believe this book is for theater scholars only. According to Mary Crane, "cognitive literary and cultural criticism continues to occupy a marginal place in our methodological tool kit because it has not so far tended to offer a hermeneutic, a mode of reading that allows us to produce novel interpretations of texts."[63] It is my intention to lay out just such a methodology for the application of cognitive linguistics to how we read stories—whether onstage or not. In order to question meaning it is imperative to understand how meaning is created. The manipulation of a category can influence literary work, performance, ideological engagement, and scientific inquiry. I take the idea *Hamlet* creates—or reflects—of an unbiased and editorializing mirror and uses it as a tool to see in the play the mechanism by which Shakespeare poses and explodes particular questions and to see how this new mirror presents some of the inquiries to come. Though I start with *Hamlet*, I hope not to end with it. With *Hamlet* as my guide, I interrogate places where cognitive science and theater and performance theory meet.

Minutes of This Night

Hamlet, a Wittenberg intellectual, home in Denmark for the funeral of his father, the wedding of his mother to his uncle, and the coronation of his uncle, is troubled by a visit from the ghost of his father claiming that he had been murdered by the new king. Called upon by the ghost to commit regicide, Hamlet thinks it is possible that the ghost is a devil sent to earth to seduce good souls into committing grave sins and wants to make sure that the ghost is who he says he is and that what he says is true. He tries many scholarly and not so scholarly assays: he acts crazy, he ponders, and he probes. Faced with this moral question, Hamlet wants to know how he knows what he knows. When a troupe of actors come to Elsinore, Hamlet decides that he will have the players play "something like" the murder of his father for the King, hoping that the ghostly apparition of the murder will spur the king to reveal his guilt. "The play's the thing" he trusts "to catch the conscience of the king" (2.2.604–5).[64] Prior to the curtain going up for this performance, Hamlet gives the players last minute director's notes, "the purpose of playing, whose end, both at the first and now, was and is to hold as 'twere the mirror up to nature; to show Virtue her feature, Scorn her own image, and the very age and body of the time his form and pressure" (3.2.21–4). Hamlet wants a "mirror" that will extract Claudius's guilt, not simply reflect it. To understand how this image could illuminate an understanding of theater, I needed a theory of language that privileged the creative over the literal.

Language in play—onstage, in speeches, advertisements, and sound bites—*works* on an audience. In Chapter 3 I investigate the historical context of *Hamlet*'s mirror, unpack the network of mental spaces evoked and blended in order to understand Hamlet's advice to the players. I trace how the technological advances in mirrors during the early modern period and the allegorical use of the mirror in writing and visual art of the time impacts the web of associations evoked in Hamlet's mirror. Because language works on the body/mind of the listener, a method of processing this language seems imperative to theater scholars.

Chapters 4 and 5 focus on the textual and performative representations of the mirror. In chapter 4 I reread the play given the linguistic and conceptual scaffolding constructed by the mirror blend unpacked in chapter 3 and argue that the mirror provides a structuring blend for the play and that unblending it, or tracking the integration network established in order to understand how the mirror is used in the play, exposes what and how the mirror as category scaffolds the play. In chapter 5 I investigate what we can learn by applying CBT to staging, casting, and directing so as to guide and analyze directorial decision making. I perform a cognitive linguistic performance analysis on the casting of the ghost in Michael Almereyda's film version of *Hamlet* and two theatrical productions of *Hamlet* and how the directors stage the conceptual mirror.

Chapter 6 folds then and now, exploring how the mirror held up to the play provides both a microscope to the past and a telescope into the future. I look at how locating *Hamlet* in the act of imitation, in what happens when the text becomes a performance—whether that performance is a radio story about a production of *Hamlet* or performance with and against video footage of an earlier performance—stages the investigation again and again. From realizing he can use the play to catch the conscience (conscious?) of the king to instructing the players how to enact this story, Hamlet's preoccupation with testing and exploring his own epistemology circulates around the mirror held up to nature. This chapter will argue that the text uses perspective as a way of compelling intellection and empathy. Hamlet's epistemological crisis is a challenge to an understanding of knowing as seeing. How do we know what we think we know? What do we do when we cannot trust what we see? What happens if what we know is not what we see? If staging *Hamlet* asks these questions, and uses the structuring metaphor of the mirror to probe and challenge our connection between sight and knowledge, how might this offer an opportunity for category shifting? In other words, what are the implications for contemporary science, scientific understanding, and scientific innovation of a performance of *Hamlet*? Traveling back in time to the methodological innovations of Galileo Galilei, Sir Francis Bacon, and Sir Robert Boyle—innovations founded on a reconceptualization of the relationship between knowledge and sight—and forward in time to The Wooster Group's *Hamlet*—a performance that locates self and other in the interplay of the two rendered visible by research in mirror neurons—I propose a rather radical bard-ering between stage and laboratory.

The divisions in our mind/brain/body are coming crashing down. It is no longer clear that there is a part of us that thinks and a part that feels, a part that remembers, and a part that dances. Indeed, many scientists believe that what we consider "thinking" happens not within our brain, but in the relationship between a body and an environment. The idea that our mind sits in our brain, watches a film of our existence, and then sends communiqués to the necessary parts to act on the processed information holds no currency. If the mind is a theater, it includes the audience, the lobby, the ushers, and the parking lot. The neurons that construct and connect the brain, body, and mind snap and flash stimulated by sensory information and creating sense information. Language and performance plays with the system that is there to make sense out of sensory. Neuroplay is the movement between meanings; it is message and reception together. Neuroplay happens in the "infinite space" of Shakespeare's Globe.

Chapter 2

Linguistic Synaesthesia

> *All our ideas are awakened in the same way that a gardener who knows plants recalls, at the sight of them, all the stages of their growth. These words and the objects designated by them are so connected in the brain that it is comparatively rare to imagine a thing without the name or sign that is attached to it.*
> —Julien Offray de la Metrie, *Man a Machine* (1747)[1]

Hamlet—dramaturg, director, theater critic—would agree with the antitheatricalists that theater makes one vulnerable, "I have heard / That guilty creatures, sitting at a play, / Have by the very cunning of the scene / Been struck so to the soul that presently / They have proclaim'd their malefactions" (2.2.588–92). Hamlet not only uses theater to expose his uncle's guilt, but views it as more permanent than the carved marble at the grave, "Good my lord, will you see the players well bestow'd? Do you hear, let them be well us'd, for they are the abstract and brief chronicles of the time. After your death you were better have a bad epitaph than their ill report while you live" (2.2.522–26). In its abstraction and brevity, the players' chronicle will live on in the language, unfolding theatrically on new stages at different times.[2] Dense and abstract language, i.e., metaphors or blends, create a linguistic scaffolding that goes on to structure, constrain, and invent future ways of seeing, thinking, and speaking.

I do not seek to reconstruct the experience of watching *Hamlet* performed at the Globe at the start of the seventeenth century, but do not need to in order to examine the cognitive process an audience member experiences watching *Hamlet* now. The tortuous textual history of *Hamlet* means that editors can compare the Folios to the Quartos to investigate mysteries that previous editors or directors had erased through choice or correction. In her introduction to the *First*

Quarto of Hamlet, Kathleen Irace notes that many words that have been corrected as spelling errors by editors might have been Shakespeare's attempts to create puns or new words. In the First Quarto the gravedigger's song refers to "such a ghest most meet" (Q1.16.34) though the Q2 and Folio emend it to "guest." Irace points out that "ghest" might be a deliberate combination of "ghost" and "guest," as, in an earlier scene, Horatio asks Hamlet to "ceasen" his admiration for awhile in order to take in Horatio's ghost report (Q1.2.106).[3] "Season"—the choice of Q2 and the Folio text—makes as much sense as "cease in" so perhaps the Q1's combination allows both meanings to come into play. In his notes on the play, Editor Harold Jenkins calls the question of how Hamlet refers to his flesh the "most debated reading in the play in recent years." Editorial preference has shifted from the Folio's "solid" to the First Quarto's "sallied" to the Second Quarto's "sullied." Jenkins admits, "The possibility of an intended play on both words cannot be ruled out; but what happens perhaps is that by a natural mental process the word (sullied), which gives at once the clue to the emotion, which the soliloquy will express, brings to mind its near-homonym (solid), which helps to promote the imagery of melt, thaw, resolve, dew."[4] While acknowledging the mystery of language's power, Jenkins abdicates a key theoretical question in literary studies—how can a word convey emotion, themes, and imagery—to scientists who study the "natural mental process."

Metaphor might be such a process. Synaesthesia is the linking of separate neurological perceptual areas. Synaesthetes, for example, might see the letter "R" as red, five as green or hear B sharp when they taste cheese. Although historically assumed to be a psychological association of sorts—i.e., the number five was green in the refrigerator magnets of a subject's childhood and the two remain associated ever since—scientists have shown that these are not creative associations but actual perceptual links within the brain.[5] When the section of the brain that registers "5" is fired, so too is the section of the visual cortex that "sees" green. Neuroscientists V. S. Ramachandran and E. M. Hubbard hypothesize that synaesthesia is a genetic mutation in which the connections between perceptual areas, present in utero and infancy, do not get pruned and compressed, resulting in a persistent experience of, say, green with "5." The cross-wiring they propose between the color area of the brain and visual grapheme area of the brain—both located in the fusiform—is similar to the "cross-activation of the hand area by the face in amputees with phantom arms."[6] They state that synaesthesia is not just metaphor but it might help to explain metaphor, as metaphors involve "cross-activation of conceptual maps."[7] In addition to presenting research that finds that synaesthesia is not just "metaphoric" but is a "genuine perceptual phenomenon," They posit a "synaesthesia-based theory of the evolution of language."[8] For some people seeing "the thisness of a that, or the thatness of a this" (to borrow Kenneth Burke's description of metaphor[9]) may not be creative but automatic. This neurological research attempts to link regions of the brain with linguistic construction and poetic understanding.

Scientists tend to think that questions in "their" field require falsifiability but that questions of art or creativity can be defended by a quote from Shakespeare or reference to Van Gogh. Ramachandran and Hubbard cite a study that found that 23 percent of fine-arts students experienced synaesthesia, "as a group, synaesthetes performed better than controls on all four experimental measures of creativity."[10] They do point out that the study did not test whether the report of synaesthesia was verified by an empirical test of synaesthetic perception, but they do not question the validity of these "measures" of creativity. It is possible that scholars in the humanities would find these measures insufficiently complicated to address the issue of "creativity"; they almost cannot discuss this question without turning to Shakespeare, "When Shakespeare writes 'it is the East and Juliet is the sun,' our brains instantly understand this. You don't say, 'Juliet is the sun. Does that mean she is a glowing ball of fire?'... Instead, your brain instantly forms the right links, 'she is warm like the sun, nurturing like the sun, radiant like the sun' and so on."[11] They go on to conclude that "we can think of metaphors as involving cross-activation of conceptual maps in a manner analogous to cross-activation of perceptual maps in synaesthesia."[12] Though they cite the work of Lakoff and Johnson, their interdisciplinary research does not involve theories within literature that have posited theories about metaphors and creativity for millennia, or ask: how does this account for the simultaneously fixed nature of language construction (abstract of time is understood through reference to the physical experience of space) and the flexibility that creates a connection between theater and the mirror once Shakespeare depicts theater as a "mirror held up to nature?"

Whereas Ramachandran and Hubbard argue that language such as Shakespeare's might be the result of synaesthesia, Philip Davis thinks that Shakespeare's language can create a kind of synaesthesia. Davis calls Shakespeare's language a physical actor on the brain and argues that Shakespeare's invention of words and his shifting of words' functions (such as using the noun as a verb) to create new meanings—as in

Antony's saying that his followers "spaniell'd me at heels" (4.10.20), for example—enriches and expands thinking. He is currently working with a scientist at his university to hook readers up to functional Magnetic Resonance Imaging (fMRI) and magnetoencephalography (MEG) machines to see whether the pattern of electricity in the brain indicates that such functional shifts excite the brain more than a less novel use of language, "to catch the flash of lightning that makes for thinking."[13] The idea is that by using a noun as a verb, Shakespeare is able to fire a noun "area" and a verb "area"—as well as the spaces in between, presumably—and that such links encourage future linkages.[14]

It would be quite something if Davis and his collaborator found an area in the brain for verbs or nouns. It is always tempting to map, to dissect, to locate. We want to see a cluster of color on a picture of the brain and say, "Here! Here's where my love of chocolate is! Or 'mom.'" Once dazzled by drawings based on visions provided by the microscope, we now look to the magic of fMRI tests for what is within. FMRI scans have been invaluable in giving us a more complete and complicated picture of how the brain works and forcing scientists to abandon old theories that are no longer viable in light of this new information. But just because our way of seeing is more sophisticated, does not make it equal to knowing. A map is not the same thing as what it depicts but we cannot find our way without imagining it first. We use maps to compress a large and infinitely detailed physical environment into a scale most useful for driving, say, or tracking wildlife. As Mark Johnson reminds us, maps are not actually there, "We do not experience the *maps*, but rather *through them* we experience a structured world full of patterns and qualities."[15] We do not experience maps, rather we experience what the maps make it possible to perceive. This desire to make fMRI scans the proof of literary merit may be more "empirical," but that does not make it more helpful. I agree with Davis theoretically: I strongly believe that Shakespeare's language facilitates and perhaps creates a linguistic synaesthesia. But I am not convinced that, at this point, fMRI studies are the best way to go about investigating it. What I am looking for is a method of exposing and exploiting Shakespeare's synaesthetic language. The question is both: how do we understand "Juliet is the sun" and also how do we think to compare Juliet to the sun? Conceptual blending theory can provide theater and performance theory with a cognitive barium milkshake, lighting up the process of creating, thinking, and understanding.

Literary theorists have had hundreds of years to make incredibly astute analyses of Shakespeare's poetry. In 1935, Caroline Spurgeon argued for the importance of the disease metaphor in *Hamlet*.[16] It is not my intention to disagree, but finding the prevalence and significance of disease in *Hamlet* would be where a cognitive linguistic reading would begin, not end. Spurgeon's reading of the disease metaphor in *Hamlet* does not question the metaphoricity of disease, or unpack the web of image schemas necessary to understand "rank" offenses or something "rotten." None of these are referring to a literal thing, but rather a metaphoric conception of illness that relies on an understanding of the body as container, illness as war, infection as invasion, seeing as knowing, etc. With the disease metaphor broken down further, it is possible to see a link between the disease metaphor and Hamlet's obsession with not seeming or with his need to write down that a man may smile and still be a villain: if the body is a container, how does the outside reveal information about the inside? By applying this linguistic method to poetry, the end game is not an explication of the image, but an explication of the integration network necessary to compose that image and therefore the spaces, connections, and images recruited for this comprehension. More often than not, it is the network, rather than the blend that provides the power of language. The goal of this chapter is to articulate why CBT is different than traditional literary analysis and to lay out the elements of the theory that will be key to the tracing of the mirror network in *Hamlet*. I begin with the important work done within Shakespeare studies on language and the early modern period. Though I will argue that my work is different than these approaches, I believe cognitive linguistics cannot be understood in a vacuum; language develops to shape and be shaped by the culture and political situation in which it lives. I will then provide an explanation of the elements of conceptual blending theory necessary to see my application of the theory to *Hamlet* and to present a method by which others can apply the theory. To do this, I will not use examples from literature or poetry but rather politics and everyday speech. As cognitive linguistics has shown, creativity is not reserved for poets—the amazing thing is how poetic our banal language is. To demonstrate the importance of applying CBT to language assumed to be "literal" I will end with a story of *Hamlet*'s (in)significance to an African tribe.

Half Cents

She...
...speaks things in doubt
That carry but half sense. Her speech is nothing,

> Yet the unshaped use of it doth move
> The hearers to collection; they yawn at it,
> And botch the words up fit to their own thoughts,
> Which, as her winks and nods and gestures yield them,
> Indeed would make one think there might be thought,
> Though nothing sure, yet much unhappily. (4.5.7–13)

Historical information on language and rhetoric suggests a clear interest in the power of language to "move" an audience. According to Joel Altman, the pedagogical theory of Erasmus—that recommended that Renaissance students write orations from the perspective of different historical and fictional characters, encouraged each student to imagine himself in circumstances utterly unlike his own and to see with eyes other than his own. In formal terms this meant composing according to the decorum of person, audience, and matter, but psychologically it involved a systematic expansion of the imagination beyond its usual subjective limitations, and fostered an awareness of other human realities.[17]

Training students to argue *in utramque partem* (on either side of an issue) led to a facility with taking different perspectives and engaged the emotions and imagination. The early modern period was profoundly interested in the power of compressed language to sway a judge, move an audience, and create something out of nothing.[18] Students studied Quintilian, who argued for the power of emotionally charged visions to persuade an audience.[19] To be persuaded through language is to be altered conceptually and physically; who we are, who we become, and what we can imagine are formed linguistically. This power, it seems to me, necessitates an ability to see the ways language can obscure faulty logic through emotional framing and compression.

Shakespearean characters use rhetoric to manipulate their audience as Shakespeare uses language to engage and shape his audience. While there are many examples of this in the plays, in *Richard III*, Shakespeare sets up two orations, one of which succeeds and the other fails. Throughout the play, Richard's language generates conceptually altered political reasoning—he thrones himself through a series of theatrical uses of rhetoric to manipulate those around him into perceiving him as the wronged friend or retiring religious figure. And yet, at the end of the play, he gives a surprisingly tepid motivational speech to his soldiers, juxtaposed against Richmond's powerful battle cry. Chris Hassel, Jr. reads the play in light of Machiavelli's work on the power of speech to motivate in war and argues that Richard's loss to Richmond at Bosworth Field is foreshadowed in the comparative power of the different motivational speeches of Richard and Richmond. While Hassel's point is that Richard loses because he is the worse orator, he does not suggest what makes a successful oration. Machiavelli's thesis that a good speech "taketh awaie feare"[20] depends on language's ability to prompt what Coulson calls "frame shifting," wherein a given circumstance is suddenly reconfigured in light of new information. That is, a speech can reframe the pending battle in such a way as to exile any doubt or fear. According to Coulson, frame shifting and semantic leaps open up a notion of nonlinear thinking or metaphoric thinking, that is, artistic or conceptual, "I locate speaker productivity in the comprehension mechanism underlying semantic leaps—natural language constructions that yield nonobvious meanings."[21] Using Coulson's work, we can expand on Hassel's point by seeing why one speech can take away fear and the other does not.

Attempting to rally his troops for the final battle against Richmond, Richard frames the speech by calling up a future space in which they have lost to an unworthy opponent. Richard tells his men that defeat means a loss of land and wives to a group of "vagabonds, rascals, and runaways" (5.3.317) vomited forth by their country:

> What shall I say more than I have inferr'd?
> Remember whom you are to cope withal;
> A sort of vagabonds, rascals, and runaways,
> A scum of Bretons, and base lackey peasants,
> Whom their o'er-cloyed country vomits forth
> To desperate ventures and assured destruction.
> You sleeping safe, they bring to you unrest;
> You having lands, and blest with beauteous wives,
> They would restrain the one, distain the other. (5.3.314–22)

He does not specify what they have done that makes them unworthy and can think of nothing worse than calling their leader a "milksop" (5.3.326): "And who doth lead them but a paltry fellow, / Long kept in Bretagne at our mother's cost? / A milk-sop, one that never in his life / Felt so much cold as over shoes in snow?" (5.3.323–27) His men probably understood this as referring to a "man or boy who is indecisive, effeminate, or lacking in courage," but may also have heard "piece of bread soaked in milk" or "an infant still on a milk diet," two definitions from the 1500s listed by the Oxford English Dictionary. Shakespeare probably wanted his audience to hear all three: he is a weak baby who is soaked in mother's milk. Richard, the master rhetorician, can think of nothing worse than falling prey to the lure of maternal love. For a group of men preparing to give their lives in battle, being a "mama's boy" hardly seems a substantial crime. For an audience who has heard Richard repeat, twist, and echo a connection between the maternal bosom/womb and the tomb might hear the slur differently.[22] Richard creates a conceptual space that does not invoke fear or motivate action. Before he lacks a horse, Richard lacks a rhetorical frame that necessitates a battle to the death.

Richmond, on the other hand, emboldens his soldiers by creating a scenario in which they have already won. God is on their side and their enemy is "A bloody tyrant and a homicide; / One rais'd in blood, and one in blood established" (5.3.247–47). Where Richard depicted an enemy soaked in milk, Richmond depicts a king seeped in blood. He does not end there, however. For Richmond, the wombs of his soldiers are not tombs, but the sacred place of the future generations that will provide immortality through progeny, "If you do free your children from the sword, / Your children's children quits it in your age" (5.3.262). Richmond's vision requires that his soldiers first call up the mental space of a threat to one's children and then blend that with the space of future children of the threatened children. In the blend, children rescued from the sword produce children who are able to repay their life's debt. In this blend, the soldiers are alive, well, and comforted by grandchildren: an image much more likely to instill courage for battle than an image of raped wives and daughters. Richmond reminds his army that who they are right now depends in part on how they will be remembered.[23] Richard fails because his language frames the battle in terms of what will happen if they lose, rather than what will happen if they win. Before he has raised a finger in battle, Richmond's rousing rhetoric moves his soldiers to "plaie the man" where Richard's rhetoric does not. In order to understand Richard's speech, the soldiers must imagine loss and in this conceptual space they are failures before they start to fight.

Cunning of the Seen

The power of rhetoric to frame a debate is more than just semantic. Lakoff (among others) has argued, for example, that calling climate change "global warming" already cedes the debate about its urgency to the opposition.[24] Compression allows speakers to frame controversial issues strategically, omitting access to contradictory or challenging mental spaces and evoking emotions helpful to the argument. There are three important elements of conceptual blending theory that I would like to clarify through examples here: mental spaces, compression, and vital relations.

In "Purple Persuasion: Deliberative Rhetoric and Conceptual Blending," Coulson and Todd Oakley examine the persuasive power of an advertisement against drinking and driving.[25] The image is of a cocktail glass with car keys where the swizzle stick would be and the caption is "Killer Cocktail." They point out that the message of the ad is to be found in the integration network, not necessarily the final blend. Taken independently, neither the car keys nor the cocktail glass suggest danger; while either driving or drinking could lead to death, the ad puts the two together to create a deadly "cocktail" from two independently innocuous items. Further, it is not making the objects dangerous, but the activity to which they refer. There is nothing dangerous about putting car keys in a cocktail glass. The combination is only meaningful when the glass evokes the drinking of alcohol and the key evokes driving. This key prompts for the mental space in which the key starts the engine of the automobile in order to drive it (as opposed, say, to just turning on the radio or rolling down the window). To read the ad is to see all of the spaces, not just the blend.

Elaboration of the blend or "running the blend" generates a mental simulation: what could happen when the two activities are mixed. Keys in a cocktail glass become a warning about future blood on the pavement; the simplicity of the ad belies its power. The "Killer Cocktail" can only be a warning in the scenario that transfers the agency of the drinker to the keys used to drive the car. A car key is the tool by which a car is started and that makes driving possible. Just as driving cannot happen without the key to start the car (on most cars), it cannot happen without the car or the driver who turns the key. In this "Killer Cocktail" blend, the keys are both: the agent that initiates the action and the object that takes the action, just as the cocktail is both the drinker and the result of the drinking. But it is the blend that gives both of these inanimate objects agency by linking them with the subjects capable of using them to cause a "killer" act.

Compression is one of the governing principles of conceptual blending theory. Our language miniaturizes the complicated into the simple to facilitate understanding. According to Fauconnier and Turner, when we compress complex relationships to human scale, we achieve "global insight, human-scale understanding, and new meaning. It makes us both efficient and creative."[26] While simplicity obscures important elements of an issue, distilling makes our language rich because it necessitates decompression. Seana Coulson and

Esther Pascaul look at how "pro-life" arguments strategically compress relationships to compel agreement with the position. In choosing this form of discourse, Coulson and Pascual show that, far from being a function of literary talent, conceptual blends are used because they make the complex (scientific and ethical issues) comprehensible to a general audience. One of their examples comes from the controversy surrounding stem cell research. In testifying about his opposition to stem cell research, a paraplegic whose daughter was a product of the implantation of an embryo that might have been used in stem cell research said, "Would I kill my daughter so I could walk again?" They point out that the rhetorical power of this question comes despite and because of its ridiculousness. In order to figure his school-age daughter as the embryo that, in a different future, created the stem cell that cured his paralysis requires complicated—but not time consuming—compression.

Arguments *for* stem cell research compress many embryos used for stem cells into one embryo sacrificed to cure a disease. The argument is: wouldn't it be worth sacrificing this embryo to make this man walk again? All the embryos in all the laboratories studied by all the scientists over many years become one embryo, one experiment, one scientist and one result. Put that way, stem cell research seems not just defensible, but not conducting such research would be morally irresponsible. This compression is already available to the audience to whom the paralyzed man asks his question. He borrows this compression to import his situation—the daughter who came from an embryo and the man who might benefit from stem cell research—to make such research not only indefensible but a case of murder. To get there, the embryo that became his daughter must be connected to a hypothetical embryo used in stem cell research. The daughter that came from *an* embryo can then be an analogy for *the* embryo. This analogy is then compressed to identity, such that the daughter and *the* embryo are one. Once these different entities (daughter, embryo the daughter developed from, and the embryo that cures paralysis) are linked to create a single identity, the different times they occupy (daughter now, embryo then, hypothetical embryo now) are compressed to uniqueness, such that killing his daughter is killing *an* embryo and killing *the* embryo that would help him walk again.

The father's question, through analogy and compression, depicts him as the scientist doing the experiment. As a potential beneficiary of the research, he has a relationship with the scientist, but is not the scientist. This is another of Fauconnier and Turner's governing principle: a blend intensifies vital relationships. This compresses individuals who share elements of an identity into a unique individual. The resulting blend gets the action from the scientist (here articulated as "killing") with the intention of the father ("so I could walk again"). The language creates an agent with intention: to walk again he must murder his daughter. The relationship between the embryos about to be discarded and the children who could result from successful implantation and gestation of those embryos is compressed so that the two are one. This intensifies the scientist's action—the cell is not related to a hypothetical person, it is a person—requiring the scientist to describe his action as murder. An act requires an agent to do the action and an intention to motivate the agent to do the action. Killing one's daughter powerfully materializes an agent ("Would I kill...") with an intention ("so I could walk again"). Coulson and Pascual conclude:

> We suggest that the blend [...] is argumentatively effective because it brings the pros and cons of stem cell research into a human scale scene involving the two most relevant elements, the paralysis victim (who would eventually benefit from it) and the embryo (who would die as a result of it). As the most likely supporter of stem cell research, the paralysis victim's repudiation of it serves as a powerful argument.[27]

Creating a powerful blend can mean the difference between winning and losing an argument, and also between gaining and losing public attention.

Two headlines side by side in the *New York Times* from 2004 provide an excellent example of the power of blending: "Bush Describes Kerry's Health Care Proposal as a 'Government Takeover'" and "Kerry Faults Bush for Failing to Press Weapons Ban."[28] While the first headline paints a dramatic picture of the government invading health care to "take it over," the second depicts an undramatic failure to push. Kerry's failure to compress did not provide the writer with a good blend for the headline. The writer quotes Kerry as saying, "And so tomorrow, for the first time in 10 years, when a killer walks into a gun shop, when a terrorist goes to a gun show somewhere in America, when they want to purchase an AK-47 or some other military assault weapon, they're going to hear one word: Sure." If Kerry had applied the governing principles of blending to compress and intensify vital relations, achieving a human-scale example of the consequences of Bush's actions his message would have been stronger.[29]

Where blending calls for compression, Kerry has used expansion. Simply reducing the number of hypothetical people and weapons in his quote, as in, "And so tomorrow, when a terrorist goes to a gun show for an AK-47 he will get what he wants," would increase the dramatic impact by achieving a more human-scale story. If he had been willing to jettison all ethics or veracity for the sake of a powerful headline, he might have said: "Bush is selling AK-47s to killers and terrorists." Figure 2.1 depicts a simplified network of mental spaces necessary to understand Kerry's potential connection between Bush and the gun seller (figure 2.1).

There are two mental spaces set up, one on the left for President Bush, a man with a unique genetic make-up, who is in the role of president and does not do anything in regards to the ban. In the mental space on the right, there is a gun seller, an identity—not a unique individual—who does something. Kerry (even in his actual quote) establishes a relationship between these two spaces, because both approve (tacitly or actively) of gun selling. Once this relationship is established—a relationship that is not at all obvious but is legible—it can be intensified through compression. By projecting Bush's uniqueness and the identity and action of the gun seller into the blended space, Kerry could have made Bush a gun seller. If John Kerry does not create a human scale scenario where one agent's actions equal the result of those actions, he will not have a sound bite that can be easily expanded or unblended to yield the dramatic and compelling story that he wants it to. "Gun seller" is not a person but an identity or

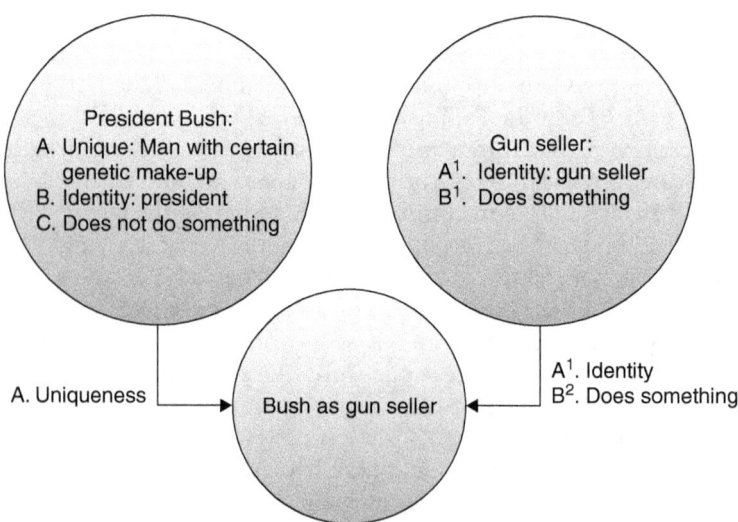

Figure 2.1 Conceptual mapping of President Bush as gun seller

"role" and Bush is a unique individual, but in the blend the "gun seller" gains uniqueness by taking on elements of the "Bush" space while "Bush" gains a profession by taking on elements of the "gun seller." Together they are more and less than they were apart.

Compression creates comprehension. Even Kerry's initial quote tells a story that masks the entrenched blend of what Fauconnier and Turner call the "causal tautology:"[30] a causal tautology blends cause and effect such that in the blended space, the cause of something is understood as the effect (see figure 2.2). President Bush's role in causing the lapse of the ban becomes the same as his being the effect of the lapse of the ban. The power of such a blend is that it highlights some information (Bush's role as cause) while masking other information (Bush is not a gun seller). Once a repeal of a ban is connected to the action the ban had meant to stop, you can turn this political act of changing a law into an apolitical act of selling guns to terrorists. Dramatic power can be illuminated using blending theory; the process of illumination also unveils the often-hidden input spaces that help construct the blend.

To read a performance, to judge an argument, one must be able to understand the elements compressed and intensified in a performance. Chapter 5 will address several specific examples from productions of *Hamlet*, but, following the political theme, I will look at a political

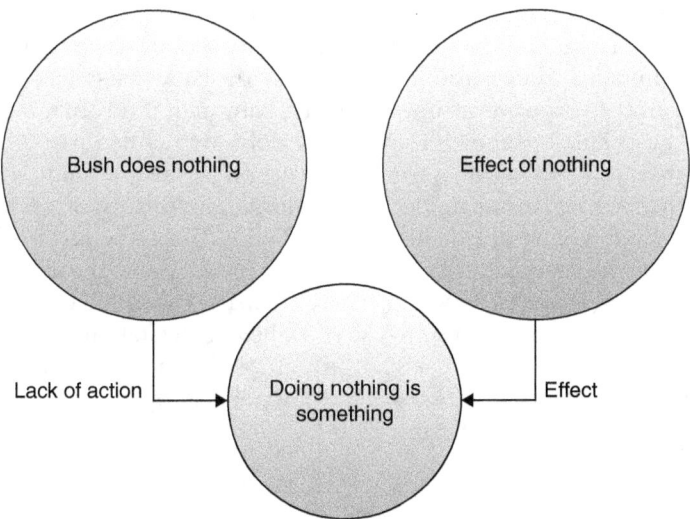

Figure 2.2 Compression of cause and effect in Bush/gun sales

performance that did not, at least for one viewer, effectively blend elements. At the controversial commencement address of President Barack Obama at Notre Dame in 2009, Operation Rescue's Randall Terry staged a protest against Notre Dame's selection of the pro-choice Obama. Terry described the performance afterward to an interviewer, "We, um, pushed baby strollers peacefully, quietly, prayerfully on campus. In the strollers were babies covered with stage blood.... And an Obama bumper sticker saying 'Obama 09: One Dead Baby at a Time. Notre Dame' To make a statement." To which the interviewer responded: "I get it." On the *Daily Show*, Jon Stewart judged the performance as not conveying what Terry had hoped. Stewart responded to the video clip of the interview by unpacking the blend, questioning how the spaces connected in the network resulted in the blend Terry intended: "You *do* get it? 'Cause I don't get it. Why are the blood covered babies supporting Obama? Wouldn't they have a McCain bumper sticker on their stroller?" The mental space recruited to understand "bumper sticker" defines bumper sticker as expressing and promoting the opinion of the driver of the vehicle on which it is stuck.

As Coulson has shown, the rhetoric around abortion depends upon the accessing of a counterfactual space: the act of terminating a pregnancy only gains meaning when understood against a future space where there is a baby where there is now not-a-baby. For pro-choice advocates, this baby represents a lack of control over one's body, an enforced life-change, a future of responsibility for a child, etc. It is not the pregnancy she wants to end, it is the future it represents that she wants to change. For pro-life advocates, the pregnancy is a future life that is missing. The counterfactual space of the baby that would be the result of the pregnancy is now a missing baby and, if missing, it must have been killed. Randall Terry's baby dolls are defined partially by their past (the blood comes from the abortion performed months ago) and their future (babies do not have political opinions). Stewart, while understanding the blend that makes bloody babies the result of an abortion, does not understand why these babies support the candidate who supports their termination. There are many complicated elements in this blend, but I raise it simply to show how understanding blending is how we unpack, and thus see through performance, whether that performance is on a traditional stage or a political stage.

Her Speech Is Nothing

CBT gives us the tools to see how meaning is made. We compose a meaning through a cognitive staging. Once composed, the connections between spaces are primed, they are ready for reapplication; this meaning does not need to be staged in just one way. If we can unblend, we can reblend. Primed and repeatable projections created through a compression to human scale and agency created through a blend organized by a generic space that finds cause where there is only effect, illuminate not just what Hamlet's mirror held up to nature means, but how it means that and what the results of that composition of meaning generates. It is not obvious or literal; there is not a clear correspondence between words and their referents and therefore CBT allows us to see as staged even meaning that we once perceived as literal. To give an example of how unveiling the blends in the unquestioned presents new avenues of research, I turn to the understanding of *Hamlet* composed by a different culture.

Laura Bohannan's 1995 article "Shakespeare in the Bush," questioned the presumed universality of Shakespeare's Danish prince from within an anthropological framework. Bohannan describes her retelling of Shakespeare's *Hamlet* to the elders of a tribe in West Africa and reports that their reactions indicate that Shakespeare's play does not express a universal human experience. During a long series of rainy days—during which the men gathered in a tent and told stories while getting drunk—the men persuade her to tell the story of *Hamlet* and she does, thinking of it as a chance to "prove *Hamlet* universally intelligible."[31] Not surprisingly, Bohannan finds that cultural traditions impact their understanding of the story. Cognitive theories of language and meaning expose more than the cultural comparisons between these two worlds; what anthropology fails to show Bohannan is that the reactions of the elders yielded more than just insight into different cultural traditions.

I should note first that Bohannan's short paper does not address her research, specifics of the tribe she is studying, the dynamics of her gender or race, her role as participant and witness, etc. Despite often being troubled by the ethnography in her work, I confine my examination to the reactions of the elders (Bohannan's term) to a couple of the conceptions in the plot of *Hamlet*. Because they are reacting to Bohannan's translation of the plot into their language, this is not a translation study or an examination of the specific poetry. However, the idea of Ophelia's drowning is not misunderstood because of a translation problem; it is misunderstood because the elders generate meaning differently than English speakers do, forming a different idea of drowning. In a culture where a king takes many wives and upon his death they are distributed among his brothers, along with the responsibility for their children, Hamlet's reaction to his mother's remarriage will—not surprisingly—seem strange. A different understanding of succession has obvious cultural and literary counterparts, but there are other less obvious differences that led the elders to a radically different interpretation of *Hamlet*. While the Africans do not understand the story of *Hamlet* the way a western-educated theater-goer might, what is interesting to me is how they compose an equally plausible version of the play and how their version illuminates ours.

The elders do not believe that people can drown unless they are bewitched. When Bohannan explains that Laertes swears to kill Hamlet because of Polonius's murder and Ophelia's madness and drowning, one of the men responds:

> one cannot take vengeance on a madman; Hamlet killed Polonius in his madness. As for the girl, she not only went mad, she was drowned. Only witches can make people drown. Water itself can't hurt anything. It is merely something one drinks and bathes in.... It is clear that the elders of your country have never told you what the story really means. We believe you when you say your marriage customs are different, or your clothes and weapons. But people are the same everywhere; therefore there are always witches and it is we, the elders who know how witches work.[32]

Females, the elders know, can only be bewitched by male relatives, and thus, the elders conclude, Laertes must have had Ophelia killed by witchcraft to sell her body to the witches for money to pay off the debts he accrued in France just as Polonius feared. Underneath this alternate story are traditions of a patriarchy that controls witchcraft, a belief in witchcraft, a family structure that defines who has power over whom in life and in death, and a different idea of the cause of death by drowning. A different understanding of dying in water necessitates a different story: in the tribe Bohannan studied, Ophelia could not have drowned because water does not have the agency necessary to drown her without the witches' help. While a belief in witchcraft obviously alters the epistemology of a people, less obvious is the effect on epistemology of a shift in how death is talked about. For Bohannan, this only reflects different cultural traditions; blending theory shows how this reflects different linguistic structures that enabled and constrained different thinking.

English language can say that Ophelia drowned in water and then Elsinore can wonder about her mental state before her death. Was it a suicide? The result of madness? English blends the effect of inhaling water and suffocating until the heart stops and life is over with the cause: she drowned. The agency this grants to water is inconceivable to the African elders, for whom such agency presumes intention. In English, water can cause death without our thinking that it did so intentionally. While the cultural traditions that lead them to say that Gertrude "did well" to marry Claudius illuminate our cultural traditions that call her marriage adulterous or incestuous (or at the very least "overhasty"), the difference between presuming that Ophelia's madness caused her death by water and blaming Laertes for selling her to the witches comes down to whether or not the language maps intention along with causal powers onto water.

While preparing Ophelia's Christian burial, the gravedigger discusses how the coroner found that her death was not suicide. The gravedigger parses out the warped legal argument that could justify her Christian burial, "if I drown myself wittingly, it argues an act, and an act hath three branches—it is to act, to do, and to perform" (5.1.10–12). The "three branches" of an act that the gravedigger refers to come from the argument of defending council in the influential 1550 case of *Hales v. Pettit*. The question of the case was whether or not Sir James Hales could have forfeited his right to his property by killing himself because, as editor Harold Jenkins puts it, "the act of suicide could not be completed during his lifetime and that at the moment of his death his wife, as joint lessee, took possession by right of survivorship."[33] Did he forfeit because he died or because he decided to die? The lawyer argued that intention is separable from action, because the act of killing oneself involves three branches:

> The first is the Imagination, which is a reflection or meditation of the mind, whether or not it is convenient for him to destroy himself, and what way it can be done. The second is the Resolution, which is a determination of the mind to destroy himself, and to do it in this or that particular way. The third is the Perfection, which is the execution of what the mind has resolved to do. And this Perfection consists of two parts, viz. the beginning and the end. The beginning is the doing of the act, which causes the death, and the end is the death, which is only a sequel to the act.[34]

The lawyer decompresses intent into conception (the "Imagination") and decision (the "Resolution") and then the act itself is pulled into two parts: the cause (the "doing") and the effect (the "sequel"). Moreover, he separates the agent into the mind and "himself," one the subject of the action and the other the object of the action. If the mind did not resolve to do it, the body cannot be guilty of completing the action: cause requires intention and cause is effect. This argument depends on a separation of the mind that thinks and the body that acts, with the agency located in the mind, not the action.

The gravedigger concludes his argument, "Here lies the water—good. Here stand the man—good. If the man go to this water and drown himself, it is, will he nill he, he goes, mark you that. But if the water come to him and drown him, he drowns not himself. Argal, he that is not guilty of his own death shortens not his own life" (5.1.16). The gravedigger's formulation gives agency to the water, but this is part of what makes his comment ridiculous. Shakespeare's language allows the gravedigger to suggest that the water intentionally sprang up out of its banks to forcefully drown Ophelia because in English, water can "come to him" without intention or agency, but to make sense of "drown him," English speakers presume intention. The presumption comes in the placement of the water as subject of the verb where it gains agency and intention. Whereas English does not presume intention on nonliving actors (such as water), it does presume intention when the actor is a human. We have an Idealized Cognitive Model for action that involves a human agent with an intention. As Coulson points out:

> Our default assumption is that all human acts are caused by intentions. If we observe a person performing an action (e.g. opening a door) we assume that the act is caused by the person's intention (the intention to open the door). We don't mention intentions in our description of actions because it is implicit to the very notion of action that it be mediated by an intention. It is not adequate to explain an action by pointing to the intention which caused it. Because all actions are assumed to stem from intentions this information is seen as trivial.[35]

The joke is in the gravedigger suggesting intention where one is assumed to be impossible.

The African elders' reading of Ophelia's drowning unveils an inseparable coupling of intention with result. If Ophelia was hurt by water it was because someone wanted her hurt by water, bewitching the usually indifferent water into causing harm. It is not that our literal definition of drowning is different from theirs, it is that our language creates a conception of death by water to which it gives a name: to drown. Death by water is no more an objective thing out in the world requiring a name than is death by witches. One language sees the effect of death in the cause (the water) and one language sees it in the intention to harm (the witches).

Reading Bohannan's essay and *Hamlet* with a cognitive linguistic lens calls attention to the different linguistic and cognitive mappings that undergird the play but that generally go unnoticed. Looking at the language we think of as "literal," such as Ophelia's drowning, we can see the mental spaces and cognitive mappings that get combined and blended to yield both obvious and nonobvious meanings: while the definition of drowning may seem clear to us, parsing its legal ramifications splits action and agency in a play famous for delay, inaction, and a search for agency. In the comic relief of the gravedigger scene, Shakespeare theatricalizes the three branches that separate in a legal sense action from intention, agency from intention, and conception from perfection. Conceptual blending theory illuminates not just the idea of Ophelia's drowning but also the split between action and agency in *Hamlet*. A complete description of the spaces within a network built by a blend is impossible, because there are an infinite number of associations. Blending theory does not need to be taxonomic in order to be valuable to performance. Its value lies in how it maps the likely spaces and uncovers connections not immediately apparent but maintaining power even in dormancy.

Chapter 3

Mirror | Mirror; Mirror | rorriM

> ...the purpose of playing, whose end, both at the first and now, was and is to hold as 'twere the mirror up to nature; to show virtue her feature, scorn her own image, and the very age and body of the time his form and pressure.
>
> (3.2.21–4)

Conceptual blending theory imagines a network of associated spaces primed for the composition of meaning on the stage of hearing; it provides a tool to explain the densely poetic and the seemingly simple. Hamlet's depiction of the aims of theater receives very little editorial comment or exegesis in the editions I have read: apparently we continue to understand what he means and thus do not need editors to explain it. The fact that it remains comprehensible suggests that although the audience at the Globe in the early 1600s might have a very different reference for "mirror" (let alone Virtue or Scorn), the process of composing the meaning of Hamlet's mirror is flexible enough to withstand such differences. CBT supports and extends other critical assessments of Hamlet's mirror, it suggests avenues of historical research and illuminates the connective tissue between ideas within the play—connective tissue that generates a cognitive scaffolding.

The cognitive scaffolding is the network of spaces and blends primed and evoked throughout the plays such that the play would not look the same without it. Uncovering the network evoked to understand "The slings and arrows of outrageous fortune" would be interesting, but the true value of the method comes when the blend selected contains, compresses, or informs other parts of the play. Hamlet's "mirror held up to nature" speech has lent itself to the titles of books, has been borrowed by acting teachers, and has been quoted by high school drama teachers; the theatrical ideal it calls for seems to require no explanation. But how can a mirror held up to nature reflect anything other than nature, reversed left to right? (grass? sky? erutan?) Who is holding the mirror? What kind of mirror? How did Virtue develop a feature and why should the feature reveal anything of substance about Virtue? An actual mirror held up onstage will reflect less theoretically rich information than Hamlet hopes; a mirror onstage will reflect the actors, backstage, lights, or the audience. Perhaps Shakespeare imagines the Ladies Virtue and Scorn in the audience at the Globe, captured in this mirror for the Groundlings to assess. Hamlet's mirror is, of course, a metaphoric mirror; he wants the player's performance of The Murder of Gonzago to reflect Claudius's murder of King Hamlet so that it extracts Claudius's guilt from nature. But what kind of mirror provides the input space for this mirror? What mirror is called to mind when we hear this directive that the players' performance should extract only the salient parts of what is placed in front of it? No such mirror exists with which to understand theater; it must be created through blending.

In Hamlet's formulation, how the mirror does what it does is not examined or illuminated, only that it is held and what is found in it. Put simply, while I might understand that Hamlet argues for a type of playing that is able to represent the most salient features of the story for the purposes of enlightenment or correction, cognitive linguistics calls my attention to *how* he means this and CBT provides me with the tools to find out. In this chapter, I argue that Hamlet's mirror doubles and troubles two deeply held models of self and other, and epistemology: agency demands intention and TO SEE IS TO KNOW. Many critics have looked in the early modern mirrors for signs of change, subjectivity, and inwardness. Critical discourse on *Hamlet* reveals how conceptions of the mirror impact not just how critics have read *Hamlet*, but how they then write about it. These critics seem to import Hamlet's historically informed, understanding of a mirror, not the contemporary object to which they look for information. I contextualize Hamlet's mirror and trace the technological advances in mirrors during the early modern period as well as the allegorical use of the mirror in writing and visual art of the period. Though it is still understood by us now, how might it have been understood then? With this in mind, I examine the conceptual integration network (CIN)[1] that makes up the conception of mirror at the center of our inquiry: what are the spaces and connections required to understand this mirror blend?

The Critical Mirror

Just as we do not see the mirror when we look into the mirror, critics seem to use the mirror to express their ideas without examining how they are holding or operating the source of reflection. Robert Weimann calls *Hamlet* the "mirror of representivity"[2] without noting that the type of mirror that creates a prototype or exemplar is a convex mirror. He does not need to, as it seems we are familiar with the mirror being used differently from our own mirrors. From simple metaphor of duplication to complicated blend of proliferation, the mirror shows up in the writings of almost every single critic of *Hamlet* that I have read. Sometimes the mirror is recognized as an unstable "trope of transition"[3] while being used confidently anyway. Stephen Orgel acknowledges that the mirror was a contradictory symbol in the Renaissance, suggesting vanity and pride as well as the way to self-knowledge and self-improvement. Still, he describes masques, known for privileging spectacle over mimesis, flattery of the monarch over unmediated reflection, as "expression of the monarch's will, the mirrors of his mind."[4] Ronald Levao argues that in the Vice plays "theatrical trickery mirrors political trickery"[5] by which he means not a reflection but a miniaturization of its subject matter, "The play itself is a typological mirror, as 'the interpretour' tells us about midway through the action, truly representing the global struggle between good and evil."[6] In exploring the relationship between performance and repetition,[7] Bert States uses the mirror to create an image of endless repetition, "Theatre is, in a sense, the quintessential repetition of our self-repetitions, the aesthetic extension of everyday life, a mirror, you might say, that nature holds up to nature."[8] Echoing Hamlet, States seems to suggest that nature disassociates itself from nature in order to hold a mirror up to itself through repeating what was already repeated. In *Great Reckonings in Little Rooms*, States blends the mirror with what it reflects, "The point is that when nature is the subject of poetry in Shakespeare, it is not perceived as threatening or beautiful in itself but as a mirror image of what is threatening or beautiful in a single soul or in the body social."[9] States's mirror is a link that connects and separates poetry, nature, a soul, the body social, and the threatening or beautiful qualities that both cause and affect them.

In separate works, new critics Rudolf Stamm and Hereward Price write about the "mirror scenes" in *Hamlet* and other plays as if the depth of the play is depicted in miniature on the surfaces of the scenes. Price insists that the scenes, "bring everything into focus,"[10] which only makes sense if he is referring to a convex mirror, which would bring diffuse things into focus in a miniaturized reflection on the surface. Price goes on to involve what seems to me to be another type of mirror in his language, "Like the mirrors in the Palace of Fun they exaggerate grotesquely. In these plays all is interconnected and there are no loose ends."[11] Mirrors that exaggerate would be concave or warp like a wave, because he has already assumed a convex mirror that miniaturizes would pull into focus rather than spread out "grotesquely." I can only make sense of the second part of the quotation if I again think of a convex mirror, which will eliminate ancillary stimuli in its tightened focus thereby removing any "loose ends."

Stamm uses a different sense of mirror in his definition of the mirror scenes. He argues that the scene in which Ophelia discusses Hamlet's insanity offers the reader more than meets the eye, "We are looking at him as through a magnifying glass."[12] While the use of the mirror would suggest projection of a surface onto another surface, in the magnifying glass, the surface is seen in enlarged detail through the glass. The magnifying glass is figured as something to look *through*, whereas the mirror is something we say we look *into*, as if it were not a surface but a container. Though a magnifying glass metaphor here may seem more literal, he does not mean this literally, as this magnifying glass functions more like Hamlet's mirror held up to nature, in that it finds features in an enlargement that had gone unnoticed looking at the subject unaided.[13] Stamm's magnifying glass here seems to combine some features of Hamlet's mirror, projecting from the magnifying glass input space the concentrated attention to a singular feature and from the "Hamlet's mirror" input space the inclusion of the holder of the object, choosing important information to angle the object at, and the social interaction blend that reads information about insides on the surface. (These elements of Hamlet's mirror will be discussed in more detail later in this chapter.)

To say that the mirror is a metaphor is only to scratch its surface. While complete and taxonomic in its excavation of the history of mirror titles at the time, Herbert Grabes's book *The Mutable Glass: Mirror-Imagery in Titles and Texts of the Middle Ages and English Renaissance* does not exhume the metaphor of the mirror, "Strictly speaking, of course, a mirror does not present something new so much as re-present something already in existence, so these mirror-titles seem to be applying the metaphor in somewhat imprecise way."[14] The application of the metaphor is imprecise *and* mirrors at the time did not "re-present something already in existence"; the shifting conception of the "mirror" in these titles evidences a shifting object; the reflection in which yielded a shifting referent. This has provided a rich source of research and analysis; new historicist and cultural materialist articles on the mirror in Shakespeare's England examine how a technological shift in mirror production intersects with a shifting notion of reflection and self. By looking at writings and paintings of the time, each scholar finds a different story about how the new mirrors were consumed metaphorically. The meaning of the object and the reflection it created is understood through its depiction in literature and art. Scholars attempt to trace back from these reflection to the Renaissance eye (or "I") that stood in front of the mirror. Debora Shuger, for example, finds in the early modern mirror not a reflection of the self but of that which is not the self; the early modern mirror is "platonically angled, tilted upwards in order to reflect paradigms rather than the perceiving eye."[15] Shuger thus argues that mirrors did not provide an experience of subjectivity, but rather a more relational or transitive experience of moral or spiritual correction.[16] For Shuger, and others, the mirror is something to look back to and in through time—attempting to locate the self that stood in front of the object.

The proliferation of different mirrors during the early modern period enables critics to see what they want to in the many reflecting surfaces. For David Scott Kastan, the mirror is significant in its production of a copy, as separated from the original. In "'His semblable is his mirror' *Hamlet* and the Imitation of Revenge," Kastan examines the idea of imitation in *Hamlet* in light of the mirror. He argues that the revenge in *Hamlet* is only "a desperate mode of imitation" and that Hamlet searches for an original act. From the Mousetrap to the ghost, Kastan sees the reflections in *Hamlet* as copies or imitations underlining the fundamentally flawed reasoning of "avenging wrongs with wrongs."[17] His reading of mirrors, copies, and imitations highlights the disanalogies between a thing and its semblable. Kastan's study does not look for the subject, but for the action; what does it mean to reproduce or imitate? What happens when one becomes two? While there has been no shortage of work on the "controversies," "invention of," or "myths" of the self in early modern England in general and *Hamlet* in particular,[18] the readings tend (as Terence Hawkes points out) to look backward through the lens of the authors' own times to find in *Hamlet*'s self the one associated with our own.[19]

Hamlet's speech to the players calls to mind theatrical realism because we see our theater in his theater just as scholars hope to find our experience of inwardness in Hamlet's articulation of inwardness. Moving across disciplines to ask what cognitive linguistics might find in Hamlet's mirror shifts the focus to the chain of agency and personification capable in this mirror. A discussion of the mirror must include what is reflected within it—in this case the personification of Virtue, an inward quality capable of causing the outward expression of that which is presumed to be inside the person behaving that way. As the gravedigger says, "Argal, he that is not guilty of his own death shortens not his own life" (5.1.16). It depends what is meant by "is"; the mind fills in agency and intention where it sees cause. But, as Bohannan's elders point out, water cannot kill people just as Virtue cannot cause virtue. Nature, broken down to its constituent parts in Hamlet's mirror, reveals the Russian Dolls of interior trait causing external action, a chain of containers so infinite as to demand a rethinking of interiority. Given that editors and high school teachers do not feel it necessary to explain how a mirror can do what Hamlet says theater does, the cognitive ability to follow this complicated and yet compressed mirror must not be a function of Shakespeare's genius, but ours.

The Rear-View Mirror

Language exists in a context; it both reflects and shapes the culture of its speakers. It is not arbitrary (ala Saussure), not generated in a language area of the brain through words memorized listening to mother (ala Noam Chomsky and Steven Pinker), and it is not cognitively determining or individually interpellating (ala Althusser).[20] Like the Dani speakers, we create the words we need for the colors we see; when we start to make a distinction between "red" and "rust," we need a new word. Like the tribe elders in Bohannan's essay, giving the water the agency necessary to kill Ophelia means giving it the intention to motivate that action. Exactly what the Groundlings imagined when they heard the word "mirror," we cannot know; we can, however, historicize this mirror, recognizing that the prototypical mirror—and thus the constraints on what Hamlet could mean by speaking of the theater as a mirror—would have been different in 1600. The early modern object that defined the conceptual category was different than it is today.

Moreover, it was in flux. The historical context and cultural materiality of Shakespeare's plays have been anatomized over the last thirty years to reveal the relationships between backstage and onstage.[21] The mirror, having been explored figuratively by the new critics, has been examined materially more recently by new historicists. Grabes calls the years between 1550 and 1670 "the Age of the Mirror" and

Benjamin Goldberg views the advancement in mirror technology at this time as reflecting the "the spirit of the Renaissance, which saw a philosophy of world reality and natural clarity overtake the metaphysical world of religion seen 'through a glass, darkly.'"[22] Adam Max Cohen includes the mirror—with gunpowder, the printing press, and the compass—as one of the most important technical advances of the age and explores the many uses of the mirror trope within the works of Shakespeare. As the technology of the mirror underwent change in the centuries leading up to *Hamlet*, so too does the metaphoric use of the word. Cohen, pursuing Grabes's call for a historical metaphorics,[23] places the image in its historical context to improve its literary clarity. Cohen connects Sabine Mechior-Bonnet's historical research on the role of the mirror as artistic object and home décor item of the nobility to the function of Shakespeare's plays in the early modern playhouse. He quotes Mechior-Bonnet in the context of Shakespeare's use of the mirror metaphor to brilliantly depict what he sees as the role of Shakespeare's mirrors as providing an

> ideal panoptic vision. But they also taught the relativity of all points of view and fed skepticism. The multiplication of incompatible gazes divides representation into smaller pieces, and the cohesion of the subject is sacrificed to the aggregate of disparate images. Man gets a piecemeal understanding of himself, he knows only bits of his singular experience and, as a fragment or shrunken image of a shattered mosaic, he loses his central and privileged position.[24]

The mirror, always both an object and a concept, is historically situated and historically defined.

In *Hamlet*'s director's notes to the actors, Shakespeare evokes a mirror that does not impartially reflect what is placed before it, as our common contemporary mirrors do. We must be told, on our sideview mirrors, that "objects in mirror may be closer than they appear" because we assume that light bounces off the surface of the mirror at the same angle it strikes it and the image reflected appears to be the same distance behind the mirror as the reflected object is in front of the mirror. Mirrors made before the fifteenth century, however, were rarely this precise. What was envisioned when an early modern audience in England heard "mirror" and in what ways was such a conception unstable?[25]

The history of glass mirrors in England was relatively short; convex mirrors were brought to England in the third century by the Romans. These mirrors could not have reflected much of "nature" because the shape produced a distorted image and the quality of the glass-backing was such that they did not reflect all of the light that entered, creating a dark and shadowy reflection. It was not until 1460 that the glass-makers of Italy had perfected their technique into a clear glass mirror. By 1569 the glassmaker industry was so large, the *specchiai*, or mirror makers, established their own guild.[26] Glass makers became highly-paid craftsmen and their fragile products were shipped throughout Europe. In her exhaustive book on the changing technology of the mirror in the fifteenth and sixteenth centuries and the concomitant change in its role in society, Melchior-Bonnet finds that despite the larger flat mirrors that the Venice technology made possible, the dangers of shipping made them relatively uncommon[27] (at least in England) until later in the seventeenth century. High-quality Venetian mirrors were very expensive and only became common household items in the seventeenth century.

Expensive and rare, the mirror became associated with the traffic in court persona of Elizabethan England. Smaller convex mirrors were worn on outfits to check one's appearance throughout the day, and were associated with vanity, narcissism, flattery, and the deceitfulness of women. Melchior-Bonnet cites a poem that equates adultery with the mirror: "Beware of being cuckolded / By a woman painting her face / Whose thoughts are far from her marriage / Carrying a crystalline mirror."[28] Presumably, these women's thoughts are on the face she sees in the mirror, not unlike Hamlet's claim that women use makeup to create a face, "I have heard of your paintings well enough. God hath given you one face and you make yourselves another" (3.1.144–45). Henry Peacham's *Minerva Britanna* includes a mirror as a representation of self-love (*Philantia*) and one in the hand of female beauty, stating that the mirror here signifies, "how we by sight are mooued to loue."[29] The use of mirrors as sartorial accessories suggests a growing fascination with a mirror that can reproduce, for enlightenment and correction, the face. I can now see me in the mirror and I am now in relationship with me. This conception of a mirror is like the pond in which Narcissus gazes to see himself and thus become himself. It reflects Narcissus, and in the gazing, Narcissus becomes the symbol of vanity.

Represented in paintings, mirrors often worked to construct what was in the frame by pulling the outside world, miniaturized, into the painting. In Jan Van Eyck's *Arnolfini Wedding Portrait* (1434)[30] an ornately framed convex mirror hangs on the wall behind a couple holding hands. The man holds his right hand up as if to bless something and the woman in an elegant green dress holds her dress up in front, creating the sense that she is patting a pregnant belly. Behind them to the left is a window, evoking the outside but not depicting it, and to the right is a partially visible red bed. In *Reality in the Mirror of Art*, Lise Bek argues that the symbolism of everything in the room works together to create the "temporal-legal act, suggested by the arriving witnesses reflected in the mirror with the artist's signature above it, and with the matrimonial fidelity represented by the dog."[31] The mirror brings the witnesses and the painter into the recording of the Arnolfinis' union, making the object a kind of legal stamp. The mirror behinds them performs their marriage by witnessing their union.

In *Hans Burgkmair and his Wife* (1527) by Laux Furtenagel[32] a frowning couple sits in front of a convex mirror held up by the woman in a pose similar to the images of vanity depicted in Peacham's *Minerva Britanna*. The mirror reflects back to the couple, not their likeness but their skeletons. The inscription reads, "This is what we looked like—in the mirror, however, nothing appeared but that."[33] Without the mirror, they are alive; in the mirror they are dead. By placing the future in the instant, the couple's identity is constrained by its future. In *The Moneychanger and His Wife* (1514)[34] by Quentin Metsys (also spelled Massys or Matsys) a man counts gold coins as his wife, sitting at his left, leafs through an illustrated book, her gaze drifting off in the opposite direction of the book. Between them on the table—and between the money and the book—sits a small round convex mirror, reflecting in miniature the window and the world outside and the author painting their portrait. Here again, the subject of the painting is captured and contained on the surface of the mirror: the space far away and unattainable by the indoor workers who deal with money gained from the outdoor traders and explorers and the painter who constitutes the couple in counterdistinction with what is on their table and what is not in the room with them. The mirror here pulls something very specific from the outside into the picture in order to change the meaning of the image. What is in the mirror is not what is in the picture but what is in the picture is in some way constituted by the image in the mirror.

Mirrors, rare and slightly opaque, were magical tools, used for fortune telling and religious worship, "pilgrims believed that mirrors were able to attract and capture the grace emanating from holy relics, despite the crowds that prevented them from getting close to the altars and relics themselves."[35] Though unable to capture a likeness, these mirrors were thought to capture a "grace" off of objects in front of them. In *Macbeth*, the witches show Macbeth the line of kings of which he will not be a part. The line is depicted as going on forever in a glass held by the last, "What, will the line stretch out to th' crack of doom? / Another yet! A seventh! I'll see no more. / And yet the eighth appears, who bears a glass / Which shows me many more" (4.1.117–20).[36] The witches use the mirror to show Macbeth who he is: in the mirror, he is the king who will not beget kings. He is Macbeth not as he is now (child-less king) but who he will be (absent from the line of kings).

The mirror behind the couple in Jan Van Eyck's *Arnolfini Wedding Portrait*, created the identity of the couple (married) in front of the mirror. It also reveals the painter, the witness of the marriage. The painter in the mirror shares the perspective of the current viewer: we look on it as he did. Just as we cannot see ourselves looking without the mirror, we cannot see the painter without it. The mirror here is a tool by which the viewer can see what is otherwise not visible. In *Hans Burgkmaier and his Wife*, the painter uses the mirror to reflect what the painter cannot: the mortality of his subjects. The inscription suggests that the mirror is a more editorialized view of the couple than the painter. The artist tells the viewer that the painter shows what *is* there—"This is what we looked like"—but the mirror shows what *will* be there—"nothing appeared but that." This mirror does not simply reflect what is before it; this mirror changes the image to show more than what meets the eye. It is less accurate and more true. In *The Moneychanger and His Wife*, the mirror shares space on the table in front of the woman with a book of paintings the woman is looking through. She is seeing, in the mirror and the book, that which she cannot see in her room. The mirror, like the book, symbolizes the exterior world seeping in through new technologies of knowing. The technologies moving the world forward, the book and the mirror, were not benign or impotent, they were editorializing tools of understanding one world through comparison with another.

Larger flat mirrors do not begin showing up in paintings until Johannes Gumpp's *Self-Portrait* of 1646 or Diego Velázquez's *Las Meninas* in 1655. As opposed to the way the convex mirror contains and miniaturizes the outside world, the lifesize reflection of the king and queen of Spain in *Las Meninas* creates a *mise-en-abîme* and a power in their absence made present, as Michel Foucault and Peggy Phelan have seen.[37] Anamorphic art of the period, such as Hans Holbein's *The Ambassadors* (1533), also call attention to the method of looking.[38] David Castillo argues that anamorphic art makes "us more aware of the fact that 'what we see' is to a certain extent a function of 'our way of seeing' and, consequently, of 'who we are and/or want to be'" (10). He begins his book (A)Wry Views: *Anamorphosis, Cervantes, and the Early Modern Picaresque* with a quotation from *Richard II*: "Like perspectives which, rightly gaz'd upon, / Show nothing but confusion,—ey'd awry, / Distinguish form!" and argues that the proliferation of these images during this period related to an idea of an absolutist state represented by an omnipresent king.[39] He posits that the work of Cervantes (among others) can be seen as anamorphic in its layers of meaning, challenging well-established views about the world by exposing an alternate reality within the anamorphosis and threatening the stable epistemology of early modern viewers. Looking at these works straight on reveals nothing strange, the world as it is supposed to be, but a change in perspective reveals something dark and different. Different tools for seeing produce different ways of knowing.

More rare than practical material mirrors in the early modern period, are mirrors that survive from the early modern period. What often remains, absent the glass, is the frame. Artisans made extravagant frames for mirrors; the frame around the Arnolfini mirror, for example, is almost larger than the mirror and is more detailed than what can be reflected in the glass. If the mirror cannot be clear and accurate, what you need is a frame that suggests what should be seen within. In other words, what the mirror can only hint at, the frame reveals. I want to show how performance can provide the frame through which to understand the significance of Hamlet's mirror; to do so I turn to two interesting "framing devices" for mirrors in the collection of the Victoria and Albert Museum in London.

Perhaps not surprisingly, critical attention to mirrors generally focuses on their frames or cases; one can be forgiven for thinking that the mirror, a product of technical mastery, was less important artistically than that which was created to contain it. The image files for pieces in storage[40] include copies of their descriptions in *Ancient Furniture and Woodwork* (1876) by John Hungerford Pollen.[41] More than once, Pollen begins his description with "This piece is remarkable for its frame." One frame, thought to have belonged to Lucrezia Borgia, spells out MALUM (evil) down one side and BONUM (good) down the other, the one the mirror image of the other. In *A Grand Design*, the Victoria and Albert Museum's book about the collection, the description of the *"Lucrezia Borgia Mirror"* (c. 1504–34) suggests that the value of the object comes from the infamous owner, "a character with a legendary reputation for wickedness and extravagant vices."[42] The frame, then, is deciphered and valued with Borgia's image imposed on the mirror's surface.

Along with the letters are various icons of either virtues or vices, "On the right of this figure [the letter Y] is that of a woman draped and kneeling. Over her is a dragon representing sin or evil, against which she is defending herself. Following to the right of this direction are various animals representing virtues, to which the kneeling figure stretches her hand" including a unicorn ("typical of virginity"). Whatever Lucrezia Borgia saw *in* her mirror, that which surrounds it loudly, if allegorically, suggests the two ways her image will appear to the world: good or evil. However, in the museum's catalog, the editors suggest that perhaps this reading was wrong:

> The frame has always been prized for the quality of its carving and abundance of symbolism, ranging from allegorical beasts to the Pythagorean "Y," signifying the choice between good and evil. However, so attached have furniture historians been to the idea of the mirror belonging to Lucrezia Borgia that they have overlooked the significance of the Virgin and Child on the other side. Recent research by Peter Thornton and Kent Lydecker on fifteenth-century Italian interiors and inventories, coupled with the moralising nature of the frame, suggest that the object served originally not as a mirror but rather as a religious icon or ancona, which would have hung in the chamber of Lucrezia's husband, Alfonso.[43]

An analysis of the frame is predicated on whom was reflected on its surface. Not unlike Erving Goffman's definition of primary frameworks as those that render "what would otherwise be a meaningless aspect of the scene into something that is meaningful."[44]

The Martelli Mirror (c. 1495–1500) was purchased in 1863 for the detailed sculpture that forms the back of the item. Here, the mirror is assessed from behind the reflecting surface and *A Grand Design* describes the piece as a "merging of sculpture and the applied arts."[45] If one were looking at a person holding the mirror up to his or her face, one would see a scene starring a satyr, a bacchante, and Priapus, "These figures, together with a Latin inscription meaning 'Nature encourages what necessity demands,' suggest that the relief is an allegory of procreation."[46] Again, the object privileges the reading of both reflection and comment, particularly because in this case the contextualizing sculpture is visible to the watcher of the gazer. Moreover, it is unclear how such an object was used as a tool for seeing the reflection of one's face and the sculpture at the same time, because, at 7–1/2 inches in diameter, it is too big to be a sartorial device. Hung on the wall, one side would be visible only to the imagination. Complicating the controversial attribution of the item (originally thought to have been the work of Donatello it was later attributed to Caradosso or Cellini), is that which was found within the mirror, "Recently found inside the mirror was a fragment of a document about enemy French troop movements written in a secret code used by Milanese diplomats." The authors cite this discovery by way of proving that "Such a discarded scrap of paper would have been available only to someone working within the Milanese court" (and therefore Caradosso).[47] What strikes me as important is the use of the mirror as reflecting glass and spy glass at the same time. This mirror did not inform on the surface of its glass but behind and within its glass. Looking in microscopically to the Virtue or Vice of the person in front of the mirror, it also telescopically informed on the military maneuverings of far off enemy troops. The integration of information about the mirror of 1600 into the network of mirror mental spaces reflects a concept of depth etched on the surface of the metaphoric glass.

Grabes argues that the manuals of correction that used the mirror in their titles presented for the reader either an ideal image or a warning against which to check one's own behavior or virtue, "a normal domestic mirror facilitates adjustment of external appearance: correspondingly, anything that facilitates improvement of the soul can be termed metaphorically a 'mirror.'"[48] The writers of these tracts generally explained how they expected their readers to use their "mirrors." *A Mirror for Magistrates*, printed several times in the second half of the sixteenth century, tells noblemen's (his) stories in order for other noblemen to learn from example. In the dedication, William Baldwin writes, "For here as in a loking glas, you shall see (if any vice be in you) howe the like that bene punished in other heretofore, whereby admonished, I trust it will be a good occasion to move you to the soner amendment. This is the chiefest ende, whye it is set furth, which God graunt it may atayne."[49] Grabes argues that in *The Mirror for Magistrates* tragedies occur due to both " 'mundane irrationality' and 'mundane retribution' " and this creates a "double mirror:" "though both serve as warning examples to the reader, they warn of different things."[50] While the title applies to all the noblemen's histories, some of them are mirrors of one part of nature (unpredictability and irrationality—chance) and some reflect another part of nature (divine justice, retribution, fortune). This mirror does not reflect, though, it predicts and then warns. Grabes examines the mirrors in these titles as vehicles of meaning and says that he wants to avoid "the pitfalls involved in seeing literary figuration as merely the outward and generally ornamental garb of thought;"[51] yet he privileges the more "literary" metaphors and dismisses others (such as the one used by Hamlet) as "anything but original."[52] If the use of the "mirror" is not to be dismissed as simply an "ornamental garb of thought," than the supposedly "unoriginal" uses should receive the most attention, not the least.

Baldwin wants the depictions to improve the ruling class; as Paul Budra puts it in A Mirror for Magistrates *and the* de cassibus *Tradition*, "Baldwin offered the Mirror as cure for the diseased and prophylactic for the sound."[53] Seeing, and thus fixing, one's traits in the stories of the demise of others can undo bad behavior as well as prevent bad behavior. In a 1609 speech to Parliament, James uses the mirror as something that provides a tool for seeing, "So haue I now called you here, to recompence you againe with a great and rare Present, which is a faire and a Christall Mirror; Not such a Mirror wherein you may see your owne faces, or shadowes; but such a Mirror, or Christall, as through the transparantnesse thereof, you may see the heart of your King."[54] This mirror operates more as a lens, used to anatomize that which is placed before it "through the transparantnesse thereof." *Through* (not *in*) this mirror, Parliament can see his heart.[55] Adam Max Cohen points out the classical models for the early modern use of the mirror as a tool: Seneca saw the mirror as a tool to learn something valuable about one's self and "St. Thomas Aquinas linked the mirror, or *speculum*, to the type of *speculation* that led to constructive meditation."[56]

The kind of theater *Hamlet* calls for—one that warns against excessive displays of gesture—is unlikely to match the prototypical "mirror" envisioned by early modern audience. Although glass mirrors did improve the quality of reflection, this was not immediately reflected in a new conceptual framework for what a mirror does. As we refer to a reflected image being "in" a mirror, medieval and early modern users of the mirror imagined that such an image was pulled into the mirror. While the technology of the mirror changed during this time, the economics and fragility of the larger glass mirrors made them rare and mysterious; few people would have had experience with a reflection of more than their face. The popularity of the object and category in book titles and paintings suggest that changing, ambiguous category, one that could do something; a mirror was a tool, a process, a verb.

In *The Literary Mind*, Turner suggests that a "blend can reveal latent contradictions and coherences between previously separated elements.... Blends yield insight into the conceptual structures from which they arise."[57] As Cohen asks: what type of mirror did the Globe audience picture in "his or her mind's eye" when Hamlet referred to his mirror? Different classes might have imagined different mirrors, "By contemplating the variety of mirror types available to different subgroups within the Globe and the different optical characteristics and cultural resonances of each mirror type we gain a more nuanced view of all the possible connotations of Prince Hamlet's famous instructions to the Players."[58] In the blends used by Shakespeare and the authors of the period's mirror-titled books, we can see images, mental spaces, and assumptions that can illuminate the fabric of blends that make up *Hamlet*. Within Hamlet's mirror we can see a history of convex mirrors used both for their functional role as sartorial accoutrements as well as their artistic function as symbol makers. Also visible in Hamlet's rich mirror are issues regarding the social presentation of self, the political necessity of reading others, the mirror as the projection of God from the scriptural understanding of seeing in the Bible (as "through a glass darkly") the path to heaven, and the mirror as exemplar or warning spelled out in manuals or handbooks. While using the blend to illuminate theater's role in societal correction, Shakespeare masks in the blend the semantically invisible holder of the mirror, responsible for choosing the angle of reflection. While rending invisible the mirror's holder, Shakespeare creates an agent through personification. In a play about epistemology and agency, Shakespeare hides the playwright and personifies the object of reflection.

The Mirror Blend

When Hamlet tells the players that the purpose of playing is to hold a mirror up to nature, he is not being particularly poetic or obtuse. The player, though not given much opportunity to speak, suggests that he understands Hamlet's direction, so he must not be translating Hamlet literally; as any actor will tell you, a mirror held up onstage will probably reflect the audience. Hamlet does not want Claudius to see his face reflected onstage literally, he wants Claudius to see his past in "the very cunning of the scene" (2.2.586). Hamlet's mirror is not a literal one, but it is also not a metaphoric one. A metaphoric mirror would project information from the source domain (flat glass reflecting object) to the target domain (theater) to illuminate the target. This type of theater would not reflect "something like the murder" of Hamlet's father; it would repeat, as a film, the original event. Hamlet's mirror is asked to see through nature to Virtue. According to Hamlet, the goal of theater is both unmediated (it reflects what it sees on Virtue's face) and intentional in its angle (because it has a goal—the "purpose"—it can be neither accidental nor random).

Rather than tell us which "dozen or so lines" Hamlet has inserted into The Murder of Gonzago, Shakespeare gives Hamlet 35 lines on theater theory and practice, at the center of which is a thesis statement on the purpose of playing that depicts a mirror that does not, and cannot, exist. This theatrical mirror provides an accurate reflection (unaffected by intention or agenda), assumes that through seeing that reflection one will know something, presents that which is normally invisible to the eye (that is, the face that surrounds the eye); anatomizes the face into internal spots representing external traits, and focuses diffuse information into a coherent picture of "nature."

Hamlet's mirror is a blend: it gains structuring information from three input spaces: a flat, perfect mirror that can show us what we cannot see without its aid (input space M1), a convex mirror that manipulates diffuse information such that it captures not what is there but what exactly it is angled toward (input space M2), and the angler or holder deciding where to look, what to reflect (input space M3) (figure 3.1) M1 is a tool we operate to gain information by reflecting what we cannot usually see. M2 is a magic tool that distorts and idealizes. M3 has agency and intention. M1 and M2 ask us to interpret and M3 takes on the agency necessary to delight and instruct through pointing the mirror toward the feature upon which he or she would like to comment. This reflection shows Virtue and Scorn the

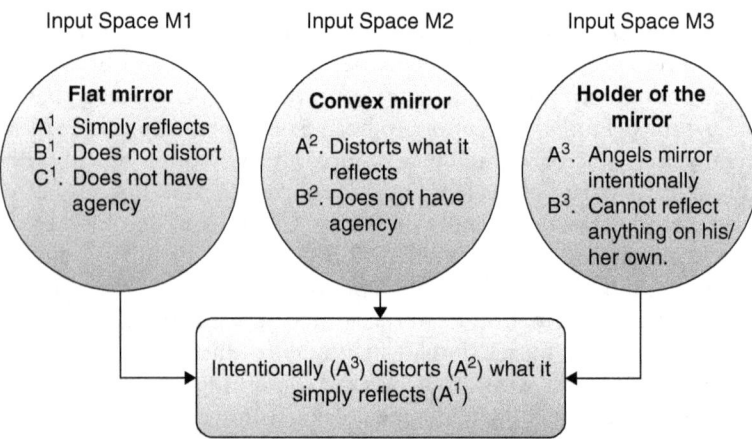

Figure 3.1 Hamlet's mirror blend

details of their outward appearance while conveying the exemplarity of one and the vice of the other. The emergent meaning in this blend is that—paradoxically—an unbiased, unadorned depiction of nature can be a didactic tract on the virtues and vices of the times.

To clarify this blend, I will focus on the first focus of Hamlet's mirror: Virtue. Virtue looks at her feature for information about her virtue. How is a trait (virtue) both a woman (Virtue) and a feature indicating a trait? Shakespeare's personification gives the trait the qualities of a woman capable of directing her gaze and, presumably, acting on the information gleaned from the perspective. Without Shakespeare, virtue cannot be shown anything; for this, virtue must be personified into Virtue. Shakespeare creates a subject (Virtue) where there was only an object (virtue). Further, cause and effect are compressed such that a person who behaves in a virtuous manner (effect) must have virtue (cause). This property is understood as residing *in* the person who behaves that way; external behavior understood as caused by an internal trait. The person did not choose that virtuous action, it was compelled by an inner trait. Our subject (Virtue) is defined by an object (virtue). To understand this one clause ("show Virtue her own feature") one must stage a scene made legible only through a series of compressions of agent, cause, and effect.

As Fauconnier and Turner have shown about personification in general, the state of no longer being alive (death) becomes the agent that caused the state ("Death") such that one can then say "Death, be not proud" and be understood. Death has a cause—"death"—and a collection of virtuous traits has a face—Virtue. An agent is created where none originally existed. Death-in-general need not have intention or agency; death occurs because humans are mortal The only evidence we have of Death is its effect. This entrenched compression is a causal tautology, "from the Event, we read off a Cause that is tautologically and exclusively defined in terms of the event category and is referred to by the very terms for that category. These causes beg the question: If we ask 'What caused this death?' and we receive the answer 'Death,' we do not think our question has been answered."[59] "Death" here is an "empty cause:" "Lust causes all events of lust, Hunger causes all events of hunger, Death causes all events of death. In the blend, the specific event of dying is caused fundamentally by Death-in-general; the specific manner of death is the means.[60] "The history of the vice characters in medieval drama is a clear example, as Good Deeds or Envy creatively and efficiently convey as people the dangers or value in the traits they personify. The language of personification creates Virtue to cause virtue: more than just useful and poetic it originates an agent where none exists.

This Virtue is looking at her own feature, presumably presented on her face but representing her internal trait. The features one might see in a mirror correspond to internal features that do not have an outward counterpart visible in the mirror. They are connected through analogy and compressed to identity and uniqueness: what is a visible feature in the mirror is now an internal trait. Virtue is not just looking at an external feature to see an internal trait: she has also metonymically compressed a part of herself (her face) with her identity as a whole. A similar blend is at work for the people Hamlet derides who, after making "mouths" at Claudius while King Hamlet reigned, now "give twenty, forty, fifty, a hundred ducats apiece for his picture in little" (2.2.361–62). While this combines the metonymy for face-identity and representation-identity, the point is the same: we quickly connect identity across disparate spaces so that what is "globs of paint" in one space is "Claudius's face" in another, "Claudius" in the third and "King Claudius" in the fourth. And the effigy, which a miniature of King Claudius becomes, is another blend where the picture/face/man is blended with the status, power, and near divinity of the monarch such that the picture itself contains the status, power, and near-divinity of that which it represents.[61] Internal virtue is also a blend of external behaviors with a feature of the insides that we imagine makes the manifestation of various features likely to occur. Once we uncover the blend, we can see that what is figured as manifesting itself externally in a "feature" was always external to begin with. Only through blending does it go inside and out, outside and in, creating the boundaries that it transgresses as it goes.

In order to understand Virtue as seeing a part of herself, of course, she must be split into two people: the person looking into the mirror and the person with the feature that represents Virtue's virtue. Here, Virtue and virtue's feature are interacting, and (by pattern completion) sharing information. This interaction is guided by the Idealized Cognitive Model (ICM) of assessing internal feeling states through external facial features. Existing in a society relies on a constant need to translate information gathered off of someone's face into information about feelings, motive, etc.[62] This interaction creates a loop where Virtue and Virtue's feature can know what they cannot see by projecting what is invisible to them on to something visible, that is, the other's face. Therefore, two people interacting are sharing information about each other; by watching how the other person's face reacts to one's own externalization of feeling states, one can attempt to adjust one's face to more accurately depict one's feelings. As Maurice Merleau-Ponty puts it "I must be the exterior that I present to others, and the body of the other must be the other himself."[63] We look into the mirror for information, information that we believe the image in the mirror can provide: how does my hair look? Do I have spinach in my teeth? In *Snow White and the Seven Dwarves* the evil Queen looks at her reflection in the mirror and asks, "mirror, mirror on the wall, who's the fairest of them all?" Young children can understand that the Queen expects to get an answer because they have a blend available to them wherein a person looking into a mirror can be seen as two people interacting and thus sharing information.

This ICM of the social feedback loop is entrenched in our reading of social situations. Though Hamlet knows that "one may smile, and smile, and be a villain" (1.5.108), his writing it down suggests that his assumption to the contrary is too entrenched to notice without a written record of its error. And, alas, he still forgets because he assumes that Claudius's guilt will "unkennel" during the Mousetrap and be exposed on his face—and while the conscience of the King might have been caught during the Mousetrap, the image of Claudius praying in the following scene is enough to make Hamlet think (erroneously) that the King is praying. The assumption that what we see on the faces of others communicates something about what lies beneath or within the other drives and defines our social life. Goffman articulates our common theory of social interchange: "as natural persons we are supposed to be epidermally bounded containers. Inside there are information and affect states. This content is directly indexed through open expression and the involuntary cues always consequent upon suppression."[64] In a striking example during a 2004 political rally, Billy Crystal joked about the man of honor, "John Kerry: if you are enjoying yourself, tell your face."[65] This joke plays on Kerry's reputation for having a stiff, sour face that does not register his internal affective states. Crystal suggests that Kerry employ an interlocutor who communicates his insides to his outsides so that others can see when he is enjoying himself. Crystal does not question his own ICM that facial expressions map to internal affective states, he assumes that Kerry's connection between internal and external has been interrupted. Critics of Kerry will similarly not question their ICM but will assume that because Kerry's expressions do not seem to map cleanly onto internal affective states, he is hiding something.

Claudius articulates a separation between Hamlet's face from his insides, concerned that he cannot read either. In explaining to Rosencrantz and Guildenstern why he has brought them to Elsinore,

Claudius says, "Something have you heard / Of Hamlet's transformation; so call it, / Sith nor th' exterior nor the inward man / Resembles that it was" (2.2.4–7) First and foremost, of course, Claudius and Crystal are looking to Hamlet and Kerry for information about Claudius and Crystal. Crystal wants to read Kerry's internal state on Kerry's face to know what Kerry feels; Crystal wants to know what Kerry feels because from that information he will gain information about his own performance as a comedian. This is not to suggest that Claudius is not vested in Hamlet's feelings (or Crystal in Kerry's), only that Claudius's reading of Hamlet (like Crystal's of Kerry) is already defined by the assumption that what he reads on Hamlet's face will indicate feelings that will indicate something about Claudius's security on the throne (or Crystal's comedy). We look to the other to know about ourselves.

Virtue looking at her feature is presumed to obtain information about herself in this gazing. Shakespeare personifies the traits he wants his audience to see and learn from—an examination of Virtue will lead, he assumes, to an understanding of virtue. What we see, we can then know. As Lakoff and Johnson have shown, we understand the abstract through the physical: thus, TO SEE IS TO KNOW. The metaphor TO SEE IS TO KNOW is so powerful that we will construct logically crazy sentences ("Virtue saw her own feature in the mirror") because it is easier to understand Virtue seeing a part of herself than to understand Virtue knowing a part of herself. For this metaphor to work, we must refer to a set of specified assumptions and entailments contained in a word. This ICM guides our understanding of seeing. Lakoff outlines the ICM for seeing as: "1. You see things as they are. 2. You are aware of what you see. 3. You see what's in front of your eyes."[66] If we say that we "see" something, it is generally assumed that we accurately perceive what is in front of us. It is "idealized" for a reason: it assumes a certain set of conditions that may not always be true. In fact, although there are many times when one or all of the above stipulations are not true, we continue to use this model for its simplicity and efficiency.[67] However, because it does structure further thoughts and articulations, it is powerful in its simplicity. It is also a powerful tool for poets, as constructing an image or example that plays with or counters an ICM illuminates flaws in our operating models. What we see is not always what we get.

Hamlet's mirror seems to have had more of an impact on our mental spaces than our contemporary embodied experience with mirrors. Harold Bloom insists that although his critics call attention to his pulling Hamlet out of *Hamlet*, what is important is not the art but what it reflects, "There is no 'real' Hamlet as there is no 'real' Shakespeare: the character, like the writer, is a reflecting pool, a spacious mirror in which we needs must see ourselves."[68] Like Hamlet's mirror, Bloom's mirror (figured here as a conflated character/writer) whose purpose and end is to show us us. Unlike Hamlet's mirror, Bloom's mirror *is* the character/writer not the "playing" that either does. Bloom's mirror/character/writer is something we look at to see backwards to ourselves. Hamlet's mirror is something that shows Virtue, Scorn, and Time something about themselves. Both "mirrors" here gain more structural information from handbooks of correction or self-help books than with contemporary experience with mirrors. It is as if Bloom—and the other critics I have read—has spent more time with Hamlet/*Hamlet* and his anatomizing and editorializing mirror than he has with the mirror in Bloomingdales which shows him how the blazer makes him look or the mirror that tells him that there is a car changing lanes behind him. Bloom is not the only one to use the mirror in Hamlet's fashion. Shakespeare's language of reflection seeps through our experience as powerfully as—more powerfully than—the mirror we see while brushing our teeth. Critics are so steeped in the blend of meanings in Hamlet's mirror, even before reading the play, they cannot read the blend without relying on it as an input space. So: is there a time before reading *Hamlet*? If so many of our entrenched blends rely on mental spaces infected and blended before by Shakespeare, then perhaps to speak English is to know *Hamlet*.

Chapter 4

Meaning Superflux—A Cognitive Linguistic Reading of *Hamlet*

This chapter begins by arguing that *Hamlet* can be productively read using conceptual blending theory and ends by analyzing the role of perspective-taking in a radio story about performing *Hamlet*. Although seemingly belonging to two different academic genres, the Shakespeare study and the performance study, I hope to show that the two parts can be linked through cognitive linguistics. The predominantly literary focus of the first part suggests the way in which the play calls into question our compression of cause and effect and our entrenched understanding of knowing as seeing. The second part uses the language of performance to understand the expansion of perspective afforded and demanded by theater. We play out our stories of who we are and how we know through staged language. Shakespeare does it in words, Hamlet does it in action and inaction, and the actor does it by embodying all three.

Compressions are powerful communication tools that can mask important logical or epistemological ruptures. The tracking of the integration network in chapter 3 exposes what and how the mirror as category scaffolds the play. Again, my focus is not the blend, but rather on the construction of the integration network as an action or verb: doing, working, and shaping. The cognitive linguistic analysis of Hamlet's theatrical mirror afforded by conceptual blending theory presents a network that exposes—and then, I believe, shapes—these very themes. As the network behind the mirror shows, (1) the compression of cause and effect obscures the often-shaky connections we create between intention, agency, and action and (2) the mirror offers a powerful—but not necessarily always reliable—visual tool that creates and constrains what we can know and imagine conceptually. Thinking of the mirror in

Hamlet and elsewhere as a blend of mental spaces, rather than a literal object or even a metaphor, displays the making and shifting of a category. Tracing the integration network required to make sense of the mirror, exposes what the network signifies, supports, and constructs.

In order for this methodology to be useful, it should complement, rather than radically upend, the brilliant and long history of *Hamlet* scholarship and ask new questions, rather than provide unassailable answers. Rather than use cognitive science and *Hamlet* to provide a radical retort to the literary theories of the last hundred years, blending theory offers a way, like the mirror, to create and constrain previous intellectual thought on the play. Mary Crane interrogates the linguistic history of "to act" to read the play's interest in interiority and intention and her work is a useful point of engagement for the cognitive linguistic reading proposed here. My unpacking of the mirror at the center of the play provides a different way in to a similar reading. I add to Crane's reading, though, the way in which the mirror operates to question our linguistic and conceptual understanding of cause and effect and TO SEE IS TO KNOW. It is not enough to say that a text says something; I want to argue that Shakespeare's use of language shapes what can be said and what can be thought.

In *Framing Authority: Sayings, Self, and Society in Sixteenth-Century England*, Crane finds that commonplace books—Hamlet's "tables"—created "a central mode of transaction with classical antiquity and provided an influential model for authorial practice and for authoritative self-fashioning."[1] Used to gather aphorisms and sayings, these books allowed a mobile social class to reassimilate or "frame" old ideas within a new context. The currency created through exchange of sayings established authority through language. Though not a cognitive reading, Crane's book provides a foundational argument for cognitive linguistic readings of classic texts: language—particularly fluid and expanding in the early modern period—shapes and creates the collective mind of a culture.[2]

In *Shakespeare's Brain*, Crane aims to create a literary theory derived from cognitive science, and sees Shakespeare's plays as representing "what it is like to conceive of oneself as an embodied mind."[3] Her use of cognitive science is grounded in the notion that it "offers the more radical idea that social and cultural interactions have materially altered the physical shape of the brain,"[4] through, in particular, "different forms of polysemy and prototype effects."[5] Crane examines how the language of the early modern period reflects and illuminates the brain that created the work. By focusing on how Shakespeare's famous wordplay relates to a shifting subjectivity, Crane finds a feedback between brain, performance, language, and culture:

> It seems possible that the process of creating fictional characters to exist in a three-dimensional stage space brought out the spatial structures of language to an unusual degree. Perhaps it is enough to say that these effects "emerge" through Shakespeare's almost uniquely rich use of language. Shakespeare (i.e., Shakespeare's language-processing functions) causes us to notice these connections—which in turn reveal information about the culture and also about the organizational tendencies of the brain.[6]

Through their language, Shakespeare's plays are a site of a construction of interiority.

Crane argues that Hamlet's concern with identifying whether action is the result of an internal process or whether it is the cause of an internal formation, creates the delayed revenge. She views the play as moving from outside to inside and back again, both in terms of a spatial location (outside the castle to the closet and back) and in terms of Hamlet's "preoccupation with what is within himself and other people."[7] According to Crane, Hamlet brings "an inner self into being by talking about it" and that he moves "toward a performative theory of self-fashioning,"[8] trying out a language of action—"O, from this time forth, / My thoughts be bloody or be nothing worth" (4.4.64–65)—that he hopes will "shape his very thoughts."[9] To some degree, he is successful: this act four soliloquy is his last and ushers in a shift in Hamlet from brooder to doer. Crane argues that Hamlet cannot take action at first because he resists his role in the play as an instrument of revenge. He is trying to figure out the relationship between agent and action—does outside action impact (or reflect) the inside or does the inside determine the outside action? The big question here (as in *Hamlet*) is: who's in charge?

This, rather than a description of melancholy as has been argued previously, was the influence of Timothy Bright's *Treatise of Melancholy* (1586) on Shakespeare. According to Crane "Shakespeare took from Bright not a specific clinical diagnosis but instead contradictory accounts of the cognitive processes 'within' that result in (or prevent) purposeful action in the world."[10] For Bright, the spirit cannot do anything without an instrument to effect something else and "the spirit [is] the verie hand of the soule."[11] The soul is, in turn, effected by the habits of the man, "butchers are 'accustomed with slaughter' and unfit to serve on juries in capital cases, while mariners are rough, bold, hardie, inconstant."[12] Because the immaterial soul cannot directly effect the actions of the man, there are spirits and habits that form a kind of semiconscious and indirect form of agency. Crane sees this in Hamlet's argument that Claudius' drinking is related to a "vicious mole of nature" that he cannot help, "since nature cannot choose his origin" (1.4.26). This internal mark, then, impacts action, "The chain of internal cause and effect—a mole of nature alters complexion, a change in complexion breaks down reason, corrupted reason destroys virtue—sounds very much like Bright"[13] but that, unlike Bright, Hamlet suggests that habit can then alter the self. Later, Hamlet will tell his mother to avoid Claudius's bed, and to "assume a virtue if you have it not," as if stopping the habit will eventually improve the self in a kind of "fake it 'til you make it" mentality of self and action. Noting that everyone in the play seems to act at one remove from action through the use of spies and proxies, Crane shows how Fortinbras is the exception that proves the rule, "Only Fortinbras's accession to the throne of Denmark at the end of the play restores a direct link between agent and action. [...] His name itself, which means 'strong arm,' suggests this ambiguity since he is indeed a powerful military leader but, like the arm to the body in Bright, not quite an independent agent."[14] Crane reads *Hamlet* against Bright as a way to see the underlying interest in the cognitive processes that move inner self into an external action that may, or may not, create an internal self.

Crane's reading is persuasive and offers an integration of literature and cognitive science that has been tremendously influential. Without challenging her reading, I want to extend it based on the unpacking of the mirror blend provided by CBT. The mirror described at the center of the play—an impossible object that is also a powerful conceptual tool—provides the instrument missing in her reading. I disagree with her claim that the mirror held up to nature is "relatively straightforward"[15] and point out the ways in which the play's concern with the questioning and creating of an inside and outside can be organized around/through/on/in the mirror. The mirror in the play is the instrument that connects sight with knowledge, knowledge with action. The conceptual integration network of the mirror creates a regression of cause and effect and internal and external, but also facilitates sight and knowledge so that through this attempt to see what cannot be seen, *Hamlet* creates it. The purpose of playing is "to hold"; Shakespeare's construction of the sentence diffuses agency such that it is unclear who is doing the holding, what the angle is or how it can be a tool for seeing internal traits and thus, presumably, altering or confirming external action. This use of the mirror is not exclusive to *Hamlet*. Indeed, as we saw in the last chapter, it is the dominant understanding both then and now: a mirror both simply reflects and also didactically presents.

Bright's problem is also a problem in neurophilosophy: how does a nonphysical thing like the mind effect change in a physical thing like the body? The extreme positions are dualism—the mind is separate from the body—and monism—there is nothing other than body/brain. Both positions present substantial problems and neither of which is particularly popular in its extreme.[16] Like Hamlet trying to assess what is possible to know for sure in a world where one may smile and smile and be a villain, René Descartes arrived at his famous "cogito ergo sum" as a the first postulate of his philosophy, because it was something about which he felt he could not be fooled. As Descartes explains, "this 'me,' that is to say, the soul by which I am what I am, is entirely distinct from body, and is even more easy to know than is the latter; and even if body were not, the soul would not cease to be what it is."[17] What Descartes is wrestling with is what can be known for sure and if knowing is located in the "mind" then that experience of knowing—the thinking—must be primary. But how does thinking about moving your arm move your arm? If the soul is separate from the body, how does it communicate with the body? Most cognitive scientists agree that there is no mind without the body; thinking does not happen separate from the body or emotions.[18] The question remains, though: is there a separation within the brain, within the "self," or even within the "self" and its environment? And, if so, where is it? While it may be clear that, as Ramachandran has quipped,[19] there is no homunculus in the brain, watching the world pass by as a movie in front of him and then ordering the organism about, it is less clear where agency exists.

Hand and Soul

Of the fourteen uses of "mirror" in Shakespeare's plays, eight of them are tools capable of presenting the internal self to the eyes of the viewer for instruction or correction. Like the mirror Hamlet offers to Gertrude, wherein she may see "the inmost part" of herself, it is a tool that creates a conception of depth on the surface of its metaphoric glass. These are the mirrors Cassius desires to find for Brutus in *Julius Caesar*, "such mirrors as will turn / Your hidden worthiness into your eye / that you might see your shadow." This is the mirror Richard II calls for when he has lost his nobility, "Let it command a mirror hither straight, / That it may show me what a face I have, / Since it is bankrupt of his majesty" (4.1.265–267). Without the crown on his head, he must be bereft of majesty internally and this internal shift must be seen in the mirror on the surface of his face. In *The*

Winter's Tale, Polixenes sees in the outward change of Camillo the inner change he perceives in himself, "Good Camillo, / Your changed complexions are to me a mirror / Which shows me mine changed too" (1.2.380–382). This is a mirror that presents information not available to the self without a tool. By creating a self on/in the mirror that is in dialogue with the self, information can be exchanged and one can affect the other. Where there is exchange of information there is influence. This mirror is the tool missing in Bright's endless loop of indirect cause and indirect effect: a mirror that can be held up between spirit and hand, spirit and soul, generating exchange and action.

Throughout *Hamlet*, Shakespeare recalls the mirror at the place between symmetry. Horatio uses the language of the mirror to articulate the similarity between the ghost and the dead King Hamlet, "I knew your father; / These hands are not more like" (1.2.211–12). The ghost was like Hamlet's father in the same way that Horatio's right hand is like his left hand: not the same (they are reversed left to right), but mirror images of each other. The use of a "mirror image" suggests a use of a mirror that privileges the differences between the image and its reflection. A "mirror image" highlights the way in which a mirror flips the left and right; it is the same and yet different in key ways.[20] Horatio's description of the ghost as the mirror image of the dead king Hamlet, as the left hand is the mirror image of the right, simultaneously confirms that the apparition was and was not King Hamlet. The ghost of the person both is and is not the person. Horatio's remark sets up the image of a mirror resulting in symmetry: what is on one side of the mirror is *symmetrical* rather than identical with that which is on the other side. It follows that if you faced two similar things toward each other, it would be like there was a mirror between them, reflecting and altering. When symmetry is evoked, then, it is linked associatively with the mirror that created the symmetry between Horatio's hands.

A visual and rhetorical antithesis is depicted in *Hamlet* as a mirror that provides, through the reflection, insight into that which is placed in front of it.[21] In action and words, Shakespeare sets up a dialectic through the comparisons and antitheses of ideas and characters. When Hamlet declares, "What a rogue and peasant slave am I" (2.2.544) he does so because he has compared himself unfavorably to the player who is able to "force his soul so to his own conceit" (2.2.553) while Hamlet "Must like a whore unpack my heart with words" (2.2.585). When he asks "to be or not to be" (3.1.56) he wants to know whether the mind's suffering justifies the body's end.[22]

At the start of his confrontation with his mother, Hamlet insists she stay and hear his words, "You go not till I set you up a glass / Where you may see the inmost part of you" (3.4.19). This glass is both a tool for anatomizing and one that cleanly maps metonymically: this inmost part *equals* the whole her. Dialogue between the two exposes the differences by insisting on the similarities.

These arguments recall Hamlet's comparing himself with Fortinbras and Laertes. The audience judges Hamlet by comparing him to the other characters in the play and Hamlet judges himself and his actions in the same way. Throughout *Hamlet*, information about the self is gained through comparison with another or through projecting an image of the inner self, outward. Hamlet compares himself to the player in an effort to understand his inaction, "What would he do / Had he the motive and the cue for passion / That I have?" (2.2.554–56). Through this dialogue about self and reflection (Hamlet with cue for passion but no action and player with no cue but action), one is turned into two; Hamlet is created in the mirror image of Hamlet. To see the truth one must look at its opposite. In act two, scene one, Polonius calls on his spy Reynaldo to travel to France where he has just sent his son to find out if his son is behaving himself. The plan is for Reynaldo, finding friends of Laertes, to impugn his character with "What forgeries you please...such wanton, wild, and usual slips / As are companions noted and most known / To youth and liberty" (2.1.20 and 22–24). Polonius hopes that Reynaldo will hear in response that the man Reynaldo describes is not the Laertes these compatriots know. Polonius explains, "Your bait of falsehood takes this carp of truth; / And thus do we of wisdom and of reach, / With windlasses and with assays of bias, / By indirections find directions out" (2.1.60–3). It is only through representing a mirror image of Laertes that Polonius hopes to see the real Laertes.

When Hamlet compliments Laertes to Osric, he does so by saying that only Laertes's mirror can match him, "But, in the verity of extolment, I take him to be a soul of great article and his infusion of such dearth and rareness as, to make true diction of him, his semblable is his mirror and who else would trace him his umbrage, nothing more" (5.2.115–20). While his language is geared to play with Osric's pretentious linguistic excess, Hamlet's use of the mirror here recalls the way Ophelia describes Hamlet:

> O, what a noble mind is here o'erthrown!
> The courtier's, scholar's, soldier's, eye, tongue, sword,

> Th' expectancy and rose of the fair state,
> The glass of fashion and the mould of form,
> Th' observ'd of all observers. (3.1.150–154)

This mirror is an ideal—platonically angled, in Shuger's terms[23]—a reflection one looks to for what the disanalogies between self and this reflection report about the self. In *Cymbeline* when Cloten uses the image of a man talking to himself in his own mirror as a justification to articulate his own strengths, he is presuming the ability of the mirror to operate as an object that separates the self in order to reflect the self. He argues that "I dare speak it to myself—for it / is not vainglory for a man and his glass to confer / in his own chamber" (4.1.7–9). For a man and his glass to confer, the "glass" must be blended with the reflection of the man, because a man can confer with another man, but not with a glass. In order for the reflection to have information to share with the man, it needs to contain information projected in from parts of the man he cannot normally see: his insides.

The disassociation between self and reflection enables a conception of the self as in a dialogue with the self. Lakoff shows how we do this in language by creating a separate self to analyze. In "Sorry, I'm not Myself Today: The Metaphor System for Conceptualizing the Self," Lakoff examines how certain cases of reflexive pronoun use ("I dreamed that I was Brigitte Bardot and that I kissed me")[24] disrupt traditionally held conceptions of semantic comprehension and provide a view to how we conceptualize the self. He argues that thinking about our selves requires a distinction between an inner thinker and a self to be thought about. His articulation of a multiple set of consciousnesses is useful in understanding how we can view the reflection in the mirror as self and not-self at the same time. As Lakoff's inner thinker must separate from the self-to-be-thought-about in order to think about himself, we look into the mirror at doubles of ourselves in order to see—and thus to know—ourselves. This may be why Claudius thinks Rosencrantz and Guildenstern will be successful spies, "being of so young days brought up with him, / And sith so neighbor'd to his youth and havior" (2.2.11–12) they might make Hamlet reveal to them that which is inside.[25] Claudius hopes Hamlet will see himself in Rosencrantz and Guildenstern and will speak freely, as if versions of himself projected outward in Lakoff's configuration or like Virtue seeing herself as separate in order to see herself. Looking in the mirror, or thinking about the self by projecting it outward, allows an interaction between self and self that facilitates knowledge through seeing. Stephen Greenblatt, for example, describes the moments in *Hamlet* when characters create a difference between oneself and oneself—Horatio saying that the ghost is like the King "As thou art to thyself," Claudius describing Ophelia as "Divided from herself and her fair judgment" (4.5.81), Hamlet's description of his madness as taking Hamlet from Hamlet (5.2.230), and "But I am very sorry, good Horatio, / That to Laertes I forgot myself"—but he does not pursue the cognitive linguistic consequences of this strange articulation of self separation.[26]

This mirror that can take a double (Hamlet and Laertes, for example) and make them into one (Hamlet as exposed through the "glass" of Laertes) or take a single (Julius Caesar or Gertrude) and turn him or her into a double (Caesar and his shadow, Gertrude and her spots) forms the active agent *not* in the one or the two but in the mirror that is held up between the two. Self is self, self constructs self, in the seeing of depth on the surface and creating connections between the two that may not actually be there. Hamlet describes his conversation with Fortinbras's captain as being an "occasion" that informs against him because Fortinbras and his men are going to their "graves like beds" (4.5.62) "for a fantasy and a trick of fame" (4.5.61) while he has "a father kill'd, a mother stain'd, / Excitements of my reason and my blood" and yet lets "all sleep" (4.5.56–58). Hamlet has motivation within but performs no external action, Fortinbras has projected outward onto his men, a fantasy that relates action to something more than a piece of straw. One acts without intention and the other cannot translate his intention into action and in this way Shakespeare hides and creates agency in the mirror placed between Hamlet and Fortinbras. The mirror Shakespeare holds up between the two men is capable of exposing this disanalogy but does not seem to "spur" anything in Hamlet—it is still two acts before Hamlet, through accidents and an indirect chain of events, kills his uncle. Although one of the first things Hamlet says is that he has "that within which passes show" (1.2.85)—[27]—he spends the next four acts of the play trying to see, and thus (he thinks) to know, images of himself in others. We look into the mirror at doubles of ourselves in order to see—and thus to know—ourselves.

Understanding the self in interaction with the self by seeing the self creates a human scale story of how perception can be intellection. If I talk about knowing myself by looking at myself, or in looking at what I imagine are images of myself in others, then the relationship created between self and reflection is one between two bodies in space and, as Newton's third law insists (for every action there is an equal and opposite reaction) one body will impact the other body with its action. Even before Newton demonstrated this, people knew that if one object struck another object, it would visually impact the target object. In the closet scene, when Hamlet sees the ghost but Gertrude does not, Hamlet is understandably upset, because previously his perception of the ghost was shared with the guards and Horatio. Gertrude, however, does not see the ghost:

> Gertrude: To whom do you speak this?
> Hamlet: Do you see nothing there?
> Gertrude: Nothing at all; yet all that is I see.
> Hamlet: Nor did you nothing hear?
> Gertrude: No, nothing but ourselves.
> Hamlet: Why, look you there! Look how it steals away!
> My father, in his habit as he liv'd!
> Look where he goes even now out at the portal!
> *Exit Ghost.*
> Gertrude: This is the very coinage of your brain.
> This bodiless creation ecstasy
> Is very cunning in. (3.4.131–139)

She sees and hears "nothing" but insists that she sees "all that is"; so then if he sees something, it must be his brain doubling or coining something. Yet this double is the same "bodiless creation" that Gertrude sees in the glass set up for her wherein she sees internal "dark and grained spots" (3.4.90). Of course, she is speaking metaphorically while Hamlet insists that he sees an actual vision of his father where there is "nothing," but the understanding of one as being "metaphoric" and the other as literal comes down to a tool that conceptually and visually duplicates. Gertrude has a mirror but Hamlet has nothing; the only difference is the mirror.

Hamlet need not place Gertrude in front of an actual mirror to create the duplication he hopes to present to her. Knowing that the conceptual integration network that understands a mirror as a tool for seeing what is not visible by duplicating what is visible is available to her, he can use his words . Gertrude's soul is depicted as if in a mirror, like one of the young women using a handbook of correction to "see" and "remove" her inward spots. In *Mirrhor of Modestie*, Thomas Salter's mirror puts on the surface of the page an inward flaw perceived in young women: just as a maid "in deakyng her self by a Christall *Mirrhor*, will be sure not to suffer...so much as a spot, if she espies it upon her face...how ought her minde, in whiche is represented the true Image of God, to be kept...from greate spot of sinne."²⁸ Hamlet assumes that she will "see" in his description of her two husbands the sins and faults on her inside that caused her to go from the "Hyperion" to the "Satyr" (1.2.140) and if she sees it, she will act on it.

As Gertrude and Salter's maids look "into" the mirror they see "into" themselves. With the picture for reference, Hamlet describes for Gertrude the magnificence of her former husband, "See what a grace was seated on his brow, / Hyperion's curls, the front of Jove himself, / An eye like Mars to threaten and command" (3.4.56–57). He then shows her the picture of Claudius "like a mildew'd ear" (3.4.64) and rather than describe what he wants her to see in the picture, as he does with King Hamlet, he asks her twice, "have you eyes?" (3.4.65 and 67), calling to mind the ICM for seeing: if she had eyes, she could see; if she could see, she would see what is in front of her; if she saw it, she would believe it. He is not suggesting that Gertrude is blind, but rather that she is blind to the difference between the brothers; it is not that she lacks eyes but simply that she has "Eyes without feeling, feeling without sight" (3.4.78).²⁹ In his anger he communicates the presumed connection between the two: perception must equal intellection. This separation of perception into modalities (eyes, feeling, sight) foregrounds the difference between simply seeing the reflection and comprehending the salient disanalogies between Claudius and King Hamlet. Throughout the scene, Hamlet tries to understand how his mother's action (marrying Claudius) could possibly reflect what she has within, because the action cannot be motivated by love or lust or judgment or sight or sense. Gertrude's choice has nothing to do with any of these things but seems to emerge from them; they are, for Hamlet, agentless and sightless action.

A play that begins with "Who's there?" asked in darkness, troubles from the beginning the idea that TO SEE IS TO KNOW. In response to learning about the ghost, Horatio says "A mote it is to trouble the mind's eye" (1.1.115). Though some editors choose the Second Quarto's "moth," the quote still evokes the passage in both Luke and Matthew of the mote in the eye:

> For with what judgment ye judge, ye shall be judged: and with what measure ye mete, it shall be measured to you again. And why beholdest thou the mote that is in thy brother's eye but considerest not the beam [log] that is in thine own eye? Or how wilt thou say to thy brother, Let me pull out the mote out of thine eye; and, behold, a beam is in thine own eye? Thou hypocrite, first cast out the beam out of thine own eye;

and then shalt thou see clearly to cast out the mote out of thy brother's eye. (Matthew 7:2–5)[30]

This image of two people facing each other, seeing in the other's eye what cannot be seen in one's own, calls attention to the role of the embodiment and embeddedness of cognition. One's vision is never moteless; we see from and through our eyes and thus must make allowances for perspective and blindspots. Only by exchanging information with our "brother"—our self projected outward as a kind of optical teammate—can we *see* and *judge* what otherwise might be obstructed. The mirror, held up to nature, creates and obscures the eye's blindspot.

Many things trouble the mind's eye in *Hamlet* and I would agree with editor Harold Jenkins that Horatio means that the ghost is an irritant that will eventually make clear its portents—as the pesky "ghest" it is.[31] Shakespeare could have had Horatio say this in many different ways; the form and contents of the phrase Horatio uses echo the biblical parable. With this image called to mind in scene one, mental spaces built subsequently pertaining to the "eye" or the ICM of interacting with another to gain information will be impacted by the biblical parable. As Fauconnier says, "What kind of meaning will actually be produced depends on the mental space configuration (generated by earlier discourse) that the sentence actually applies to."[32] This is not to say that spectators will *consciously* connect Hamlet's articulation of suspicion to Rosencrantz that he "has an eye" of him with the "mote" in Horatio's eye, but the mental spaces primed or evoked by both lines share networks of associations, for that moment. The gradual buildup of these connections creates a scaffolding of meaning. Shakespeare's image of a speck in the mind's eye recalls the story of blind judgment at the start of the revenge play and suggests that the differences between the person looking and the person reflected are as salient as the similarities.

Knowing through sight means that the one thing we can least see (our face and thus our own internal states as reflected thereupon), we most want to know. The ability to understand the relationship between self and image or between a three dimensional physical object and its two dimensional representation requires blending. The mirror is the instrument thought to expose the self because it is capable of displaying the face to the self. First, the face is metonymically understood as being the self. Second, the self must be blended with the reflection in order to see the reflection as the self. This is possible because the two share vital relations[33]—that is, the same features—and despite the fact that there are differences between the two—one is the left-to-right reverse of the other. In the mirror blend, the similarities and differences are compressed and we see one identity where there are two images. The reflection in the mirror becomes the "self" so quickly that we have to work to see it simply as a reflection.[34] Or, we need a few hours traffic on the stage to perform the integration network, perform the framing and reframing of a blend, to see what is hidden through linguistic and conceptual compressions.

Enactures

While examples of the mirror in the literature of the sixteenth and seventeenth centuries are numerous, below I focus on a series of examples from Shakespeare's plays, in which the mirror most often reflects the meaning one might expect from a convex mirror: an idealization and miniaturization of many examples into one. What we see in the convex mirror on the moneychanger's table is not just a distorted image of another part of the room: what is condensed in the mirror is more than the trees and window it reflects, but the significance of those items within the frame of the painting. Seen in this mirror, in this context, the window cannot help but equal social and physical separation. The convex mirror compresses vital relationships between "windows" and "separations" into one so that we see the impenetrability of the room in which the lenders sit and count their money by seeing the outside penetrating the room in the mirror. In this image we start with the object that we can see is convex and move to what such a physical object allows the painter to say or represent. In Shakespeare's plays, we must unpack how the meaning is made in order to see the focal length of the mirrors described. As discussed in the previous chapter and as others have pointed out,[35] the technology of the mirror changed during this period. Shakespeare's language reflects these changing focal lengths and this instability informs a reading of *Hamlet* that uses the conceptual integration network found in the mirror at the center as a lens to re-see or un-know the play we cannot stop talking about.

In *Henry VI, part 1*, Lord Talbot compliments Salisbury by calling him the "mirror of all martial men" (1.4.74) and the Chorus in *Henry V* similarly praises Henry as "the mirror of all Christian kings" (2.0.6). This mirror is like the one Ophelia uses to compliment Hamlet ("the glass of fashion and the mould of form"), not like the one Hamlet uses to compliment Laertes ("his semblable is his mirror and who else would trace him his umbrage, nothing more"). In one, the mirror presents an ideal; in the other, the mirror creates a duplicate of that which stands before it. An ideal image in the mirror shares structuring information with the convex mirror mental space. A convex mirror reduces that which is in focus and therefore presents an editorialized version of that which stands before it. This highlighted feature of that which is in front of this mirror, came to be understood as an ideal—like the Bible or manuals of correction—or a warning—like the deaths of noblemen in *The Mirror for Magistrates*. A mirror capable of such focus must have a different focal length than one capable of reproducing Laertes more clearly than his shadow. The convex mirror instructs; held up to nature it will differentially reflect certain elements, seeming to prioritize relevant elements within nature. The other mirror creates a mirror image of that which stands in front of it—important for its differences as well as for its similarities—placing the responsibility for judging with the person reflected. This assessment takes the form of a dialogue with the duplicate, granting the image access to an unseen truth.

After killing Polonius, Hamlet moves from words to images, from mirrors to miniatures,[36] focusing Gertrude this time on "this picture, and on this, / The counterfeit presentment of two brothers" (3.4.53–54) and attempting to show Gertrude what he would like her to know. The two pictures of the brothers are like Reynaldo's description of Laertes and the true Laertes (or so Polonius hopes); the two are held as against a mirror to call into being that which is not there: the difference between the two. In the comparison between the two miniatures, Shakespeare's language creates a blend of King Claudius—who in the blend is all that King Hamlet is not—with King Hamlet—with his godlike qualities and exemplary behavior. This blend is like the "nonthings" created through counterfactual blends described by Fauconnier and Turner, "Counterfactuality is forced incompatibility between spaces, and when one is thinking about reality, counterfactuality is often a vital relation between spaces that involve some of the same people and the same events."[37] The "forced incompatibility" comes from an attempt to make one input space reflect the other; the ways in which they do not fit creates a nonthing. Hamlet's mirror, his words that construct nonthings in the gap between what should be and what is, works to bring Gertrude's sins to her eyes—"O Hamlet, speak no more. / Thou turn'st my eyes into my very soul, / And there I see such black and grained spots / As will not leave their tinct" (3.4.88–91)—figuring herself in front of the mirror created in Hamlet's words and finding spots on the face of her soul like Virtue looking for virtue in her features. The soul, like the face that requires a mirror to see and correct, can only be seen in a mirror.

Crane points out that the speech that Hamlet prepared for the player king—or the speech that Shakespeare wanted us to hear—is not about killing the King but about the relationship between action and agent, "he [the player king] argues that various internal factors can alter willed intentions: 'purpose is but the slave to memory'"[38] and that bringing the motivation for action to an actual completion is an "enacture" (3.2.197). Crane notes that Shakespeare must find a new word for actions—enactures, "to express intended action that is carried through to completion...It is as if by this point in the play *action* had become so distanced from a concept of successful completion that a new word was necessary to convey this idea."[39] This is the same separation of intention, ability, and action used by the gravedigger—who is referencing a contemporary court case as discussed in chapter 2—to parse out the difference between being the subject of the verb "to drown," the agent that can drown, and the object of the verb. Both the player king and the gravedigger try to equivocate about a past or potential crime: the player queen's stated fidelity but ultimate infidelity and Ophelia's intended and accidental suicide. Crane finds that the graveyard scene works to "define intentionality from the outside,"[40] as the gravediggers examine her outward action without reference to that which may have been within her when she drowned, just as "Gertrude's oddly lyrical description of her drowning, with its transposition of agency to surrounding plants and her clothing...similarly leaves Ophelia's inner state opaque. She is only '*as* one incapable of her own distress' (4.7.178, my emphasis)."[41] What I want to focus on here is not the attempt to locate intentionality as either being on the inside or outside—though as I argue above, I agree this is a key point in the play—but on the compression that obscures differences between cause and effect and that defines something or someone in terms of an event or diffuse set of qualities.

Crane understands *Hamlet* as revolving around the question of whether the self is formed by an internal trait or external actions and connects this with Bright's interest in understanding the "stable, essential, and unchanging center for the inner self" as a "complex chain of impulsive and instrumental actions that lead to both involuntary and purposeful acts"[42] that creates a self that emerges through action and intention. Like the tanner whose body will last nine years before rotting because of what he did in life, Bright points out that butchers are changed by what they do, "butchers are 'accustomed with slaughter' and unfit to serve on juries in capital cases, while mariners are rough, bold, hardie, inconstant."[43] As Crane points out, "*Frailty* is another name for 'woman' because women's inner selves can be so easily molded or altered by what they do."[44] But "frailty" and "woman" are, of course, not the same; "Frailty" is personified as a woman, as Virtue is, by connecting traits shared between the two into one identity. The gravedigger presents his coworker with a riddle about profession and identity, "What is he that builds stronger than either the mason, the shopwright, or the carpenter?" (V.i.41–42). In presaging Hamlet's announcement 217 lines later that he is "Hamlet the Dane," the gravedigger insists that profession is identity; from the play's initial interest in "*who*'s there?" act five, scene one returns again and again to "*what* is he?" Interestingly, the gravedigger is never referred to as "gravedigger" in the text of *Hamlet* (a text that is also unstable and, despite repeated efforts by editors, not unique[45]), but rather "Clown." He is defined not by who he is as a character, or what he does as a character, but what he is to the playing company. As with the attempt to understand the self by splitting it into two that share information, or taking two people similar in some way and imagining them as one person learning from a duplicate in the mirror, there is a complicated cognitive process—that is both profoundly creative and banal and basic—to make Frailty and Woman identical.

Bright's, and Hamlet's, interest in defining a unique self, formed and stabilized either internally or externally, are seen by cognitive linguists as a conceptual issue illuminated by the language used to speak of it. There is no unified self that is essential, objective, and stable; I understand today's "me" as the same as the "me" that lost my tooth when I was five while eating an apple even though very few of the cells are the same, the memories are created anew each time I recall an event, and my environment, perspective, and accumulated knowledge are all different. We need a way of stabilizing the self conceptually and cognitive linguists argue that this is revealed in and created by language. As I showed in the introduction, Lakoff sees this happening through metaphors that create similarity, as much as they reflect it. According to Fauconnier and Turner, the conceptual construction of the self happens by compressing vital relations—that can be imagined here as metaphors, because target and source are related in some way that allows target to be understood through reference to source (TIME IS MONEY)—such that identity becomes uniqueness. Put simply, identity is our ability to perceive sameness whereas uniqueness is seeing two as one. Uniqueness is when the body of the tanner *is* the tanning, when the butcher is not just changed by the slaughter but is so identified by it that the man underneath the profession is not available for jury duty. Like Virtue, this butcher is defined exclusively based on external behavior; he *is* slaughter and thus cannot serve on a jury because there seems to be no part in him that is not his behavior.

To unpack this relationship between cause and effect and the events hidden within them, I turn to Mark Turner's example of the conceptual integration network that forms the Christian understanding that "Jesus died for our sins."[46] In one space, Jesus is without sin and in another, humans have sins. The event of his death transfers his lack of sins to humans such that we are now relieved of them. But how can our sins go with Jesus when he dies? The event of his death is an effect and effects have causes. Once perceived as having a cause, the integration network of Jesus' death includes the possibility that something else can be caused by this event. This is necessary in order to imagine that the event of his death could *do* anything. There is also a network of spaces called upon to understand sins moving from one place to another. Like the personification of virtue, sins become objects and objects—unlike a sin, which is an action understood to be counterfactual to defined rules of behavior—can be transferred from one agent to another. As objects, they are also material things that can be held, and therefore, by transferring them to Jesus, they go with him when he dies. This is the emergent structure created by the blend but inexplicable without information from both input spaces. All of this is necessary to understand that the event of Jesus' death causes the transfer of our sins. There is no other way to make sense of "Jesus died for our sins," a statement so universally comprehensible and also extraordinarily complex and strange. His death becomes dramatic, meaningful, and iconic because we understand it not literally but as a blend; the blend then shapes how Christians think of the cross, suffering, death, and sin.

In *A Mirror for Magistrates,* identity is seen through the perspective of death, like a convex mirror warping while reflecting. Jim Ellis argues that *A Mirror for Magistrates* writes the doom of the men on their bodies, externalizing internal sins in its attention to the details of the, often gruesome, deaths.[47] Their stories are told for the way in which they operate as a compression of traits into a unique man; who they are is also why they are there. What he did in life becomes who he is and who he is kills him. This compression of vital relations also operates to obscure the difference between cause and effect, because the effect—the death of Jack Cade, for example, one of the men depicted in the book—is equated with the cause—the fortune that he had, or did not have, in his life. Important people do not stop living: they die because of something and this cannot be explained by "fortune," because, as Paul Budra argues, "It is a form of paganism to invoke fortune as the cause of our miseries, for this denies the agency of providence."[48] God has power; the individuals are either positive or negative exemplars of the hands that obey God's ends.

Budra notes that the descriptions of the deaths of women in *A Mirror for Magistrates* are written in the form of:

> autobiographies addressed by the ghost to the recording poet. They are first-person narratives delivered, often in a vision, to the writer. The poet plays both character and audience, both deceased, lamenting woman, and living, recording man. The poet grants both voice and text to the woman, and that text is history itself. As the women in these stories are dependent upon men for whatever political power they wield, so are their fictive ghosts dependent upon men for articulation.[49]

Budra's point here informs our reading of *Hamlet*: the ghost has no power without the poet and the poet is constituted by the story he is instructed to tell by the ghost. They are both constituted in the relationship, not in the individual, like Virtue seeing virtue in the mirror or, indeed, Hamlet becoming the character in a revenge tragedy of his name by being called up to do so by his dead father.

Assessing whether man is at the mercy of an all-powerful God or whether he controls his actions in life and therefore must take responsibility has remained a keystone question within philosophy and literature and thus, what causes the effect is (and must be) obscured by a compression of cause and effect, This, indeed, is the surrender Hamlet finds to his role in the revenge tragedy, "as theatrical character and as instrument of a revenge plot."[50] As Hamlet tells Horatio to explain why he will not avoid what is clearly a rigged fencing match, "Not a whit, we defy augury. There is special providence in the fall of a sparrow. If it be [now], 'tis not to come; if it be not to come, it will be now; if it be not now, yet it will come—the readiness is all. Since no man, of aught he leaves, knows what is't to leave betimes, Let be" (5.2.219–224). Whatever causes the effect matters little in light of it.

Yet this is not the perspective that instigates the revenge tragedy. As David Scott Kastan points out, revenge is an imitation of a prior act.[51] Fauconnier and Turner show how revenge is a blend of a future event with a past one, because the second murder does not become revenge without information projected from the initial murder space:

> the result is not one loss versus one win but instead a true integration in which the elements of the revenge situation are elements of the original situation. Enacting the integration network does not change the facts of the original situation as an input, but it does change the overall

defining context in which it sits, and it also eliminates the possibility that losing is a permanent or fundamental feature of the avenger.[52]

Revenge is defined not by the effect (death) but by what causes this death: murder two in response to murder one. What *Hamlet*'s revenge highlights, like the tales in *A Mirror for Magistrates*, is the importance of cause in determining effect. The ghost's instructions to Hamlet to act on behalf of him initiate a play in which Hamlet attempts to understand his role as actor or agent in life's tragedy and yet the idea of revenge paradoxically obscures agency by displacing it from the person who has been killed and wants to right it by wronging his murderer to the proxy he calls on to do this for him. Further, the ghost in *Hamlet* is unwilling to cede his material power on earth. As Crane notes, he does not tell Hamlet the "secrets of his prisonhouse" (1.5.14) because of what it would do to Hamlet, "The ghost argues that his discourse, if poured into Hamlet's ear, would have material effects on both soul and body."[53] Yet if the immaterial words that come from his immaterial being have this power, why does he need Hamlet to affect his revenge? Why not visit Claudius and pour his words into Claudius's ears, harrowing up the soul of his enemy? Because the ghost is not interested in Claudius dying, he is interested in Hamlet murdering.

The cause is more important than the effect here because if Hamlet causes the death of Claudius it is because he *intended* to, choosing his dead father's request over material, spiritual, ethical, and intellectual obstacles. Claudius dies due to blood loss—but without a focus on the cause of this blood loss, we do not have an agent with an intention. Someone, due to internal features or external behavior, must want to cause the effect, creating a causal chain and a human scale story. By calling attention to the difference between cause and effect, Shakespeare pulls apart their tight compression. Just as "to drown" means ceasing to be animate due to water inhalation: it is one word because we no longer think we need two. By troubling the single by making it a double, Shakespeare forces us to see where we create and deny agency, suggesting that perhaps we have more invested in obscuring the holder of the mirror than in inventing the single in the double reflection.

The dispersion of agency created by Hamlet's mirror is also found in his first articulation of the power of theater, "I have heard / That guilty creatures, sitting at a play, / Have by the very cunning of the scene / Been struck so to the soul that presently / They have proclaim'd their malefactions" (2.2.424–9). A scene capable of moving an audience member to confession is "cunning." The OED lists three definitions for cunning that also contain examples from Shakespeare's works. Under definition 2a, "possessing practical knowledge or skill," it cites *Twelfth Night*, "And if I thought he had been valiant and so cunning in fence" (3.4.312). Under definition 3, "possessing magical knowledge or skill," it cites *2 Henry VI* "A cunning man did calculate my birth, / And told me that by Water I should die" (4.1.34). And under definition 5a, the pejorative sense most commonly used today "skillful in compassing one's ends through covert means," it cites *Henry V*, "And whatsoever cunning fiend it was / That wrought upon thee so preposterously / Hath got the voice in hell for excellence" (2.2.111). In the three examples cited above, "cunning" describes a person who either has or wields a particular skill either for good or ill. In *Hamlet*, it describes a theatrical scene, as if the *scene*—by which he might mean the dialogue or the performance of dialogue or the situation of dialogue—acquires the agency necessary to plot or manipulate. Not unlike the mirror held up to nature, capable of being both biased and nonpartisan at the same time.

Crane calls Hamlet's mirror up to nature "relatively straightforward"[54] and yet deploying its complexity against *Hamlet* reveals a play that operates conceptually and linguistically to create the meaning found historically in this incessantly studied text. While Hamlet may be telling the players that theater should "simply" reflect, Shakespeare—or, to borrow Crane's useful phrase, "Shakespeare's language-processing functions"—uses the play to expose this impossibility.[55] The Mousetrap itself is an immediate example of the power of meaning superflux[56]—there is more than shakes easily off this mirror. We are not told which lines exactly Hamlet added, he objects to the dumbshow—which clearly telegraphs more than the mirror he had in mind—the Murder of Gonzago is done by the nephew to the king, not the brother, etc. We see in Hamlet's mirror what we hope to see: a whole body with an overflowing interiority just barely visible on the surface. Through the difference between what is reflected and what is experienced we imagine and fill in a self, capable of making sense of the visible pieces. *Hamlet* is a play that continues to contain more meaning than is dreamt of in our theory and philosophy. If *Hamlet* "reflected nature" the way Hamlet wants the Mousetrap to, we would have long ago stopped discussing it.

Hamlet's an Old Minnow

The perspective Shakespeare gives his audience of Elsinore is never singular. As Crane points out, Shakespeare leads the audience from outside the castle to the inside, moving from the watchmen guarding the castle in scene one to Gertrude's closet at the "center" of the castle in act three, scene four. Almost every character gives us his or her perspective on the prince, forcing TO SEE IS TO KNOW into conflict, because every character seems to have a different perspective on Hamlet. Shakespeare introduces the title character to his audience with a monologue extolling the virtues of questioning an assumption that outward appearances match internal truth:

> Seems, madam, Nay, it is. I know not "seems."
> 'Tis not alone my inky cloak, good mother,
> Nor customary suits of solemn black,
> Nor windy suspiration of forc'd breath,
> No, nor the fruitful river in the eye,
> Nor the dejected havior of the visage,
> Together with all forms, moods, shapes of grief,
> That can denote me truly. These indeed seem,
> For they are actions that a man might play;
> But I have that within which passes show,
> These but the trappings and the suits of woe. (1.2.76–86)

Shakespeare stages a play that self-deconstructs: scene after scene reminds us that things are rarely as they seem.

Shakespeare's language accretes perspectives as it goes along, vividly depicting what is not there. The sunrise in act one, scene one— "the morn in russet mantle clad / Walks o'er the dew of yon high eastward hill" (1.1.171–2), the depiction of the murder of King Hamlet and the description of Laertes by Reynaldo are all perspectives created by words. The ontological status of each (morning, murder, reputation) is very different, and this seems to be what Shakespeare's play aims to suggest, testing out the senses evoked by language for accuracy in intellection. The perspective the ghost could give Hamlet would, he warns, "harrow up" his soul and (as Jenkins notes) the OED lists this as the first example of the fourth definition of "harrow" (lacerate or wound the feelings of). Shakespeare could also be suggesting that the ghost's tale is like the "harrowe" defined in *Heresbach's Husbandry of* 1586, "The Harrowe, is an instrument crosse lettused, to break the Cloddes withall, and to cover the seedes." The noun (the instrument) used as a verb suggests a corporeality of the soul (capable of having clods), as physical as the young blood that might "freeze" or the eyes that could "start from their spheres." Rather than churning up Hamlet's soul or disconnecting his eyes, the ghost shifts Hamlet's perspective on a story he already knows, that of his father's death. The ghost's tale would dismember poor Hamlet, as Crane observed, and so he tells one *like* it.

There has been much interest in examining the early modern concern with the power of rhetorical perspective shifting to change minds.[57] Jonah Barish, Joel Altman, Louis Montrose, and Bryan Reynolds[58] all focus on the compelling argument for the power of the theater in the words of the antitheatricalists. Montrose cites a letter from Edmund Grindal, bishop of London, arguing that plays cause "infection," and notes, "The language of the letter suggests that the act of playgoing is itself the material source of the 'contagion,' that the youthful auditors quite literally take their 'infection' from the 'impure mouths' of the players."[59] As Reynolds argues, "Early modern antitheatricalists ascribe to the theater, as an open terrain where the imagination runs wild, a devilish power to alter transgressively the minds and wills of men and to foster demonic possession."[60] Although the antitheatricalists assumed themselves safe from contagion (because they generally did not attend the theater), they understood that exposing oneself to unsavory perspectives risked being infected. Today we speak of being "moved" by theater without questioning where we have been moved to or how long it will take us to get "back." In her essay on the "performance of self," Emily Bartels argues that in Shakespeare's plays, playing constitutes being, "the potential to speak and act as an independent subject comes through—and not despite—the embrace of prefabricated roles."[61] She uses Weimann's distinction between *locus* and *platea* to situate Shakespeare's characters and their internal selves. *Platea* figures, (such as Edmund, Iago, and Richard III) align themselves with the audience and in so doing bring the audience into their perspective. To explore the impact on an actor of this perspective shift, I want to look at the language used by a nonactor to describe his experience playing the role of Horatio.

Ira Glass, the host of *This American Life*, introduces a segment on *Hamlet* as performed by prisoners by asking what any of us can relate to in *Hamlet*: who among us has a father killed, a mother stained, or is plagued by a revenge-obsessed ghost? Instead of exploring the play based on a performance at one of the preeminent Shakespeare Festivals, reporter Jack Hitt suggests that there is much to learn about *Hamlet*, a play about a man contemplating a violent crime and its consequences, from people who have committed such a crime and are currently living with the consequences. His "Act V" story follows the rehearsals and production of *Hamlet*'s Act V within a maximum-security prison in Missouri.[62] With very little education and no acting training, these inmates make sense of Shakespeare's play because of where they have been and what they have seen. The piece tracks the perspective of the actors as they attempt to "get into" their characters and argues that their individual perspectives, their crimes and victims, were powerfully present in their performance. While the story is enchanting and their insights into the play refreshing, Hitt's argument that their perspectives make them uniquely qualified to perform this play seems less persuasive to me than the idea that their backgrounds make their performance deeper or more interesting to an audience. It is not surprising to me that Derrick "Big Hutch" Hutchison found it so easy to slip in and out of his character of Horatio; what is surprising is how hollow Horatio is without Big Hutch.

Big Hutch is one of the stars of Hitt's piece. He is the "killer whale," the top of the prison hierarchy, in an acting company composed mostly of "minnows." Hitt describes him as "the type of guy that if you met him you would think 'he's probably serving 120 years for armed robberies,' and that would be correct." Hitt's tape punctuates Big Hutch's comments with Hitt's laughter in the background; Hitt sounds so affected by the size and threat of this actor that his respect for Big Hutch's "literary criticism" seems tainted by the slightly patronizing surprise that someone so physically threatening could also provide insight. That being said, however, Big Hutch does give Hitt a compelling reading of Horatio, his own character:

> I think he's a chump for real...I mean, he's supposed to be cool with Hamlet, and they're best friends, but I think Horatio's somebody that...a sounding board for Hamlet. I mean a majority of his lines is "eh my lord...yes my lord." I mean if we're friends, we're going to communicate better than that. I mean: you're going to tell me your deepest secrets. You know, I wanna know what you and Ophelia did last night.

In addition to picking up on one of the longstanding mysteries about *Hamlet*—what did Hamlet and Ophelia do last night?—Big Hutch's rumination on Horatio and Hamlet's relationship exposes the ease with which Big Hutch is able to be Hutch, Horatio and Hamlet all in the same sentence.

The first thing he says is that he sees his character as a "chump," defined by www.urbandictionary.com as "Someone who does not understand the basics of life on earth. Confused easily" and "A sucka that tries to act cool, but is really a fool and tries to act tough, but really isn't."[63] Most actors (at least American-trained actors) avoid judging their characters objectively like this, because they are taught to get "inside" the character and view the character's perspective from within and such criticism might "block" identification with the character. Big Hutch looks squarely at Horatio from the distance required to assess a friendship that seems to him unequal and disconnected; he's judging his character as a character in a play, serving the plot, rather than requiring a back story, inside, and feelings. However, as soon as Big Hutch speaks a couple of Horatio's lines—even if they are "eh my lord" and "yes my lord"—he switches perspective. He goes on to refer to Hamlet and Horatio as "we," now speaking from Horatio's perspective.

In a smooth and effective rhetorical move, he then puts Hitt, the interviewer, in the perspective of Hamlet, "I mean, you're going to tell me your deepest secrets. You know, I wanna know what you and Ophelia did last night." Big Hutch has prompted Hitt to build a space where Big Hutch and Hitt are friends talking about Hitt's sexual escapades with Ophelia. Convict and interviewer are now in Shakespeare's play, navigating secrets and friendship. Hitt's tape again includes his laughter, and it is unclear to me if he is laughing at Big Hutch's casual reference to the Hamlet/Ophelia mystery, the idea of his being Hamlet and having such a secret or the idea of Big Hutch—the killer whale, the violent criminal—rhetorically establishing a friendship with Hitt, the NPR journalist and scholar.

Though Hitt credits Big Hutch for his "gift for literary criticism," suggesting that having such intelligence brings out his "inner minnow,"[64] I am interested in the rhetorical skills that Big Hutch wields by shifting perspectives.

> I don't see the conflict. I don't see what Hamlet is dealing with, man. "I should kill the king now, I shouldn't kill him now." Nah...you knew that once your father said revenge him, you knew you was going to do this. So what's the hubbub about? That's the same way I couldn't see someone raping my daughter or something and just sitting around...nah nah nah nah nah. I got to do you man, and that's just...you done. That's why I think Hamlet's an old minnow too.

Here Big Hutch has trouble taking Hamlet's perspective, and that difficulty helps to communicate the incomprehensibility of Hamlet's problem to Big Hutch. He interrupts his attempt at speaking from Hamlet's perspective ("I should kill the king now, I shouldn't kill him now") and quickly makes Hitt take the perspective of the wavering son ("you knew that once your father said revenge him, you knew you was going to do this"). He tries again by analogy with his own daughter and again cannot complete the thought without returning to Big Hutch's perspective.

Big Hutch then creates a corollary to Hamlet's dilemma by placing Hamlet in Big Hutch's situation, where revenging the death of a friend in prison could result in losing parole and thus a longer prison term. Here Big Hutch starts with Hamlet and moves at the end to talking about himself in the third person, "if he [meaning Hamlet as prison inmate] let that killing go, he have the roughest three years of his entire life. So I mean, he got this dilemma: will he be strong enough to survive that, to get out there and…Hutch wouldn't. I ain't going to lie…Hutch…." As his voice trails off, thinking about what Hutch would do from the perspective of the dramaturg/director he is playing in his conversation with Hitt and projecting Hutch onto the role of Hamlet, he sounds moved by his clear-eyed assessment of the type of man Big Hutch is. Hutch would kill the murderer of his friend, losing parole but protecting his status. In this last rhetorical formulation, Hutch is not Hamlet and is not Horatio; he is being not-Hutch in order to see Hutch.

At the final performance of Act V, Hutch "nails" his final speech to Hamlet, overcoming what Hitt calls his Jack Nicholson syndrome, wherein the "actor's persona is bigger than any role he might play," and in this performance "Horatio has Hutch under control and the audience in his hand." Underneath the cliché of a good performance that stipulates that the audience be reduced in size, swept up by the performers, held in their hands, Hitt intimates that part of what made the performance powerful to him was the blend of Big Hutch and Horatio that Hitt saw in the performance. The audience does not come to the theater to see Horatio; it comes to see Big Hutch's Horatio. Big Hutch learns to see his own story through the rehearsal of Horatio's; his embodied enaction of the character is profoundly effected by the experience of living in Horatio's environment. Horatio comes into being through his enaction: he *is* because Big Hutch *does* him. The relationship between the two, character and actor, performs what we need to know about perspective and language, self and other.

Hamlet's mirror held up to nature is Big Hutch's performance of *Hamlet*: both use language to decompress cause and effect, seeing, and knowing. Theater theory requires a constant taking and shifting of perspectives; talking about "house right" or "Polonius's line" encodes perspective into discourse immediately. Directors work to shape a performance from the protagonist's perspective, while ensemble actors color their performance to expose their characters' backgrounds and perspectives. For method actors (and therefore most of contemporary American actors), at least, the goal is to bring as much individual perspective to each character, as if only through a stage full of perspectives can the audience see the whole. Despite an assumption of difference between self and other, the ability to take on multiple perspectives breaks down that distinction, enables us to understand each other's parts, and makes us feel whole. Theater shows audiences a vision of a self in its play. Theater can create "that within which passes show," which may be why Hamlet, and so many since him, have found in theater's mirror a hidden inside and an internal sense of self. Theater provides an illusion of depth in a network of stories and truths. Theater constructs what it then reflects.

Chapter 5

Play's the Thing—A Cognitive Linguistic Performance Analysis

Conceptual blending theory seeks to understand the way in which language creates emergent structure—novel ideas, creative leaps, and powerful associations. But, as Fauconnier argues in "Compression and Emergent Structure," this comes not from the blend itself but from the way the final blend remains connected to the network of spaces evoked to understand the blend. He looks at complex numbers as something that can be taught to kids really quickly, the idea/blend in itself is simple, but the way it connects to past theories of numbers, space, and math is what makes it genius:

> The complexity lies in the construction of the entire network, i.e. in building links, projections and compressions from familiar inputs to novel but simple ones. This shows in turn that when we speak of "emergent structure" we don't mean the structure of the blended space by itself, but rather the dynamic structure of the entire network, and in particular the compressions and projections that link the input mental spaces to the novel blended spaces.[1]

A particular blend might vary from individual to individual. The network of spaces prompted in a given situation is more powerful as a process in flux, a series of variables, than simply a final blend. Almost by design, a complete description of the spaces within a network built by a blend is impossible, because there are an infinite number of possible associated spaces. The value of applying blending theory to a text or performance does not lie in its taxonomic abilities, but rather in how it maps the likely spaces and uncovers connections not immediately apparent, though maintaining power even in dormancy. Blending theory offers theater practitioners and scholars a tool to improve staging and design because it provides a way to understand what is meant when we say one thing "works" and another does not.

Literary critics and English teachers can read and experience the nuances and brilliance of Shakespeare's language, but the audience watching it must see it in the staging. The mirror held up to nature in *Hamlet* becomes the frame through which we view the play. The performance shows us how to read what's within the text based on an embodied language. A cognitive linguistic performance analysis reveals the frame that constitutes the mirror: a director who understands not just the play's metaphors or themes but who makes choices based on a rich understanding of the whole *network* of spaces required to make the structuring blend in the play will stage the play better. A staging informed by CBT will provide a foil for the play, revealing the cogency in what is a complicated and often ambiguous text. It will condense the diffused textual information into a production capable of finding virtue in nature. While it is uncontroversial to say that plays are not literary relics but dynamic prompts for production, I hope to persuade theater scholars and practitioners that meaning is not accidental in its artistry or mathematical in its semiotics, but is both profoundly creative and banal. Through reading performance as a site of meaning, I hope to persuade literary scholars and cognitive linguists that all language is embodied and that therefore a study of one must include a study of the other. I explore the meaning making in two different productions of *Hamlet* to show where CBT informs staging. I analyze the casting of Sam Shepard in Michael Almereyda's film, *Hamlet* (2000). Finally, I show how a cognitively inflected reading of performance—particularly manifested in actors' gestures—opens new avenues of research, theory, and practice.

Inexplicable Dumb Shows on an Unworthy Scaffold

Piece out our imperfections with your thoughts;
Into a thousand parts divide on man,
And make imaginary puissance;
Think when we talk of horses, that you see them
Printing their proud hoofs i' the receiving earth;
For 'tis your thoughts that now must deck our kings,
Carry them here and there; jumping o'er times,
Turning the accomplishment of many years
Into an hour-glass

As the Chorus reminds us at the start of *Henry V*, the power of theater is in the work of our imagination, seeing horses in galloping words and many years in an hourglass. The power of compression and imagination has been known long before Fauconnier and Turner; their contribution has not been to articulate the power of rhetoric or poetry, rather, they explore the creativity of every day speech; provide a tool for unveiling the elements both masked and highlighted in the language; and argue that understanding how the brain accomplishes these feats illuminates both how—and what—we think. Analyzing how meaning is made is important because it illuminates the scaffolding that structures the play. This scaffolding can be of vital importance to directors.

In *The Literary Mind*, Turner provides an excellent example of the importance of performance in reading Shakespeare's text. When a messenger arrives in *King John*, the king perceives the bad news on his face, "A fearful eye thou hast: where is that blood / That I have seen inhabit in those cheeks? / So foul a sky clears not without a storm / Pour down thy weather" (4.2.106). Turner unpacks the language that understands weather as news and also the way the king is simultaneously submitting himself to his powerlessness over the weather while maintaining an ability to command it to begin.[2] The full meaning of the line requires performance, as we must see the messenger kneeling before King John, lower than him, to understand the clashing construction of the weather being poured down from below. This may not be the type of performance element generally noted by theater critics and theorists ("a bold innovator, this director staged the messenger kneeling before the king!"), but the relationship of text to its performance is important to consider when examining how meaning is made in Shakespeare's plays. The performance of language onstage changes the dynamics of meaning through the networks of spaces evoked and blended in the process of understanding. Watching theater, we see a depth to ourselves created in the blending of actor/character, backstage/onstage, and house-space/stage-space.

Staging Shakespeare's plays involves rendering visual a selection of images within the language in order to tell the story to contemporary, and more visual, audiences. The language of black and white in *Othello*, for example, will find expression in costumes, lights, and props and such decisions—is the world in high-contrast black and white or Technicolor? How white is Desdemona's nightgown?—will guide the audience's interpretation of the play. While the image of the mirror in *Hamlet* may not be as central as black and white in *Othello* or night and day in *Macbeth*, Hamlet's description of a theatrical ideal that holds "as 'twere the mirror up to nature" does offer a director an opportunity to integrate reflection into his or her staging of the play. The mirror forms an important pivot point in the play, around which meaning (I argue) is either made or lost. However, this does not necessitate the presence of a mirror onstage. Any set designer could explain the practical difficulties of designing with mirrors—unlike the mirror described by Hamlet, a mirror onstage indiscriminately reflects what is before it, often diffusing light meant to focus the audience's attention, reflecting characters or offstage business not meant to be seen, and/or reflecting the audience itself, bringing them onstage. A mirror onstage complicates the relationship between actor and character, surface and depth. Below I trace the use of the mirror onstage and investigate how new meaning emerges with the object in performance.

For Tiffany Stern, areas of the stage take on meaning in one production and carry it forward into the next, such as the trap door, "The trap presumably came to represent a cumulative evil. Much in the theater, props particularly, worked in this way, borrowing their natures partly from the collective character they had built up through use in many plays."[3] For Stern, this impacts the reception of the ghost of King Hamlet: because his voice is heard below and the actor (presumably) entered through the trap, the audience would associate the ghost with hell and the devil.[4] Not surprisingly, the meaning of the text is complicated by the meanings evoked through performance. Though Stern does not use the language of cognitive linguistics, she articulates an accretion of meaning that can be explained using blending theory. As Stern argues in her account of the way props, stage areas, and actors accrued meaning through performances, leading all performances to be an amalgam of past performances, "In making one play gesture towards another, Shakespeare upsets the difference between one separate text and another."[5]

The players in *Hamlet* do not belong in the rotten world of Denmark created by Shakespeare up to that point. They are commenting on the theatrical moment in London contemporary with the first performance of the play—boy players sending the professional companies into the countryside—not to further the spectator's understanding of *Hamlet*, but to further the spectator's experience in the Globe at that moment, privy to inside information that enriches these players by displaying the players playing them. Shakespeare's use of ironic anachronism occurs again before the Mousetrap, when Hamlet asks Polonius about his acting past. Polonius says, "I did enact Julius Caesar. I was killed i'th' Capitol. Brutus killed me" and Hamlet responds, "It was a brute part of him to kill so capital a calf there" (3.2.101–4). Editor Harold Jenkins notes that the original actors of Hamlet and Polonius probably played Caesar and Brutus in the 1599 production of *Julius Caesar*.[6] Shakespeare plays with the similarities—the same "Globe," the same actors—while the audience puts the similarities together with the differences.

The network required to construct the meanings of a particular casting choice (e.g., Burbage as Hamlet or Polonius as Julius Caesar) constantly gestures beyond the play to an extratextual dialogue.[7] Stern's analysis of the *Julius Caesar* conversation in *Hamlet* points out the particularity of the theatrical reference: Shakespeare could have had Polonius refer to a role not included in the plays of his own writing (e.g., Polonius could have played Herod), but then Shakespeare would have been referring to another text, not just another performance. If, as is assumed, Burbage played Hamlet in 1600 and Brutus the year before, Polonius is simultaneously speaking to both Hamlet and Burbage. Burbage, onstage in 1600 as Hamlet, cannot completely slip the roles he has played in the past; in fact, Stern recounts Burbage's elegy that states that he was so important to the roles he played that they died with him, "No more young Hamlett, ould Heironymoe / Kind Leer, thee greved Moore, and more beside, / That lived in him; have now for ever dy'de."[8] Stern's argument views this gesturing as an example of a kind of contingent meaning, where a full understanding of the moment depends upon an understanding of the performance history of *Julius Caesar*.

Andrew Sofer's *The Stage Life of Props* looks at the evolution of meaning around specific stage properties as they moved across the stage and into different plays. He insists on the "vitality" of props onstage and that:

> Theater colonizes reality for its own ends, and in the case of the prop it does so by appropriating the object's prior symbolic life. As a result of this theatrical appropriation, each prop I discuss revises or attempts to revise the way objects signify for spectators.[9]

Tracing the handkerchief from early liturgical drama through to Othello's ocular proof, Sofer shows how Shakespeare used the accumulated meaning to his advantage. Sofer's position that "The Elizabethan playwrights who wrote for a nascent commercial theater were eager to exploit the rituals of the old religion"[10] relies on the assumption that the rituals of the old religion would transfer from church to theater and that the objects associated with the rituals would maintain their meaning.

Sofer's account of how the cloth from the early liturgical drama became associated with Christ even though a symbol of His absence could be productively expanded using theories of cognitive science. How does that symbol operate? Bruce McConachie, for example, points to Pierre Jacob and Marc Jeannerod's theory of "visual intentionalism" wherein visual information is processed based on how we intend to use the information. Information that does not require, depict, or suggest intentional action is a "visual perception" (McConachie uses the example of the landscape above the skene at the Theatre of Dionysus) whereas information that does engage intentional attention generates a "visuomotor representation" (e.g., Oedipus stabbing his eyes or the usher handing us our program).[11] He applies this as a counterargument to a semiotic understanding of theatrical elements because they are not processed just based on their "sign" but based on the character's intentions:

> When they [spectators] want to understand what an actor/character is doing with a particular costume (e.g., Malvolio in cross-gartered stockings wooing Olivia or Stanley in red pajamas taunting Blanche), viewers engage their visuomotor representation. In this instance, because spectators are primarily interested in an actor/character's intentions, cross-garterteredness and redness are secondary effects, not the focus of attention. Semioticians often use this "costuming" and "color" as general categories for signs related to an actor/character's clothing, and this category has a certain common sense validity for theatre people. But these categories, like many semiotic categories, try to account for the meaning of a group of signs that are processed very differently by the mind/brain; they are not cognitively coherent. Saussurean semiotics does not account for the differences between visual perceptions and visuomotor representations.[12]

A different conception of how we process visual information, like a different conception of meaning composition, requires a different method of performance analysis.[13]

From the rise of the curtain to the bow of the actors, theater prompts for blends. Hamlet walks onstage and the space that is "Hamlet" has already been blended with the input spaces of the actor playing the role, the character, and the character's role in the play that bears his name.

Fauconnier and Turner depict dramatic performances as blends:

> The character portrayed may of course be entirely fictional, but there is still a space, a fictional one, in which that person is alive. We do not go to a performance of *Hamlet* in order to measure the similarity between the actor and a historical prince of Denmark. The power comes from the integration in the blend. The spectator is able to live in the blend, looking directly on its reality.... The importance and power of living in the blend would be hard to overestimate.[14]

Embodied in the actor's body, "Hamlet" can become Hamlet. The actor is never invisible, never wholly subsumed by the identity of the character, "While we perceive a single scene, we are simultaneously aware of the actor moving and talking on a stage in front of an audience, and of the corresponding character moving and talking within the represented story world."[15] McConachie applies this to an understanding of actor/character as "a blend of real people and fictional people whom audiences readily credit with real intentions and emotions when they live in the blend while watching a play."[16] In order to live in this blend where Kevin Kline or Peter Stormare is the most famous dramatic character in theater history, an audience member can (but may not) forget how much she paid for her seat or whom she is sitting next to or what happens next onstage. While the body onstage playing Hamlet is already a blend, *Hamlet*, the play, prompts for a blend, because theatrical representation necessarily must blend that which is being represented (Hamlet's story of revenge) with people on a stage speaking lines.

Ingmar Bergman brought his theatrical production of *Hamlet* to the Brooklyn Academy of Music (BAM) in 1988.[17] In Swedish, Bergman's *Hamlet* was well received by the critics. Even without speaking Swedish, the BAM audience recognized the places where Bergman shifted the staging to alter the play. Ophelia (played by Pernilla August) and the ghost (played by Per Myrberg) haunt many scenes; in half-light they watch as Hamlet (played by Peter Stormare) talks to Rosencrantz and Guildenstern (played by Johan Lindell and Johan Rabaeus) or as he plots with the player king (played by Per Myrberg). At the end, Fortinbras's (played by Joakim Westerberg) army arrives like the Marines, carrying the bodies upstage and tossing them into a mass grave. For Bergman, Hamlet's attempt to examine, to anatomize the facts before taking action, is a form of action and only a knife's edge separates thought, feeling, and action.

Bergman literalized the idea of a mirror with the reflecting side of a stage knife. Stormare's/Hamlet's anatomizing knife is first used during his advice to the players: the purpose of playing speech with the mirror at its center. He picks up the players' stage knife and holds it up when he talks about a mirror that can "show virtue her feature, scorn her own image, and the very age and body of the time his form and pressure" (3.2.22–4). Stormare's/Hamlet's gesture calls attention to the knife's reflective abilities and its trick nature: it retracts like a fake stage knife. Soon after peering into it as the theatrical mirror, he demonstrates it as a representation of a knife in a passionate stabbing of the Myrberg/player king meant to seem strangely serious. As Stormare's/Hamlet's emotions get the better of him, and he begins plunging the knife into the Myrberg's/player king's back, the audience is reminded of why stage knives are used in the first place: passion or carelessness aside, a fake knife will not hurt. A stage knife represents a knife without actually being a knife; a stage knife represents a thing that can kill by being decidedly something that cannot kill. Bergman's use of the stage knife as a mirror allows him to represent a mirror with an object already notable for privileging the representational by denying the actual.

Bergman creates the image of a mirror onstage through the use of symmetry in his staging. The coronation scene, the Mousetrap, and the final fencing match are staged symmetrically, duplicating members of court in a *mise en abîme* of red-robed men or reflecting the image of Laertes (played by Pierre Wilkner) with sword drawn in

Figure 5.1 The duel begins, Ingmar Bergman's *Hamlet*
Produced by Brooklyn Academy of Music, 1988; photography by Bengt Wanselius.

the image of Hamlet with sword drawn (figure 5.1). Throughout the duel, Bergman calls attention to how the fighters can only stay alive if they maintain symmetry; the mirror becomes a scale, held in balance only as both remain on either side of the mirror. Stormare/Hamlet and Wilkner/Laertes must mirror one's thrust with the other's parry as a "palpable hit" results from an imbalance. In fact, even as the fight nears its end, the stage picture holds up the mirror between Stormare/Hamlet and Wilkner/Laertes as long as possible (figure 5.2). Through

Figure 5.2 The duel ends, Ingmar Bergman's *Hamlet*
Produced by Brooklyn Academy of Music, 1988; photography by Bengt Wanselius.

the doubling of images, Bergman locates the mirror onstage in an absence, in the place equidistant between the doubles where the reflecting occurs. In this way, he is able to stage the idea of a mirror in the lacuna between images.

The Mousetrap occurs up on a long table, with Gertrude (played by Gunnel Lindblom) and Claudius (played by Börje Ahlstedt) sitting in chairs upstage of the actors on the table and Stormare/Hamlet and August/Ophelia sitting on the floor downstage of the performance. As the Myrberg/player king and queen (played by Marie Richardson) perform a silent courtship, they do indeed form the mirror that Stormare/Hamlet suggests theater should be, with a watching couple on one side of them being reflected in the couple on the other side of them. The players are placed midway between the Ahlstedt/King and Lindblom/Queen and Stormare/Prince and August/Ophelia, exactly where a mirror would need to be to reflect the image of one to the other. While the reflection is clear in the staging, it is left open who is assessing whom in the reflection being performed. And the play within the play is already a mirror within a mirror, because the audience is either reflected in the performance of Ahlstedt/Claudius and Lindblom/Gertrude watching the players, Stormare/Hamlet and August/Ophelia watching the Ahlstedt/Claudius and Lindblom/Gertrude watching, the players watching the courtiers, or all three, seeing our watching in the watching we are watching.[18]

The one time an actual mirror is used onstage, it is used to communicate through symbolism, rather than reflection. The closet scene begins with Lindblom/Gertrude holding a small hand mirror up to her face. The audience does not see the mirror or the reflection, but Lindblom's/Gertrude's pose (her bent right arm holding the mirror, tilted head, long dress, and outstretched left arm) immediately suggests classic images of vanity.[19] Even though the scene begins with a mirror, Stormare/Hamlet holds a knife up to Lindblom/Gertrude when he talks about the glass capable of reflecting her inner parts. Neither of them looks into either of the reflecting surfaces, satisfied with the idea of the reflection rather than the specific image reflected. This representation of a mirror conveys the idea of reflection without being big enough to actually show her (or the audience) enough to distract with actuality of reflection. The knife also suggests the kind of threat such an invasive examination would be, making explicit the idea of a mirror that can be a scalpel capable of beginning an autopsy. The mirror Hamlet's language evokes is similar to the manuals of correction popular in the sixteenth century; yet Bergman's use of the knife to symbolize this mirror echoes the movement in the seventeenth century toward the use of "anatomy" or "anatomize" to represent an unveiling of hidden sins.[20] While Bergman rarely uses an actual mirror onstage, he unpacks the mirror blend and stages the spaces that make up our conception of a mirror. His staging is successful because he does *not* stage a mirror; he stages the ideas that make up the idea of a mirror prior to being condensed into the image or metaphor we know so well we no longer think about it.

Reviewing the production, Mel Gussow claims that although Bergman's *Hamlet* is entirely in Swedish, with no subtitles, "our familiarity with 'Hamlet' leads us to think that we know some Swedish."[21] Bergman's representational mirror helps an audience understand Swedish by physicalizing the main conceptual blend of the play. He does this by playing with the liminal space between representation and real as exhibited through the mirror and through symmetry that creates a mirror at the place of duplication. Though we may not be conscious of the degree to which mirroring structures the language of the play, Bergman's production is proof that a rich and varied representation of the structuring metaphor can enable an audience to hear *Hamlet* in Swedish.

In 1986, Livliu Ciulei directed Kevin Kline in a production of *Hamlet* at the New York Shakespeare Festival Public Theater. Ciulei's production was dark and politically charged—Gussow called it "Bismarckian–more German than Danish"—turning the focus away from Fortinbras and the dangers from without to the corruption within. Ciulei used a vanity mirror in several scenes to focus attention on the troubled surface—the outward presentation of self that one perfects while sitting in front of a vanity, applying makeup or fixing hair—and the corruption within the state of Denmark. Kline/Hamlet uses it to put on clown makeup while he instructs Horatio (played by Richard Frank) to watch his uncle's reaction to the play and also as he begins his advice to the players. Here Ciulei's mirror focuses attention on the masks put on to generate and circulate power.

Ciulei's mirror seems situated to reflect more contemporary theories of power, corruption, and performance. As Clifford Geertz has shown, the performance of power is also a masking of the making of power, "The very thing that the elaborate mystique of court ceremonial is supposed to conceal—that majesty is made, not born—is demonstrated by it."[22] Greenblatt pursues Geertz's argument finding that the creation of courtly charisma occurs through exposing and then repairing a charismatic center.[23] Similarly, Montrose explores the "performativity of sovereignty" of the Elizabethan court and the power of performance, both within and outside of the theater.[24] This mirror creates the outward show hiding an inner power and also can be used to see in to Gertrude to reveal her inward spots. Once staged, however, this mirror does not reflect with the theoretical clarity of Geertz or Montrose. Ciulei's actual mirror has a slippery reflection onstage and does not communicate a single meaning.

At center stage, Kline/Hamlet prepares for his role—as trickster clown, perhaps—while the actors prepare on stage left and the court prepares stage right. Ciulei stages Hamlet/Kline and his mirror as the mirror of one preparation for the other, suggesting that the performance of the role of performer is similar to the performance of the role of audience. Of course, this underlines the flaw in Hamlet's logic about the exposure of Claudius' (played by Harris Yulin) guilt: if everyone is creating a performative mask prior to the performance, there is no reason to believe that Yulin's/Claudius' face will be free from masks—and thus display his internal feelings of guilt—during the performance. Gussow finds this scene particularly effective, "In one of the director's most vivid images, while the players don their costumes for their performance, on the other half of the stage the members of the court dress to play their roles in the theatre of life. Anchoring both halves is Mr. Kline's mesmeric Hamlet. Instructing the players, he puts clown makeup on his face and then acts as interlocutor for 'The Murder of Gonzago.'"[25] In Gussow's description, Kline/Hamlet and the mirror are located at the vanishing point of both reflections. Placed between two sets of actors performing identical tasks, Kline/Hamlet as interlocutor physicalizes the mirror he hopes the coming theatrical presentation will be.

The vanity mirror also appears in the closet scene, though Kline/Hamlet does not refer to the mirror when he mentions finding his mother a mirror to show her inward spots. In fact, the mirror is not used or touched by either of them. Upstaging Gertrude (played by Priscilla Smith) and Kline/Hamlet, the mirror takes on a charged meaning, despite, and maybe because, it is not used by the actors. The mirror is angled down, as if Smith/Gertrude sat in front of the mirror in order to see her stomach. The angle seems chosen for its ability to avoid reflecting the lights or the audience, rather than its usefulness. Unlike the magical X-ray mirror proposed by Kline/Hamlet, this mirror can only show what is below; it only reflects a different angle on what can just as well be seen without it.

Ciulei's attempt to manage the reflection in the mirror calls attention to the star playing his Hamlet. In his review, Gussow comments, "Mr. Kline has not settled for one face of Hamlet, but offers a variegated version—devoted son, avenging angel, devious actor." Though Gussow means that Hamlet's character also contains a "devious actor," it is also true that Kline's Hamlet deviously puts forth the face of the film star playing him. Kline's/Hamlet's application of another face in the Mousetrap scene calls attention to the performativity of state and the corruption and masking within this Denmark. In performance, though, the mirror he looks into complicates this reading. Ciulei stages the scene so that the audience is shown Kline's/Hamlet's face as it transforms with the clown makeup, but not the reflection of his face in the mirror. Though the audience watches the character apply stage makeup, the mirror calls to mind the actor, not the character. Because the character of Hamlet is not applying makeup or looking into the mirror, but only the eyes of the actor, only Kline can be reflected in the mirror. Kline cannot see Hamlet's reflection and so the audience sees Kline in the looking; what was combined into one—Kline/Hamlet—becomes two in the mirror: Kevin Kline playing Hamlet.

As several of the commentaries and reviews of this production note, Kevin Kline is the face that launched the production, the film star surrounded by actors "not in his solar system."[26] As is often the case with productions of *Hamlet*, the star gets better lighting, special placement onstage, and often carte blanche for upstaging other actors. The first scene, where the guardsmen encounter the ghost, is practically not lit at all and the second scene gets brighter only when Kline/Hamlet enters. Ciulei gives Kline/Hamlet a special entrance at the beginning of the court scene, having him enter before Yulin/Claudius and receiving the bowing and deference by courtiers onstage that we would associate with the King. Because this is Kline's first entrance—as well as Hamlet's—Ciulei and Kline can be forgiven for assuming that the entrance would occasion applause. Kline/Hamlet takes in the honor with surprise and humility—the character responding to the clapping courtiers and Kline responding to the applauding audience. Ciulei stages the entrance so that both Hamlet and Kline can take their time receiving the adoration from both audiences. The moment disconnects the identity of the actor and character, so the audience sees him as both. Like the mirror that reflects an editorialized version of what stands before it, Ciulei's production of *Hamlet* uses the star power of one to comment on the star power of the other. From the start, the face of the star and the face of the character are welded together; not merged, but rather combined—Janus-faced—separate but equally visible. It is not that the casting of Kline as

Hamlet creates a rich *Hamlet*, it is that this *Hamlet* oscillates between presenting the face of the star and the face of the character.

Both Bergman's and Ciulei's productions of *Hamlet* stage the language of the play's mirror blend. How they do so shifts the meaning of the language. An embodied theory of language suggests that there is a link between our experience of our body interacting with our environment and the concepts, metaphors, and blends that shape how we think and talk about our world. The mirror comes to represent a tool for seeing that which is hidden or internal because of how we use it physically and then how that use is blended with other mental spaces for seeing, self, depth, and so on. How we understand the mirror in the poetry is impacted by information gained in the staging of the play. In Ciulei's *Hamlet*, the mirror's impotence reflects the power of the star's presence to upstage the character; in Bergman's *Hamlet*, the mirror—present representationally while absent practically—reflects the poetry's ability to communicate through the indirection of its images. As Polonius explains to Reynaldo, there is more truth in a network of biases, than an accurate summation of qualities.

Directors and playwrights have relied on rich networks of associations and blends in their storytelling and staging, yet no one has studied this in relation to cognitive theories of linguistics or perception. Fauconnier and Turner point out that analyses of individual blends can be found across the academy, but what has been missing is an appreciation for the banality and cognitive complexity of blending. Whether or not Bergman shaped his *Hamlet* around symmetry because he saw its relationship with the mirror at the play's center or not, the success of his staging suggests that conceptual blending theory can assist a director in choosing which image to depict. While I am not suggesting that cognitive linguistics can provide an equation for good directing, it might provide new experiments to try. Blending theory allows us to see meaning as a rich web of spaces that may not always make sense, but seem to help the play to work. Cognitive linguistics calls our attention to the contingency in all meaning. Tracing the spaces within the integration network that produce a blend—Kline's entrance as Hamlet, for example—illuminates the relationships between ideas tacitly or overtly evoked by the final blend. Where traditional literary and theater theory focuses on understanding images, metaphors, juxtapositions, and meaning in general, conceptual blending theory provides a methodology that connects seemingly disparate moments into a scaffold that gains power as it grows.

Casting—to out-Herod Herod

There has been tremendous interest in casting and celebrity in theater and performance studies. Marvin Carlson argues that celebrity performance is "ghosted" by past performances and that "each new appearance requires a renegotiation with those memories."[27] What is this renegotiation process? How are performances calibrated to constrain some ghosts and not others? Stern suggests that certain characters in the plays bear the marking of the actor used to play him, such as the clown roles written for Robert Armin versus those written for Will Kempe. Like the trap, "actors may have had a series of composite character types built up over years of performance which affected every play they were in by every author."[28] Michael Quinn's semiotic reading of casting says that there is "something about dramatic performance that causes spectators to seek information about the personal life of the performer" and he finds that celebrities intrude in the "creative genius" of the author or director, without examining the creativity of the casting or the rich ways a director can use the "intrusion" to complement his own "genius."[29] Bert States's phenomenological explanation is to find in the "competition" between actor and character a kind of electrical charge.[30]

Joseph Roach has exploded notions of performance in his work, examining "how culture reproduces and re-creates itself by a process that can be best described by the word *surrogation.*"[31] In theorizing about the role of actor as effigy, Roach cites George Farquhar speaking about a performance of Thomas Betterton: "Yet the whole Audience at the same time knows that this is Mr. Betterton, who is strutting upon the Stage, and tearing his Lungs for a Livelihood. And that the same Person shou'd be Mr. Betterton, and Alexander the Great, at the same Time, is somewhat like an Impossibility, in my Mind."[32] It is *exactly* like an impossibility in his mind, because an impossibility is a counterfactual blend: it is a thing defined in relation to its relative possible-ness. These multiple understandings—he is an actor strutting on a stage and Alexander the Great—are held up together to form a constellation of things that define what is being watched. What Farquhar finds to be "somewhat like an Impossibility" is the same cognitive ability that children use to understand the talking mother fisherman bunny. Isolating something as one thing, rather than an amorphous assemblage of potentials is actually a far more complicated cognitive task.

Roach's recent work on "It" examines the mysterious "charm" or presence that "we know when we see" but has not been bottled, sold, or taught at BFA or MFA programs. He defines "It" as "the power of projecting contradictory essences in the same role, even in the same gesture.... Theatrical performance is the simultaneous experience of mutually exclusive possibilities—truth and illusion, presence and absence, face and mask."[33] This focuses on a quality of the actor or actress, separate from any particular role, yet describes a process of balancing sometimes "impossible contradictions" in the processing of performance.[34] It is deeply attractive, though not necessarily beautiful; It is vulnerable and combustible; It is seductive and yet "unbiddable."[35] This It blurs the boundaries between self and other, "Perhaps then,... actors with It are not merely there *for* us; they are there *instead* of us—there to live the sort of lives we can imagine and desire but for which we lack the courage, the gift, or the luck—in short, the It—to live for ourselves. In that sense, we are also there for them."[36] To experience this "vicarious It," this "surrogacy," is to be in more than one body at a time, to see from several perspectives at the same time, and to exist in a space where truth, illusion, fiction, nonfiction, face, and mask cease to be in opposition.

Roach's work tends to focus on moments of great theatrical interest: the theoretical shift in acting theory of Diderot's *The Paradox of Acting*, the funeral processions of New Orleans jazz musicians, and the powerful charisma of Marlon Brando, for example. These extraordinary events have led Roach to extraordinary theoretical work; yet, what is the relationship between the extraordinary and the ordinary here? While Marlon Brando might be special, any actor performing a role allows a spectator to be simultaneously herself and himself at the same time. The pretend play of children and the rich performance strategies of a funeral procession depend upon similar cognitive abilities. McConachie's formulation of the actor/character blend is tremendously productive, as it compels a reexamination of the phenomenology of spectatorship and our engagement with fiction. For McConachie the actor/character is never a fixed and stable entity but a fluid organism, created and manipulated by the audience:

> To create an actor/character, spectators take knowledge from three different mental concepts—certain qualities from the conceptual primitive "actor" (that he/she is alive, can move, has certain vocal characteristics, etc.), some knowledge about the "character" (that he/she has a certain past, faces specific situations in the present, etc.), and the cognitive concept of "identity." [...] All conceptual blends are

selective in these kinds of ways. The imaginative process of creating actor/characters begins for spectators with the conceptual universal of identity as a kind of template and then transforms it to create a new, more specific, and complex identity, such as Brando/Stanley in *Streetcar*.[37]

Seen from this perspective, Roach's "It" is a blend: contradictory information is projected from different spaces to generate emergent structures. Marlon Brando's "desperate vulnerability that underlies the male drive toward sexual domination" may be unpacked differently by each audience member, but to experience Brando's performance (e.g., in *A Streetcar Named Desire*) is to integrate a network of perhaps previously disconnected spaces. Perhaps Brando is able to excite a wider network of associations in the spectator's brain than Karl Malden,[38] but both of these performances require a complicated processing of perspectives, identities, associations, emotions, and bodies. I want to take up his argument about how spectators oscillate between seeing the actor and seeing the character to question the ways in which the blend is created and constrained by the director's casting.

> I am thy father's spirit,
> Doom'd for a certain term to walk the night,
> And for the day confin'd to fast in fires,
> Till the foul crimes done in my days of nature
> Are burnt and purg'd away. (1.5.9–13)

Anytime an actor plays a character an audience creates a blend to read the performance. Perhaps more exciting than the rare cases of "It" is the simultaneous banality of blending to create the actor/character perceived onstage or on screen. In fact, deploying conceptual blending theory to directorial choices can unveil It in the collision of actor/character. Whether or not Sam Shepard has It, cast as the ghost of Hamlet's father in Michael Almereyda's *Hamlet* (2000),[39] he brings more to the screen than seems possible to fit in the time and space allowed. This casting choice provides an excellent example of how a cognitive linguistic performance analysis can uncover some of the sources of impossible contradictions held together in a theatrical/cinematic space.

Almereyda films his *Hamlet* in a modern panoptic city, making Elsinore a corporation and Hamlet's father the previous CEO. Shakespeare's Hamlet is a scholar and Almereyda's Hamlet is a videographer. Shakespeare's Hamlet takes in information via "words,

words, words" (2.2.192); Almereyda's Hamlet takes in information televisually, by recording, watching, and projecting the world around him on a video. Ethan Hawke plays Hamlet and Sam Shepard plays his father. Throughout the film, Hawke/Hamlet watches pixilated, black and white eyes stare back at him on his monitor, looking for understanding not only with his eyes, but in the eyes. One of his video memories of his father that he plays and replays on his screen is of Shepard/CEO-Hamlet pushing away the son's intrusive camera lens. To say that Shepard's performance is "ghosted" by his persona fails to capture the presence of the absence.

In "The Ghost of Anyone's Father," Mark Turner counters Greenblatt's claim that the ghost in *Hamlet* is unlike any other ghost. Just like all conceptual ghosts, Turner avers, the ghost of King Hamlet conforms to the same "ghost physics" commonly understood to control other ghosts. Ghosts share some properties with the living (they move, talk, think) and some properties with the dead (they cannot die). A ghost is "a concept for which there is no referent, no evidence"[40] and thus it must be created through blending. He looks at the blend that has given human beings a soul, which comes from "our most familiar conceptual frames, called 'Caused Motion' "[41] wherein that which does the motion is seen as separate from that which motivates it. Because the body, conceived of as a container, requires a force to cause motion, there must be a soul that resides in a living body and out of a dead body. That which causes the body to move, separated from the body, can then be understood as another version of the self, the soul:

> since a person appears to have a body that is identical to the body we see after the death of the person, we can make a blend in which the disanalogy connection between the person and the body is compressed to create an *absence* in the blend of the cause of the movement and the sensation. In this blend, the human body becomes a *corpse*—that is a *lifeless* human body, a body whose animation is *absent*.[42]

This blend yields emergent structure that can be seen in many of the ways death and self are manifested in language as well as in the plots of Shakespeare.[43]

If the soul, a nonthing created through blending, is present in the person and absent from the corpse, then, "when the soul is absent from the body, it is because it is present somewhere else; that the soul is in single space-time location; that death is the departure of the soul from the body as it journeys to another place."[44] The soul separated from the body becomes the ghost, often figured in the shape of the body it came from, but without the constraints of "earthly" physics. These constraints drive the "ghost physics" wherein the ghost maintains elements of the dead King (his appearance, his memory, his intentions), but not others. While neither a dead body nor an alive body can move through physical objects, the blended "ghost" space can move through physical objects. The ghost takes the shape of the body it once resided in, but not its physical materiality, "In the same figure like the King that's dead" (1.1.41). It can talk and walk, but cannot effect material change directly; that is, the ghost cannot get his own revenge.

Of course, Turner is not speaking of the actor/character "ghost" here; he refers to the conceptual ghost created by Shakespeare. Once staged, the ghost (generally) gains an actor's body, one that cannot escape its materiality. Certainly stage directors can use tricks to suggest the ghost physics Turner points out, but the meaning of the ghost in a particular production requires that the spectator selectively project information from their "ghost" mental space (e.g., Halloween costumes or the noise in the attic) with information from their interpretation of the ghost in *Hamlet* (e.g., a devil sent to tempt Hamlet to commit a sin) with the mental space created by the performance of this ghost in this performance (e.g., lights, costume, casting). On film, directors have more power to stage the ghost physics but the emergent meaning of the particular actor/ghost remains a blend.

Leonard Maltin opens his short biography of Shepard with a description of his talents: "While his rugged good looks, sinewy frame, and pleasant drawl seem to make this actor an all-American hero in the Gary Cooper mold, Shepard's background renders him something more than that. He is also a highly regarded playwright who won the Pulitzer Prize for his 1979 play 'Buried Child.'" For those unfamiliar with Shepard's playwriting career, his evocation of the "Gary Cooper mold" might suggest Marshal Will Kane from *High Noon* (1952), or simply the cliché of the strong, silent type. If one is only familiar with Shepard from *The Right Stuff* (1983), his ghost will remind one of Chuck Yeagar. If, however, the audience is familiar with Shepard's literary output, they might think of him as "the elusive cowboy of American theater"[45] or as the anatomizer of family disfunction who favors San Francisco's Magic Theatre over Broadway. While there are many possible inputs to the Sam Shepard mental space, Shepard's value for Almereyda comes in the cogency of his persona.

Though each casting choice carries meaning based on the elements of the actor automatically brought to the screen with him (age, race, physical type, vocal mechanics), not all actors come with such precise personas. Shepard's biography is free of roles or details that conflict with the image above. Particularly for a smaller role like the ghost, where audiences are not given the same amount of time with or information about the character, casting Sam Shepard is casting that persona. Casting a star with a concise persona allows a director to enrich a small part by strenuously projecting information from the star's real life onto the character; such a casting choice provides a director with a short hand. Casting Billy Crystal as the gravedigger in his *Hamlet* (1996), Kenneth Branagh could be assured that the scene would be perceived as funny before anyone speaks a line. The power of the blend is more clearly articulated in these roles because the performance depends on so much more information from the "actor" space to build the "character" space. The tradition of the cameo also allows actors to reify their persona by playing their persona in a movie. Playing a small role in a film should not be attractive to an actor who is accustomed to being the star or the lead. But actors get to use cameos to shore up their personas (Robin Williams as slightly foppish comedian with a strenuous language sense in Branagh's *Hamlet*) and/or complicate their personas (Tom Cruise as the ugly and despised film executive in *Tropic Thunder* (2008)). I would not want to argue that Cruise has what Roach calls "It," but maybe when combined with Les Grossman he has "them."[46]

Almereyda juxtaposes Shepard with Ethan Hawke and thus foregrounds thematic elements in the relationship between Hamlet and his father. With Shepard as the CEO father that Hawke/Hamlet is supposed to avenge, it is no longer ambiguous whether or not Hamlet is mad for being passed over for succession. What this makes explicit that the play (at least to contemporary audiences) does not, is that Hawke/Hamlet—a grungy video artist—does not wish to follow in his father's footsteps. This setup relies on cultural (or folk) models of the father/son relationship wherein if they are not alike, they are at odds. Almereyda exploits the audience's assumption that a slacker/artist son like Hawke/Hamlet would hesitate to avenge his father's death because he does not want to be like his father and he does not want to take over the corporation from his uncle. At the same time, Almereyda exploits Sam Shepard's persona to make Hawke's/Hamlet's desire to follow his instructions understandable to an audience familiar with Shepard's oeuvre. Shepard, the "strong, silent type," is not a man to ask favors lightly, if he needs his son's help, it has not been easy for him to reach this conclusion. With Shepard as the dead father returning to seek revenge from his dawdling son, there is an added pathos to Shepard's/Ghost's disappointment and Hawke's/Hamlet's anxiety about revenge: this is probably not the first time Shepard/Ghost has found his son Hawke/Hamlet lacking in strength, action, or integrity. When Shepard first appears to Hawke, he charges him, intimidates him, and silences him. Sam Shepard is the strong cowboy to Hawke's disaffected Gen X intellectual. Shepard is action and Hawke is talk. With Shepard as Hawke's father, the complexity and pain in the father/son relationship is made clear.

The more information one has about Shepard and Shakespeare's play, the richer this blend becomes. Just as the ghost seems grieved to find himself a ghost, Shepard seems trapped in his good looks, using his grudging film persona as a way of communicating his real pull toward the elevated status of playwright that he has only temporarily abandoned. According to an interview posted on his Web site, "'There was this feeling,' he says, 'that my credibility as a writer would go in the toilet if I suddenly became Robert Redford. I didn't want to be a movie star. I didn't want to have that thing of being an icon. It scared the *bleep* out of me.'"[47] Moreover, because Shakespeare was thought to have played the ghost onstage originally, in Almereyda's film Sam Shepard becomes the modern actor/creator hybrid. With these mental spaces evoked, Almereyda's King Hamlet is the spectre of greatness temporarily walking in the shoes of a bit player. Familiar with Shepard's reputation for preferring the Magic Theatre in San Francisco over more commercial theaters in New York, Almereyda's King Hamlet has been felled by his brother's commercialism and his son's preference for videos over theater. Shepard has written about his own father's alcoholism and many of his plays involve the ghosts of absent fathers in sons' lives. Through the confluence and clashes between the mental spaces evoked by Sam Shepard and the ghost of King Hamlet, Almereyda tells a rich story of high and low art, dead and alive, father and son, film and video, stage and screen, in an instant.

Almereyda does more than just cast Shepard; he primes these associations through how he films him. Almereyda could have filmed Shepard/Ghost as a disembodied voice or bellowing spirit. These choices would have primed ghost representation spaces (Caspar, horror movies, history of ghosts in Shakespeare plays). By presenting Shepard/Ghost full bodied and not ghostly, the camera can concentrate on his Shepard-ness, not his ghost-ness. Shepard/Ghost smokes in a long leather trench coat, recalling the Marlboro man cowboy type Shepard has played in the past. Almereyda has Shepard/Ghost disappear by walking through a Pepsi machine, which does convey the "ghost physics" controlling Shepard's character, but also primes the corporation responsible for such product placements—particularly powerful given the similarity between the Pepsi logo and the "eye" logo of Almereyda's Denmark corporation—and therefore Shepard's persona as outsider, moving through, as if by magic, the constant imposition of commodity capitalism.

Casting Shepard as the ghost of Hamlet's father, Almereyda is able to translate the terrifying quality of the dead to a modern audience. Shepard's ghost is the specter of disappointment that floats over all of us.[48] He does not sell out and yet succeeds. He is the outcast whom everyone wants to join. As the ghost of Hamlet's father, Shepard is the death of theater, replaced by a video artist who rents old movies to understand how to feel. He is crying for revenge to a son who we know will only disappoint him. He is the old west and high art looking to disaffected New York arty intellectual for salvation. He is the past left homeless by the apathetic, postmodern present. Sam Shepard is only on screen for a few minutes, yet based on the mental spaces he evokes, he tells the story without speaking a word. Like Roach's "It," this "poignant antiphony"[49] could describe good casting, good staging, or good art. A cognitive analysis aims to understand the relationship between language, bodies, movement, story, and perception.

Gesture and Performance—"tweaks me by th' nose"

> *the tongue, without the hand, can utter nothing but what will come forth lame and impotent.*
> —John Bulwer, *Chironomia* (1644).[50]

> *The head is not more native to the heart,*
> *The hand more instrumental to the mouth,*
> *Than is the throne of Denmark to thy father (1.2.47–49)*

Claudius spells out a chain of embodied dependencies that are about 380 years before his time: there can be no feeling without thinking and there can be no speaking without gesturing. Though it is more likely that he means the hand that acts is at the command of the mouth that instructs—an image that will go on to prove contentious in this play—he introduces another important relationship: the one between language and gesture. The ghost tells Hamlet that it was his "brother's hand" that dispatched him and it is then the hands of Horatio and the guards that are held against the sword in a pledge to contain their speech. Hamlet's director's notes to the players begin with the relationship between hands and words: his words should not be mouthed but bounce off the tongue "trippingly" and they should not "saw the air too much" as he knows that such gestures do not "suit the action to the word, the word to the action."[51] Thought and action, language and gesture, do not always go hand in hand in *Hamlet*, but aspire to. Below I want to focus on the relationship of gesture to meaning; how gesture relates to imitation and perspective; previous integrations of gesture into theater history and theory; an example from an anthropological-linguistic study of how gesture can depict thought; and, finally, how gesture can import the argument of the play.

Language is embodied and performed. For Maurice Merleau-Ponty, speech is inseparable from the body and for Giacomo Rizzolatti and Laila Craighero gestures are linked to speech through the mirror neuron system.[52] David McNeill's research on gestures and language demonstrates that gestures:

> coexist with speech. They are tightly intertwined with spoken language in time, meaning, and function; so closely linked are they that we should regard gesture and the spoken utterance as different sides of a single underlying mental process. Gesture provides a new perspective on the processes of language.[53]

Gestures are not just linguistic add-ons; just as verbal language evidences our conceptual metaphors, so must our physical communication. These findings demand an extension of cognitive linguistics into the visual realm; not only is language always embodied, the body is language. McNeill finds that while some gesture depict that which is being said, some present abstract ideas not explicit in the speech, and some help the listener follow a through-line of a story. Any dramaturgic or performance analysis should include the understanding of language as performed.

McNeill credits Quintilian and Bulwer with earlier focus on gesture, yet their work looked at how gestures could be added to prepared speech or acting in order to facilitate meaning or communication, whereas most of McNeill's research looks at the communicative system that is spontaneous speech and gesture. For McNeill, gesture is figured as theater:

> The hand and its movement are symbolic; they present thought in action. The hand represents something other than itself. The hand is not a hand, but the character; the movement is not the hand moving up, but this character climbing up; the space is not the speaker's space, but a fictional space, a narrative space that exists only in the imaginary world of the discourse.[54]

To "stage" meaning with one's hands requires different types of gestures, the three most useful for my purposes are "iconic," "metaphoric," and "cohesive." These gestures communicate and manipulate perspective as well as convey the context of the scene—or "discourse system"—rather than just the sentence.

Iconic gestures are those that most clearly depict that which is being said. These are the ones we use when we are trying to describe, for example, how a character in a cartoon takes a tree and "bends it way back" by pulling one hand away from the space above the other hand in an arc.[55] The speaker highlights this particular object and action in his story. Though it is not conscious—unlike a Quintillian-trained rhetorician he has not added this gesture in for clarity—it is meaningful. It communicates the action/event of the tree as slingshot, and also exposes "the particular point of view that he [the speaker] had taken toward it. The speaker had the choice of playing the part of the agent or the tree. He was 'seeing' the event from the viewpoint of the agent performing the act."[56] Here, our hands "stage" the meaning of the word or phrase, as the speaker views it and how he would have us view it.

Metaphoric gestures, on the other hand, "present an abstract idea rather than a concrete object or event. The gesture presents an image of the invisible—an image of an abstraction."[57] McNeill gives the example of a speaker introducing what will be his description of a cartoon. To introduce the subject, the speaker begins by holding his hands out, as if presenting the subject for conversation. This is a metaphoric gesture, rather than a concrete one because, "A particular cartoon event is concrete, but the speaker here is not referring to a particular event: he is referring to the genre of the cartoon. This concept is abstract. Yet he makes it concrete in the form of an image of a bounded object supported in the hands and presented to the listener."[58] The cartoon is now a "bounded, supportable, spatially localizable object."[59] This gesture does not operate at the level of the sentence but of the discourse more generally.

A "cohesive" gesture aims to help the listener understand the narrative; it "serves to tie together thematically related but temporally separated parts of the discourse."[60] If the speaker sets up the gesture space in one area, then moves it briefly to the side while explaining a piece of background information, for example, the listener tracks the subject of the story without losing the timeline of the story. Like a quick scenic element taken on and then off stage, these gestures move us from place to place. What all three types of gestures do is depict the particular and the general—we see in the detail both the presentational meaning as well as the representational concept of the speech or play.

Because they can manipulate perspective, they are integral in political or persuasive speech. Gestures can indicate and create unity through imitation. Research by Amy Franklin finds that gestures are used in deception: when a speaker is attempting to lie to a good friend, the friend will attempt to help the deceiver by adjusting the gestures to clarify the story the listener is telling, but lying about. She concludes, "Gestural mimicry, which surprisingly increases during deception, provides the best evidence of coordination between speakers concerning both the dyadic sense of rapport as well as a shared mental representation."[61] In other research, subjects who were asked their opinions about a new sports drink were far more likely to like it and believe it would be successful when the interviewer imitated their gestures and body positions during the conversation. The imitation was delayed by a few seconds to avoid a conscious perception by the subject, "the idea is to be a mirror but a slow, imperfect one. Follow too closely, and most people catch it—and the game is over."[62] This rough mirroring of the other leads to social bonding, trust, and an increased incidence of collaboration. The article acknowledges that this is something that skilled salespeople and con artists have known and practiced, "subtle mimicry comes across as a form of flattery"; reflecting me to me creates a pleasurable feedback loop. The experiments suggest more than pervasive narcissism: subjects who saw themselves reflected in the tester's gestures were more likely to see things the way they thought the tester wanted them to see things. In other words, gesture and imitation seems to shift the perspective of the subject through a creation of a sense of kinship with that which is reflected.

As McConachie points out, McNeill's (and others') "understanding of speech and gesture as a single communicative system has profound implications for theatrical spectatorship."[63] But how do we apply this new understanding? McConachie integrates it into his study on spectatorship, understanding the language presented on stage—infused with gestures linked to speech through rehearsals—as an integral part of that which is perceived and therefore, according to the embodied cognition and mirror neuron research that informs his study on spectatorship, literally moves the audience. Tobin Nellhaus explores the role of gestures in creating an emotional feedback loop onstage in the eighteenth and nineteenth centuries. These gestures are historically situated and thematically meaningful. Based on the primacy placed on the communicative power of visual signs (such as a handwritten letter or gesture) at that time, "gestures and facial expressions were necessary and immediate representations of a person's feelings, thoughts, and even intrinsic merit...Gestural language was a confessional tongue in which one always admitted something—or had to be seen as admitting something."[64] The gesture, then, communicates and creates; the spectator perceives the "internal" feeling exposed in the gesture and empathizes, "Thus, we arrive at the cycle of sentimental response, in which the emotions and behavior of one person produced sympathetic feelings in the observer, and the reflex of sentiment reflected the observer's inward self. By reading and reflecting on *The Spectator*, the reader looked into a mirror of his or her own inner being."[65] Nellhaus depicts a theater deeply fascinated with the relationship between the "inside" and the "outside" communicated through gesture. Moreover, as the research on imitation and gesture shows, Nellhaus's "cycle of sentimental response, in which the emotions and behavior of one person produced sympathetic feelings in the observer,"[66] seems to have a neurological corollary in the mirror neuron system. Both studies fundamentally integrate McNeill's argument that *"gestures are an integral part of language as much as are words, phrases, and sentences—gesture and language are one system"*[67] into their analysis of theater history and practice.

If an actor comes up with a gesture for a sentence given to him by a playwright, would it be the same as if the semantic or aural meaning was his and spontaneous? McConachie points to the way this research illuminates why "amateur actors focused on their memorized lines [...] appear 'wooden' on stage," and professional (western) actors discover more organic gestures in rehearsal, once memorization occurs, "they rarely plan specific gestures ahead of time, although they may consciously shape some of their gestures after they have arisen in rehearsal."[68] And yet, gesture research suggests that because some gestures occur on the level of the discourse system, the organic one might not be the one the actor comes up with absent a study of gesture and speech that forms an "inorganic" method. We use gestures to communicate information that is not available on the level of the sentence, and so actors would need to integrate a very close reading of the text as a whole—not just his or her lines—to imagine gestures that do more than point or convey intentions. Given McNeill's research on the deep (as well as meta) level at which gestures embody meaning, perhaps gestures should be fashioned consciously by the actor in collaboration with the director. These gestures would not speak to the character but the discourse system or concept and narrative of the play as a whole.

This is a particularly ripe area for the kind of empirical study of theater called for by David Saltz and Bruce McConachie in their articles for the performance and cognition issue of *Theatre Journal*. Given the same sentence and the same actor but two different gestures, what is the difference in narrative or conceptual understanding perceived by a subject/spectator? Does repetition of gesture change meaning? In other words, if a gesture in act one is repeated in a different context in act four, are the two ideas or moments linked in the subject/spectator's mind? To what degree are gestures "mirrored" in the minds of the subjects/spectators and what kind of gesture is the most emotionally rich given that embodiment? McConachie points to the important difference between contemporary western actors and performers of kathakali:[69] are mudras[70] more like sign language, and thus do not fall under the conception of gestures studied by McNeill? Or are they perceived differently given the theatrical conventions of Indian dance-drama? Theater scholars and practitioners, experts in the performance of language, have a lot to offer the linguists studying gestures in the laboratory.[71]

David McNeill points out that gestures convey content, not culture:

> The gestures of different speakers can present the same meanings but do so in quite different forms. Moreover, the gestures of people speaking different languages are no more different than the gestures of different people speaking the same language. [...] This nonstandardized quality of gestures is important for theoretical purposes. Precisely because gestures are *not* obliged to meet standards of form, they are free to present just those aspects of meaning that are relevant and salient to the speaker and leave out aspects that language may require but are not relevant to the situation.[72]

Gestures convey thought, not environment. This is not to say that inhabitants of Spain might have a different offensive gesture than the inhabitants of New York City; McNeill's research here does not refer to hand slang, but rather the gestures that sculpt in front of us that which we imagine within us. Rafael Núñez and Eve Sweetser studied the Aymara Amerindians in the Andean Highlands of South America, finding in their language a conceptual difference that they then confirmed through watching their gestures. Unlike almost everyone else on earth, the Aymara see the future behind them, an image schema visible in their gestures. Although there are many interesting facets of this research, I want to focus on how the gesture renders visible what the speaker sees.

Like everyone else on earth, the Aymara situate time in space;[73] unlike almost everyone on earth, they locate the future behind them. When the Aymara speakers speak of events in time they use nayra (eye/front/sight) to speak of events that are past such as "nayra mara" for "last year" and "ghipa" (back/behind) to refer to events that are yet to occur, such as "qhipa uru" for "a future day."[74] The perspective of the Aymara is clear from the wording—if something is in front of me/within my eyesight, I am facing that direction. The Aymara face the past as they move backward toward the future. Núñez and Sweetser found this perspective demonstrated in their gestures as well: 70 percent of Aymara speakers produced gestures with expressions involving future or past times and all of the participants who spoke Aymara fluently but did not speak Spanish fluently used gestures that mapped the future behind them.[75] They found a correlation between the perspective taken and the age and Spanish fluency of the speaker. In other words, the younger speakers tended to have more formal Spanish education and interaction with the urban centers and this made them less likely to communicate past-behind and/or future-front through gestures. Many still did so, however, confirming for Núñez and Sweetser that "the cognitive linguistic claim that conceptual metaphor is not a 'mere' linguistic phenomenon but [rather] a much deeper cognitive one"[76] because speaking in Spanish did not preclude gestures in the Aymara directional schema. And yet the deeply embedded cognitive experience of self, movement, time, and space shows signs of erosion through exposure to the more modern, Spanish-speaking urbanites.

Just as engagement with the Spaniards begins to erode the Aymara's construals of time, perhaps an engagement with Shakespeare's language holds in place conceptual structures. As Crane finds evidence of Shakespeare's brain in his metaphors, Núñez and Sweetser look for a kind of cognitive archeological trace in the Aymara metaphoric mapping of the future is behind. If current thinking within cognitive linguistics is accurate and language evidences conceptual structures, one might use this trace to imagine the Aymara worldview that supports this conception of the future is behind. Their essay analyzes the linguistic data alongside gestural data to understand the cognitive construal of the Aymara speakers and "the embodied nature of human everyday abstraction."[77] Núñez and Sweetser unpack the mapping of placing the future ahead versus behind and find that the biggest difference seems to be movement: if you imagine yourself moving through space, then what is behind you is what you know and what is in front of you is unknown. If you are still, then you can see—and thus know—what is in front of you, but not what is behind you. As soon as you start moving, that which is in front of you includes more unknowns than knowns. It may suggest a culture that envisions a fairly stable present. Like Hamlet going out of doors without the use of his eyes, the Aymara move backward through time, and therefore imagine movement happens slowly. Either that, or the Aymara ascribe no agency to their own movement, but imagine they are moved gently through time while facing the direction they came.

Though the Aymara language encodes information about the perspective, the embodied performance of time discourse exposes the depth of the conceptual framework. As Núñez and Sweetser study the gestures of the Aymara to get an "eye of" them, I turn to Almereyda's *Hamlet* for information about the play in the hands of the actors. There are important differences between actors speaking someone else's words within a discourse structure they may not understand and asking people to speak about their past and future in front of a camera. I do not want to argue (nor could I) that the actors' gestures were conscious choices meant to further the comprehension of a deeper metaphoric structure of the play. I will not argue that the gestures make the film successful or unsuccessful. I want to ask: what can be understood by an attention to gestures informed by McNeill and others? If gestures are an integral part of language, convey metaphoric conceptual structure in addition to semantic units, and often refer to the discourse system of the whole rather than just the immediate sentence or phrase, then the hands become central to a dramaturgic analysis of the play.

I use a film version of the play for several reasons. It is easier to study and does not change every night. I can point to stills from the film, inviting counterarguments from readers who can see the same images and read them differently. Because film actors use fewer hand gestures than stage actors—though perhaps more facial ones—the gestures chosen take on a greater significance. Moreover, the director has a choice about how to film each scene—when the hands are filmed or not—and which take to include in the final cut. Almereyda's *Hamlet*, in addition to being discussed above in reference to Sam Shepard's performance of the ghost, was an obvious choice for someone interested in hand gestures, because the image selected for the poster is of Ethan Hawke's hands holding the top of his head.[78] I am interested in the relationship established by the poster between hands and head.

To narrow the scope of investigation further, I will concentrate on two gestures used by Shepard/Ghost. In one scene, there is only one brief manual gesture, fleeting, but powerful and in another our attention is drawn to his hands because the whole scene is interested in the "wringing/ringing" of hands.[79] Shepard/Ghost uses his hands infrequently. We see him smoke, but for the most part his hands are out of the camera or obscured by his long coat. In the two moments discussed here, his hands become central to what he is communicating, and, I want to argue, the larger metaphoric discourse structure of the film.

In the first scene between Shepard/Ghost and Hawke/Hamlet, the stillness and control of their movement adds to the tension between father and son. Hawke/Hamlet seems just as afraid of his father as he is of his father's ghost. Similarly, Shepard/Ghost does not seem ominous because he is a ghost on a mission, larger than life because he has no life; he is ominous in the way he stalks his son. Though he mostly keeps his distance from his son, when he tells Hawke/Hamlet that "I could a tale unfold whose lightest word/ Would harrow up thy soul, freeze thy young blood, / Make thy two eyes like stars start from their spheres" (1.5.15–18) he rushes his son, seeming to threaten him with his power, not just the power of his story and certainly not expressing the horror of the experience for him. As he attacks him, he thrusts his two hands up, both pointer fingers aiming at Hawke/Hamlet's eyes. This gesture calls attention to the many moments in the film when the camera focuses on Hawke/Hamlet's eyes, either on his video recordings of himself, obscured partially behind orange-tinted glasses, or pushing his fists into his eyes after the murder of Bill Murray/Polonius. These are his weakness and his strength, forced to see what he would rather forget. This gesture seems to make no sense from the perspective of the sentence or the character: a deictic pointing gesture is not needed to place Hawke/Hamlet's eyes and an iconic gesture that depicts the particular meaning simply confuses it, because Shepard/Ghost explicitly says that the danger to Hawke/Hamlet comes from the story entering Hamlet's ears, not what Shepard/Ghost is going to "show" him. What this gesture does is connect the ghost as threat to Hawke's/Hamlet's own insistence on knowing through sight—on his incessant watching.

Further, Shepard/Ghost need not use both fingers. A pointing gesture is rarely doubled like this and, from the perspective of the character, it makes him seem a bit off, and does not convey the kind of military or cowboy strength that one strong arm pointed at his son would convey. By pointing with both fingers, Shepard/Ghost echoes Horatio's comment that he recognized the ghost because he knew the original, "these hands are not more like" (1.2.212), because one pointing finger mirrors the other pointing finger. Further, the doubling isolates Hawke's/Hamlet's two eyes, as if one could see something different from the other, as if eyes were not a unit, but could be a controlling singular, like the panoptic emblem of the company Kyle McLaughlin/Claudius has taken over from his dead brother or Murray/Polonius's missing eye as he stumbles out from the mirrored closet door, shot by Hawke/Hamlet. The gesture does not need to be doubled, but by being doubled it connects Shepard's/Ghost's story with other doubles and mirrors throughout the play, not least of which is the called-for revenge, duplicating his murder.

In the closet scene, the camera calls our attention to the hands of all three characters.[80] Again, each gesture is doubled, so that what is done with one hands is done with the other. Diane Venora/Gertrude holds both hands up as she falls toward the mirror, showing two hands reflected into two. She then turns and puts the hands up in the same position around her face. She clutches the phone with both hands, as if one wasn't enough to hold its weight. She holds her face in her hands when she asks Hawke/Hamlet, "what hast thou done?" (3.4.25). Shepard/Ghost does almost nothing in this scene except sit and stare at his son, chiding him in silence. He is filmed, however, so that his hands convey what Shakespeare does not give him the lines to say. When we first see him, he folds his right hand under his left, one loose fist held in the other. When he tells Hawke/Hamlet not to forget and chides him for a "blunted purpose" he holds them at chest level with his fingers interlinked, a bridgelike gesture that suggests support but also impotence, because his hands can do nothing in that position but hold up his chin, if he were to rest it on them, or mask something on his shirt. Or, perhaps, to convey an interconnection between two things—he and his son, perhaps—as if linked like the two hands are linked. When Hawke/Hamlet then asks his mother if she sees Shepard/Ghost, the camera cuts to Shepard/Ghost sitting on the chair with his hands forward over his knees, almost strangely large and floppy. Shepard/Ghost's gestures here, again, speak to the play's interest in language versus action. This gesture is then echoed by his son after the murder of Murray/Polonius: as he prepares to "lug the guts," he holds his bloody hands forward off his knees. Yet, in counterpoint to the same gesture made earlier by his father, these hands are not floppy, but blood red.

The gestures examined here are hardly the kind of air-sawing movements feared by Hamlet or employed in the sentimental theater studied by Nellhaus. Yet, not unlike the Mousetrap's dumbshow, gesture here silently "imports the argument of the play" (3.2.135). The importance of gesture in cognitive linguistics expands the field of focus for what language and cognition is, because it is not a stylistic add-on but a physicalization (in many cases, at least) of the cognitive structures reflected in and created by the language. Gesture is where language, performance, cognition, and the body are most visibly united. Because meaning is embodied and performed, performance analysis benefits from a rich engagement with cognitive linguistics. Such an approach offers a method of understanding performance and connecting it with work being done in other disciplines. It is no longer adequate to say about good theater that, "we know it when we see it." Making meaning is not magic; it can be studied, applied, and demonstrated.

Chapter 6

Past/Future, Microscope/Telescope, Performance/Science

In the last two chapters, I moved from the relationship between cognitive linguistics and rhetoric to the relationships between cognitive linguistics and practical issues of staging. This chapter argues that Shakespeare's troubling of the mirror blend offers a reconceptualization of cognition and intellection: how do we know what we think we know? In the century following *Hamlet*, philosophers (who we refer to retrospectively as scientists) were asking and positing new answers to that question. Sir Francis Bacon, Renè Descartes, and Sir Robert Boyle changed how data were gathered and examined; they understood knowledge as mediated and thus changed the tools used for seeing and the performance of their results. From realizing he can use the play to catch the conscience of the king to instructing the players how to enact this story, Hamlet's preoccupation with testing and exploring his own epistemology circulates around the mirror held up to nature. The research on mirror neurons in the brain provides exciting new ways to think about perspective, imitation, and the self; it also provides some evidence that our metaphoric conception of TO SEE IS TO KNOW has a literal corollary at the neural level. I believe that what we do as theater practitioners and academics—indeed as humans—is move from question to question, not focusing on the answer, but on what is the next question posed by the results of the last asking. Rehearsing and remaking *Hamlet*—from the performance at the Globe at the beginning of the seventeenth century to a performance by The Wooster Group at the end of the twentieth century—asks the questions the community is interested in answering and poses new ways of approaching and pursuing the answers.

To represent the previously invisible, to perform the seemingly impossible, is vitally important to creating the visible and the possible. The early modern period learned from the language of the hypothetical and the performance of the important discoveries of the seventeenth century depended on performance and spectators to make them true. Mary Crane has found in *King Lear* echoes of debates at the time about divisibility and argues that *King Lear* exists in light of an "epistemological rupture"[1] where the breakdown of Aristotelian physics also calls into question basic mental concepts of weight, space, divisibility, and existence. In addition to turning to the history of science for circulating debates at the time, Crane suggests that Shakespeare's basic mental model of weight and wait, "woven into the fabric of poetry" provides a "shaping presence" or "frame that supports plot, characterization, and theme."[2] Henry Turner, imagining Shakespeare's language as a kind of genetic code, articulates a tight relationship between science and poetry: "We should regard genetic engineering and biotechnology not simply as a new application of scientific knowledge but rather a new mode of poetics, and that Shakespeare's own work provides a model for just such an approach."[3] Before one can do an experiment to test a hypothesis, one must have a hypothesis (or theory); before one can have a hypothesis, one must imagine. This is where representation of the previously invisible, performances of the seemingly impossible, are vitally important.

Telling and understanding stories—embodied and perspectivized language—teaches us to see and thus to conceive and then to test, and finally, perhaps, to know. Several theorists have found the shoreline between cognitive science and theater productive in reconceptualizing the work of theater. Many cognitive scientists see cognition as embodied simulation and this provides Bruce McConachie (among others) with a tool for retheorizing the relationship between performer and spectator. With new theories of perspective, empathy, and narrative come new arguments for the purpose and importance of theater as an instrument with which to alter and expand our relationship to each other and our environment, as investigated recently by scholars such as Naomi Rakotnitz, Ellen Spolsky, F. Elizabeth Hart, Lisa Zunshine, and others.[4] This chapter asks about the role of dissection in rehearsing previously unimagined territories and the role of performance in projecting perspective and seeing beyond ourselves. Specifically, I turn to remakes of *Hamlet* to ask how the same play can be deployed against different epistemological questions. The tool Shakespeare, through *Hamlet*, finds in the mirror was the rhetorical tool of the sixteenth century and the scientific tool of the seventeenth century. The rehearsal of investigation is central to results.

An Eye of You

> *Our meaning is human meaning—meaning grounded in our human bodies, in their humanly encountered environments. All of the meaning we can make and all of the values we hold grow out of our humanity—interacting with our world.*
>
> —Mark Johnson[5]

Just as the hand is the initiate of action, the eye is the foyer to the brain: what is to be known must first "trouble" the eye. Hamlet wants to know if the ghost "fix'd his eyes upon" the guards, as if to ascertain whether the ghost was interested in investigating them, more than simply seeing them. In a strange panoptic echo, both Claudius and Gertrude refer to the "eye" as controller of knowledge in a precarious state. Gertrude asks Hamlet to stop acting so dour and "let thine eye look like a friend on Denmark" (1.2.69) as if his eye were his assessment and judgment in one. Claudius responds several lines later that it is his eye that can both control and assess Hamlet, using the repetition of the royal plural as a reminder of just whose eye should be judging whom, "And we beseech you, bend you to remain / Here in the cheer and comfort of our eye, / Our chiefest courtier, cousin, and our son" (1.2.116). Ophelia knows that Hamlet is out of his mind because he is able to know the way out of the door without seeing the way: "He seem'd to find his way without his eyes, / For out a' doors he went without their helps / And to the last bended their light on me" (2.1.95–97). Shakespeare uses the image of the "eye" thirty-three times in *Hamlet* and "see" ninety-four times; I begin with the eye here because Shakespeare grounds his epistemological play in the eye. The ability to take on multiple perspectives enables us to see others by seeing through others; theater facilitates this perspective shifting through embodied storytelling.

When Hamlet first sees Rosencrantz and Guildenstern he calls them his "excellent good friends" and trades bawdy jokes with them. When he asks them why they are there, their seemingly selfless answer fails to convince him and he presses them, "Were you not sent for? Is it your own inclining? Is it a free visitation? Come, deal justly with me. Come, come! Nay, speak" (2.2.274–6). They dodge his questions and when he continues to press for a verbal admission, Rosencrantz asks Guildenstern in an aside "what say you?" In his own aside,

Hamlet tells the audience that he is onto their betrayal, "Nay then, I have an eye of you" (2.2.290). Harold Jenkins notes that Hamlet means "I have an eye of your meaning"[6] and J. Payne Collier notes that it is only one of many times Shakespeare uses "of" for "on."[7] While Shakespeare may have simply meant to say "I have an eye on you" as if to convey "I have my eye on you," he also may have meant to suggest something different from what editor James Boswell (1821)[8] argues is "still a common phrase": *"To have an eye upon any one."* Again, conceptual blending theory explores what entailments are involved in how the meaning is made and applying it here allows us to unearth another network of associations in Hamlet's brief aside.

Again, according to Lakoff, the Idealized Cognitive Model (the rules by which we understand an idea) for seeing is: "1. You see things as they are. 2. You are aware of what you see. 3. You see what's in front of your eyes."[9] Our understanding of "to see" comes from an embodied experience with seeing: we see that which is in front of our eyes. If we see what's in front of our eyes, how could you see what your eye is "on"? When our eye is literally on something—like pressed down into a pillow—we cannot see it, because there is no light coming in. Our eyes are on our head, yet that is exactly what we cannot see (without help from a mirror). How is it that having an eye on something facilitates sight? Given how we understand seeing, isn't "I have my eye in front of you" more appropriate? Both theories of extromission and intromission connect the eye with the object of sight through rays; either sent by the object to the eye (intromission) or by the eyes to the object (extromission). With extromission—proposed by Plato—the eyes are imagined to maintain agency over sight, because they send the rays to the object upon which they aim to focus. With Aristotle's theory of intromission (generally agreed upon by the sixteenth century), the objects send information to the eyes—rather than reflecting light—and the eyes are the passive receiver of this information, though the eyes/seer can control sight by decreasing the distance between object and eyes (because distance is in inverse proportion to an object's apparent size). Increasing the size of the object, here, decreases the distance between the eye and object and thus suggests a greater degree of focus on the object in question. Regardless of the physics of sight, or the spectator's understanding of "an eye of" for "an eye on," the language used to discuss sight calls attention to the acquisition of knowledge and the role of perspective and agency in knowledge.[10]

The part of the eye where the optic nerve attaches to the retina at the back of the eye does not have photoreceptors because it is where all the information comes together to travel to the rest of the brain. Paradoxically, this place of all sight is the eye's blindspot. The eyes work together, the sight of the left eye covers the blindspot of the right eye, and vice versa, which is why the lacuna are not visible unless "revealed" by optical tricks.[11] Further, the eye and brain compensate for the missing information by filling in what it thinks should go in that spot. V. S. Ramachandran and Diane Rogers-Ramachandran suggest that the filling in is:

> probably a manifestation of what we call surface interpolation, an ability that has evolved to compute representations of continuous surfaces and contours that occur in the natural world—even ones that are sometimes partly occluded (for example, a cat seen behind a picket fence looks like one whole cat, not like a cat sliced up).[12]

Our eye fills in the missing cat: it is not that we deduce that it must be a cat, we "see" the whole cat.

Experimental psychologists have tested the extent to which humans have nonvisual "bias blind spots," ways in which we ignore any information—not just visual—that does not fit with our expectations. This bias blind spot allows everyone to think he or she is above average. Studies have shown that even when subjects are warned that such biases occur, most do not—cannot—see their own blind spot. Despite the psychological bases of these tests, the blindness is not just "in their head." Research on "inattentional blindness" suggests that our brain will ignore information that does not fit with the narrative we are attempting to create or a particular optical task we have set ourselves. In an extreme example of this, patients with brain damage in a particular area (usually the result of a stroke) will ignore a part or whole side of their body or field of vision. Patients with hemisphere neglect will only apply make up to the right side of their face, or draw only the right side of a flower.[13] As Ramachandran explains it, the brain will not rewire its conception of itself and thus perceives itself the way it always has.[14]

In language chosen to include the reader in the experiment—to give the reader the perspective of the subject—Ramachandran and Rogers-Ramachandran describe one particular study:

> Pretend you are a member of an audience watching several people dribbling and passing a basketball among themselves. Your job is to count the number of times each player makes a pass to another person during a 60-second period. You find you need to concentrate, because

the ball is flying so quickly. Then, someone dressed in a gorilla suit ambles across the floor. He walks through the players, turns to face the viewers, thumps his chest and leaves. Astonishingly, as Daniel J. Simons, now at the Unviersity of Illinois, and Christopher F. Chabliss of Harvard University learned when they conducted this study, 50 percent of people fail to notice the gorilla.[15]

More than just proving the old adage that we see what we are looking for, this test (and others) seems to suggest that the brain privileges its stories over information. Once it takes hold of a story that fits, it does not want to let go in order to make a gorilla fit: "things that do not quite fit the script or that are not relevant to a particular task occupying our interest are wiped wholesale from consciousness."[16] The story that holds our focus on the dribbling basketball or the cat behind the fence is powerful enough to see what is not there and to not see what is there.

Our ability to process the visual/conceptual information coming from the object/concept of the mirror is highly complicated. It seems self-evident that a mirror presents us with a reflection of us, but how do we turn that flat, left/right and front/back reversed image into something we call "us?" We do not fully project ourselves into that body otherwise we would be confused when the reflection lifts what seems to be his or her left hand when we lift our right. Facing the mirror, my face in the mirror is facing me. We compensate for the fact that what we see in front of us in the mirror is behind us in front of the mirror—otherwise we could not use the rearview mirror as a safety tool. Ramachandran studied a woman for whom this simple cognitive task stopped working. After a stroke that made her "blind" to (or neglect) objects in the right side of her visual field, Ramachandran presented her with a mirror, to test whether she would see the left side if it was projected on the right in the mirror. She knew it was a mirror and could describe what she saw in the mirror, but her ability to act on that information was strangely disturbed. Asked to grab a pen held out behind her, within the neglected visual field but reachable with the good side of her body, "Ellen lifted her right hand and without hesitation went straight for the mirror and began banging on it repeatedly." When the task was repeated later she reached around the mirror and then later she looked over the mirror to find the pen.[17]

Absent previous experience with this condition, Ramachandran turns to literature to understand it:

> We decided to give a name to Ellen's condition—'mirror agnosia' or 'the looking glass syndrome' in honor of Lewis Carroll. Indeed Lewis

Carroll is known to have suffered from migraine attacks caused by arterial spasms. If they affected his right parietal lobe, he may have suffered momentary confusion with mirrors that might not only have inspired him to write *Through the Looking Glass* but may help explain his general obsession with mirrors, mirror writing and left-right reversal. One wonders whether Leonardo da Vinci's preoccupation with left-right reversed writing had a similar origin.[18]

Our comprehension of the object is as constructed as our understanding of the concept. I look into a mirror because I understand it as presenting on its surface that which is in front of me and inside me. But we have created that story and we could create another one. The mirror is a tool for seeing and a thing seen. The mirror can reflect, condense, and bisect. I want to argue that Hamlet's description of a theatrical mirror is important to understanding the play, but it can be so only because the integration network that creates our concept of a mirror—as object and as concept—is so rich and extensive.

Hamlet enacts a "story" of his father's murder hoping to see the truth on Claudius's face. Polonius sends Reynaldo to Paris to present a false story of his son in the hopes that the falsenesss will be remarked upon by the acquaintances comparing Reynaldo's Laertes to the one they know. Through the disanalogies mapped across spaces (Laertes as Reynaldo describes him versus Laertes as his Parisian friends know him), Polonius will confirm Laertes' true character, "Your bait of falsehood takes this carp of truth; / And thus do we of wisdom and of reach, / With windlasses and with assays of bias, / By indirections find directions out" (2.1.63–66). Telling stories is how we know what we think we know.

Eve Sweetser points out that mental perception is understood (across languages and cultures) using conceptions of sense perception. Just as mental intellection is acquired through vision (TO SEE IS TO KNOW: "I see your point"), "receptivity" or "heedfulness" is often expressed through hearing (TO HEAR IS TO HEED: "you are just not hearing me!"). Consider the final couplet in sonnet twenty-three, a sonnet about a lover unable to communicate his feelings, "O, learn to read what silent love hath writ / To hear with eyes belongs to love's fine wit." The mystical power of being able to hear with eyes is endowed on the intellect of the lover, as they often must transcend the folk models of perception that associate the eyes with intellection and the ears with emotional comprehension. Of course, it may depend on what you mean by "hear." Bruce Smith argues that in the early modern period, "green" was something one sees or hears *with* rather than sees or hears. Hearing green is hearing passionately and longingly, "to hear green would mean then, allowing rhyme, alliteration, and assonance to divert the sense of hearing from its rational work."[19] This challenges not just our reading of early modern verse, but our *way* of reading early modern verse, because hearing green "dissolves words, not into other words, but into nonsemantic sound. It does not just break down words into phonemes that can be recombined with other phonemes in new and interesting ways; it *liquefies* words."[20] Shakespeare's exercising and troubling of our basic metaphors—hearing the love expressed by a lover by seeing it—melts one into the other and offers a kind of conceptual and linguistic neuroplay.

What Hamlet wants to know about Rosencrantz and Guildenstern is, of course, not visible to the eye. Hamlet wants to know their motivations for being there, their secret intentions, generally understood to be internal. Just as when Hamlet tells Gertrude he hopes to find a mirror with which to show Gertrude her "inmost parts," Hamlet's desire to obtain a perspective from which to see Rosencrantz and Guildenstern is a desire to see, and thus to know, that which is invisible. This further complicates the question of whether to read Shakespeare's "of" for "on," because having an eye on them requires a mapping of that which is internal onto external features, a solution that Hamlet repeatedly discovers is not a reliable method.[21] Of course, to have an eye of Rosencrantz—as in to take Rosencrantz's eye to see *through* it—suggests not that Hamlet will be able to "see" the truth, but that he relies on a knowing of the truth that comes from taking Rosencrantz's perspective. Having "an eye of" Rosencrantz and Guildenstern is a violent dismembering of self into perspective. Hamlet hopes to transfer not the eye, but the information available to the perspective of that eye—not from seeing what lies *ahead* but from experiencing what came *before*.

The First Quarto has Hamlet convey his comprehension of his friends' motives by saying, "Nay, then I see how the wind sits" (7.228). Though ultimately conveying similar information, the sight metaphor in the Folio echoes the play's complicating how seeing can be knowing. Whereas there is nothing complicated or potentially misleading about seeing where the wind sits, having "an eye of" Rosencrantz—whether one imagines *seeing* him or seeing *as* him—*does not guarantee that Hamlet will have the knowledge, experience, and secrets of Rosencrantz*. Through this eye, though, Hamlet can see their scene play out from the perspective of Rosencrantz and Guildenstern as the King's spies. He uses this perspective to direct the scene that follows to manipulate what *they* see. Indeed, as soon as he gets "an eye" of the duplicitous friends, he begins a monologue about losing his mirth—performing the prologue of the play he wishes them to see. Through this "eye" of Rosencrantz he now "has," he is able to frame the rest of the act in order to view his situation in a new light.[22]

Cognitive linguist Brian MacWhinney places the process of "mutual perspective taking" at the center of communication. His work coheres with that of Lakoff, Turner, Fauconnier, and others in privileging the role of imagination in language comprehension. Perspective taking—"at the very core of language structure and higher-level cognition"[23]—is evidenced in the way we comprehend and discuss social roles, seeing in a simple word like "libel," for example, a drama played out among the person who perceives that a rumor has been spread, the person spreading the rumor, and the society that the victim assumes will be reading the allegedly false information. In order to understand what libel means, one must be able construct a scenario that involves multiple perspectives, "a complex set of interacting and shifting social perspectives. To evaluate whether or not a statement is libelous, we have to assume the perspective of speaker A, speaker B, and audience C to evaluate the various claims and possible counterclaims. All of this requires continual integration and shifting of social roles and perspectives."[24] Language facilitates perspective taking and perspective taking enables conceptual leaps.

MacWhinney draws on a wide range of research, from developmental psychology experiments to neuroimaging studies and from cognitive linguistic corpus studies to more theoretical philosophy. This is not contradictory to CBT but a useful corollary. MacWhinney does not offer the tool I am looking for to unpack language the way CBT does but he grounds a linguistic study in research on the body and cognition and approaches cognition and the body through language. The core of our language ability is perspective taking, seeing from another vantage point—in essence, role-playing. Though Fauconnier and Turner would imagine this in terms of blending, MacWhinney's argument allows us to include in a cognitive linguistic analysis of drama and performance the importance of perspective—of taking on an embodied experience of someone else's experience—to how we understand not just language, but performance as well.[25]

It is relatively uncontroversial in the cognitive sciences to say that thinking is an embodied and embedded process. We think *with* and *through* a very particularly environmentally situated body. In their highly influential book, *The Embodied Mind*, Varela, Thompson, and Rosch explain the cognitive paradigm shift that is the change from thinking that there is a world out there with particular features and properties that we represent in the brain in order to think about and then refer to symbolically in order to speak or write about. They call the traditional approach the "Chicken position" wherein what comes first is this objective reality that must be represented linguistically/symbolically, but they argue for an "Egg Position" wherein "The cognitive system projects its own world, and the apparent reality of this world is merely a reflection of internal laws of the system."[26] Of course, just as their reference makes clear, there is not one without the other, "chicken and egg, world and perceiver, specify each other." Although they site scientific studies to support their position, the terrain of their argument is defined by philosophers, specifically Maurice Merleau-Ponty and Martin Heidegger. It is Heidegger who insisted that interpretation is, according to them, "the *enactment* or *bringing forth* of meaning from a background of understanding."[27] Here is the same useful distinction between action and enaction needed by Shakespeare. Shakespeare's player king (reading the lines, perhaps, given to him by Hamlet and, of course, written for both by Shakespeare) needs to invent the word "enacture" to find the space between agent and action just as philosophers and cognitive scientists at the end the twentieth century need enaction to understand a result of thinking that is *in* the body and *of* the world.

Replacing "cognition" with "action" allows Varela, Thompson, and Rosch to avoid the trap of reinscribing a body/mind separation implicit when one speaks of embodied cognition: to say thinking is embodied is to tie them together instead of reformulate what both of them are together:

> By using the term action we mean to emphasize once again that sensory and motor processes, perception and action, are fundamentally inseparable in lived cognition. Indeed, the two are not merely contingently linked in individuals; they have also evolved together.... the enactive approach consists of two points: (1) perception consists in perceptually guided action and (2) cognitive structures emerge from the recurrent sensorimotor patterns that enable action to be perceptually guided.[28]

Their philosophical framework can be seen in several of the important (though not mutually exclusive) areas of cognitive science today: embodied simulation and extended or distributed cognition.

Most famously set out by Andy Clark and David Chalmers, extended cognition is the idea that elements in the environment can be "coupled" with the brain in order to become a part of the mind (David Chalmers uses his iPhone as an example in his foreword of

Clark's *Supersizing the Mind*). Mark Johnson takes apart a traditional understanding of thinking by changing how we think of the things we are thinking about. Percepts, concepts, propositions, and thoughts are not "quasi-objects," they are "not mental objects locked up in the theater of the mind, trying desperately to make contact with the outside world. As we will see, thoughts are just modes of interaction and action. They are *in* and *of* the world (rather than just being *about* the world) because they are processes of experience."[29] Embodied cognition, for Johnson, has the following qualities:

- is the result of the evolutionary processes of variation and selection;
- is situated within a dynamic, ongoing organism-environment relationship;
- is problem-centered and operates relative to the needs, interests, and values of organisms;
- is not concerned with finding some allegedly perfect solution to a problem but, rather, one that works well enough relative to the current situation;
- is often social and carried out cooperatively by more than one individual organism.[30]

This last point, also explained as distributed cognition, locates the process of thinking in the organism created by a community of individuals (a company of players, perhaps), the elements of their environment that they use to take actions, and the actions taken.

Evelyn Tribble provides an interesting application of this theory to the environment of Shakespeare's Globe. Tribble applies the idea that organisms can function as cognitive units and that therefore, the players and environment of the Globe can be thought of as a system that creates and perpetuates cognition, rather than assuming (as scholars have) "that the properties of the system as a whole must be possessed by each individual within it."[31] The elements of the playing environment of the Globe that she sees as contributing to the intelligence of the whole are the "plots" used back stage to map the entrances and exits of the players, verse, and the writing and distribution of parts. She concludes that the very form of the theater provided a cognitive "prosthetic": "Such a theater can best be understood, in other words, through a framework that takes group practices seriously, that assumes that systems can work well, and that sees individual agency as constrained but not contained by these practices."[32]

Henry Turner foregrounds the disperse elements of *Hamlet*—the many ways that *Hamlet* is not a singular source or unchanging unity—in his analysis of how the play works as operating instructions. Whereas Tribble places the meaning-making machine of Shakespeare's play in its historical and geographical origins, Turner sees the play as a process, as an always shifting code:

> The 'source' of the Shakespearean code resides less in the hand of a once-living, human person than in a distributed network of many different agents, from actors and other people involved in the production of the plays in the theaters, to the censoring and approving authorities, to the publishers, printers, proof-readers and compositors who actually set the type, and even to the physical printing machine itself—a material or non-human agent—whose 'characteristics' as a particular kind of technology introduced certain parameters on how the text could be assembled and printed and thus on the way that the play actually appeared on the page.[33]

The play is not a singular object "out there" in the world to be captured, its meaning is bodied forth in a particular time and place and through a particular mode of enaction. As Johnson defines thoughts, so might we understand *Hamlet*, as a process of experience. *Hamlet* is embodied, embedded, and distributed anew each time it returns. Like the ghost, it does not leave us alone; unlike the ghost, it asks different things of us each time it returns. Embodied simulation focuses on the individual internal processes that are emotion, perception, and knowledge. Simulation insists that the organism is always doing: imitating to learn. Niedenthal, Barsalou, Ric, and Krauth-Gruber correlate imitation with emotional knowledge and experience. In experiments, most people will unconsciously mirror the emotional postures of another; when told to amplify the imitation response, subjects experience greater emotional embodiment (empathy) than subjects told to inhibit imitation. They point out that the pain-related neurons that are activated when a subject's hand is pricked are also activated when the tester's hand is pricked.[34] Presumably, the subject's sensory cortex would inhibit a reaction, noting that this time it is not his/her hand that is in trouble, but nonetheless, the initial neural reaction is the same. While watching expressions of sadness, fMRI scans will reveal activation of the neurons that control the "pain" muscles of the subject's face. Subjects will imitate prosody when asked to recite emotional content. Niedenthal and her colleagues argue that this imitation is not separable from perception: the "embodiment or simulation of others' emotions provides the meaning of the perceived event."[35] According to embodied cognition, perception/cognition does not exist as thought; it is an internal action. We imitate in order to feel, and we feel in order to know.[36]

Expanding Varela, Thompson, and Rosch's conception of embodied action for our purposes, who we are—what we feel, what we do, where we are, and what we remember—is then best seen as an embodied, embedded, and transactional *performance*. I do not mean that our identities are performative as Judith Butler argues, but rather that there is nothing other than enacting. Sweetser looks at the performance of ritual as an embodied metaphor, performed not simply to convey meaning, but to *enact* a specific result. She argues that rituals—such as an Italian tradition of carrying a newborn baby up a flight of stairs to ensure a successful life, and representations such as the French cave paintings of hunted buffalo, are done to bring about good luck in life or the hunt, not to describe such good luck. Carrying a newborn baby up a flight of stairs to generate good luck is a metaphoric mapping of GAINING STATUS IS RISING onto a performed action. The metaphor structures how we think and talk about status, as being "higher up the corporate ladder" or "he's below you," but in the case of the newborn ritual, the performance is an attempt to bring the metaphor into being, "By changing relations in the source domain (height), the relations in the target domain (status) are to be changed."[37] Ritual can both represent and create the reality it believes in, "Does kneeling to a divinity metaphorically represent the already extant differential in power and status between worshipper and god (a depictive use), or help to bring the worshipper into the right state of humility (a performative use)."[38] Of course, both. Whatever one feels about the person he kneels in front of on the way down, on the way back up he will discover that the performance of submission has altered his perception—and the perception of other audience members. The performance of the action does not signify, it creates. Something comes into being at the moment of performance and continues to scaffold our understanding long after the curtain has fallen, the ritual has been completed, the gesture faded.

Neuroscientifically, a performance that activates imitation in an audience is likely to be (almost literally) moving. Research on the mirror neuron system (MNS) suggests that certain neurons in the brain themselves do not discriminate between an act performed and an act as witnessed.[39] Because watching is—at least for some neurons—the same as doing, drama *inspires* the imitation of an action, rather than, as Aristotle suggested, *being* the imitation of an action. In some scenes, such imitation might be the simulation required to understand the emotions expressed onstage. This system is thought to provide intentional attunement so that the action of the other is understood with its intention. In some scenes this imitation might take the form of understanding the goal of the action performed onstage—the broadly congruent mirror neurons alert the spectator to the fact that the character picks up the gun in order to fire the gun. And in some scenes, the spectator will find that he or she is tensing muscles, crying, breathing differently, leaning forward, smiling, or turning away. It is the power and pervasiveness of *audience* imitation that is central to theater. So perhaps the rehearsal of actions and feelings that this generates allows us to respond to current or future experiences *as if* we had experienced them before, even though only a few of our neurons *actually have* experienced this before.[40]

Not unlike Hamlet's mirror, the mirror neurons do not map the entire other onto the entire self: they map part onto part. As one monkey grabs a banana, another monkey perceives a connection between the gesture of the other's hand and his own. While the language used to describe the impact of the mirror neuron system often relies on the metaphor of the self as container—"put yourself in the place of the other"—what these mirrors do is put the other's hand in place of one's own. The other does not become the self, but his hand might become a part of what one experiences as one's own. Just like Hamlet's mirror, which selectively reflects a part of nature rather than the whole messy category, the mirror neurons depict us as a system of parts, looking for connections, alive in the scaffolding between self and other, visual and motor, banana and phone.

Shakespeare shapes and shifts his audience's perspective, building a facility with perspective taking, "as if" thinking, and critical thinking. *Othello* presents the perspective of both the rhetorician and his audience, allowing a kind of backstage view to meaning construction. Every time Othello refers to Iago as "honest" the audience is reminded that he is not. Othello is operating on an Idealized Cognitive Model for ordinary communication that Lakoff outlines "a) If people say something, they're intending to help if and only if they believe it. b) People intend to deceive if and only if they don't intend to be helpful."[41] Othello will have to conceive of a self-interested and dishonest friend in order to enact a different meaning. As Donald Freeman points out, Othello assumes that what one sees is true, "What Othello knows is what Iago sees—or purports to have seen, and Othello acts on that vision with the same certainty that he would act on his own."[42] Iago directs the action that he wants Othello to see and presents how he wants him to see it, relying on Othello's unquestioning reliance on cognitive models to do the rest. He sets up a dumb show for Othello, tells Othello to judge what is happening in conversation with Cassio based on what is on his face: "mark his gesture" (4.1.89). Shakespeare calls attention to the "gestures" of rhetorical game-playing for the audience at the theater through Iago's villainy and Othello's gullibility. He wants us to see the construction of "truth" through language and gestures, in order for us to conceive that it might not always be what it looks like. Seen from the perspective of the audience, the "duping" of characters through linguistic trickery ("Till Birnam wood remove to Dunsinane") or rhetoric ("for Brutus is an honourable man") seems fairly clear. By giving the audience a view of the theatrical and linguistic manipulations as well as the tragedies that result, Shakespeare educates his audience in performance analysis.

In Rob Reiner's 1987 film, *The Princess Bride*, Vizzini (played by Wallace Shawn) responds to each unexpected plot turn by exclaiming, "inconceivable!" Of course, that which he finds "inconceivable" is occurring right in front of him, so it is less "inconceivable" than it is "unfortunate" or "unlikely." Indeed, Fezzik (played by Andre the Giant) finally responds, "I think you should look that word up. I don't think it means what you think it means." Shawn/Vizzini fashions himself an intellectual—even a scientist/philosopher—so if something happens that he did not expect, it is impossible. But it is inconceivable only because he had not predicted it. It was not part of the imagined possibilities. This calls attention to the mind/body that needs to conceive of the possible in order to run through the thought experiment necessary to assess the likelihood of such an outcome.

If Shawn/Vizzini did look up "conceivable" in the OED, he would find the following definition, "That can be conceived, imagined, or thought of; imaginable, supposable." The first use of this sense of conceivable is Sir T. Browne's *Pseudodoxia epidemica or enquiries into very many received tenents* (1646): "that he remained ignorant of this account it is not easily conceivable." If Shawn/Vizzini had looked up "conceivable" in the OED, he would also notice that prior to 1646 "conceivable" meant, "That can be received or taken in," as in, "That...we might finde therein apt and conceiveable foode" (from Thomas Bowes's *De La Primaudaye's French academie*, 1586). Of course, he would be referencing the first definition, but the relationship between the two—from a physical taking in, suggested by the earlier, to a cognitive taking in, communicated in the later—suggests conception as always an action that has a simultaneous separation of the body that eats with the mind that imagines. According to current theories, such a separation is a chicken/egg argument: neither can be first because they are not separable.

Surpassing Show

Literary texts are not, of course, merely passive conduits. They actively shape what the technologies mean and what the scientific theories signify in cultural contexts.

—N. Katherine Hayles[43]

Pascal Boyer suggests that, "Our intuitive ontology is not the only one possible."[44] Just like we could imagine slumber as something other than a container—not something we are *in*, as Johnson points out (something we travel *through* or a dance we *do* with our eyes closed), perhaps we could imagine the body as something other than a container. Research on cognition continues to expand where "thinking" actually happens (Damasio showed that thinking included emotions, others proved it was embedded in the body, Barsalou argues that it is in the simulation of the environment, Clarke presents it as operating with and through the environment); maybe we need to reimagine our conception of the body, not cognition. If so, I want to imagine that it is within the theater that this can happen. The Wooster Group's *Hamlet* envisions a conception of the self at odds with a deeply entrenched notion of the individual as a unique, discreet container. Situated in this *Hamlet*, which resides at the intersection of live performance and videotaped memory, is a clear explication of current theories in cognitive science. Theater can, and occasionally does, stage new stories that help us understand ourselves differently.

Michael Feingold begins his *Village Voice* review of the Wooster Group's *Hamlet* with the line, "O Hamlet, thou turn'st mine eyes unto the VCR, and there I see such black and grainy tape as will not leave its tinct."[45] Feingold refers to the 1964 film version of Richard Burton's production of *Hamlet*, a production that, according to the Wooster Group program, "was recorded in live performance from 17 camera angles and edited into a film that was shown for only two days in 2000 movie houses across the United States." A theatrical production could suddenly be seen by tens of thousands of people at the same time, rather than by the far smaller audience of a single Broadway house. Like Feingold, Robert Brustein also dismissed the Wooster Group's *Hamlet*, finding that it was more interested in "technical gesticulations"[46] than text, "In this production, LeCompte has left Elsinore for Media City, a technological complex that is located out of literature, out of culture, indeed out of history."[47] The intellectually astute criticisms of both Feingold and Brustein have spotted the game but missed the point: we are out of history and in a kind of wormhole[48] that links us both to the past and to an ironically erasing videotaped recollection of a previous production.

Josh Abrams and Jennifer Parker-Starbuck find the production "breathtaking" and shift the terms of debate from what this *Hamlet* says about *Hamlet* to what it says about theater and history:

> For them, the question is not merely why do *Hamlet* today, but how does theatre matter? How does theatre continue to exist and why? Through the interplay between them and the Burton/Gielgud film they pose theatre as the site wherein to capture not merely the conscience of the king, but the understanding of history, representation, and of life as well.[49]

While those of us who try to teach theater 101 to undergraduates realize that seeing a filmed version of *Hamlet* does not count as bringing "a live theatrical experience to thousands of viewers simultaneously through a new form called 'Theatrofilm' (made possible through the 'miracle of Electronovision')"—as the Wooster Group program articulates the goal of the 1964 project—the (arguably unrealized) point of the original Burton film project, it seems to me, is not the particular production of *Hamlet* that was filmed but the thousands simultaneous *Hamlet*s screened and viewed by film audiences. Theatrofilm would be both and neither but would potentially illuminate what is rarely "center stage" among theater or film critics: what happens at the meeting point between audience and media, or audience and actors?

The Wooster Group's *Hamlet* was neither a new staging of the classic play nor a screening of the 1964 film. Rather, the production focused on the space in between the film and the play, the media and the live event, the self and the other. Scott Shepherd plays Hamlet, but more accurately he plays Burton/Hamlet; his performance aimed at imitating, as precisely as possible, the filmed archive of Burton's *Hamlet*. His imitation foregrounds the character/actor blend. Always read through Burton, Hamlet loses his critically cherished "corrosive inwardness" and finally becomes a character requiring—like all others—an actor to embody him. Shepherd is not imitating Burton, though, as becomes clear the first time the film footage skips and Shepherd imitates the stutter of the archived Burton/Hamlet. Indeed, Shepherd/Hamlet mirrors Burton/Hamlet behind him, without watching him, which makes it seem almost as if Burton/Hamlet is imitating him. The original is lost forever in this fun house of bodies ghosting bodies—archived, repeated, and ghosted again.

At first, the Wooster Group's imitation of the actors in film seems to point out an evolution in acting styles; seen in the reflection created by the actors' imitation, Burton and others chew up the scenery, as if projecting to a large house rather than for the camera. Soon, the audience notices the live actors performing what Steven Leigh Morris of the *LA Weekly* called the "microballet of little bounces backward while walking or descending stairs, as though they too are figurines on an aging celluloid strip that occasionally slips a sprocket."[50] Kate Valk, playing both Ophelia (via the 1964 performance by Linda Marsh) and Gertrude (via Eileen Herlie), is particularly stunning in this regard: she forges the performance at the seams of the technical interruptions to the model performance she imitates. Her Herlie/Gertrude *is* the jumps and skips and this performance of technical interruption gains humanity in her embodying them. By the end of the production, the skips and jumps that interrupt the film performance come to constitute a meeting point between live actor and archived performance, creating a dislodging of self/character/actor. When Valk/Gertrude imitates of Herlie's/Gertrude's slightly exaggerated pose, the precision and commitment evidences a kind of empathy between the two women/characters, across time, media, and place. In the end, the imitation of the archived performance seems to project the actors—those filmed in 1964 and those performing in front of a live audience in 2007—out of their temporally situated bodies and toward the location where screen and stage meet, like brilliant puppeteers throwing their voices. The self is what hovers in between.

Feingold faults the Wooster Group for choosing the production of *Hamlet* that they did, saying that Burton's production was not "legendary" as the program asserts, and was actually not even worthy. Further, he goes on to complain that the Wooster Group did not point out the historical elements that Feingold would have found interesting:

> But the Woosters apparently aren't interested in theatrical tradition any more than they're interested in *Hamlet* the play and what it might mean for today's audience. They don't even explore the links that the Burton production extends: Backstage at it, ensemble member Gerome Ragni was busy dreaming up the work that would ultimately become *Hair*, also produced in the Public's first season—a connection you might think would be of interest to the people who found the subterranean ties between Flaubert's *St. Anthony* and Lenny Bruce.[51]

The production was not an attempt to look backward historically at theater or at a play. It was a *manifestation* of theater's ability to constitute us by, in, through, and in between performances.

The *New York Times*'s Ben Brantley called the production an "aching tribute to the ephemerality of greatness in theater" and a "sometimes ravishing, often numbing homage to a fabled theatrical event."[52] The review's focus on the disappearing act of theater, of the performance the actors stand in front of, seems off the mark, however. Though the program aids this reading, comparing the production to "an archeologist inferring a temple from a collection of ruins," the production seems less interested in the architecture of the temple *qua* temple than in the spirit it once housed. Indeed, the final paragraph of the short "Program Note" suggests the more complicated reading I am arguing for, "Channeling the ghost of the legendary 1964 performance, we descend into a kind of madness, intentionally replacing our own spirit with the spirit of another." This theatrically induced madness exhibits the kind of permeability of self—"spirit"—supported by recent research on mirror neurons. This is not to argue that the Wooster Group has been impacted by or reflects scientific research in their work—indeed, one might point to their slightly misleading program notes as evidence—but that the performance nonetheless evidences current thinking across and between the sciences. If the sum total of what a playwright or director wants to convey could be listed in a program note, then I do not want to see the play. I need the play to organize or reorganize my thoughts and theories about my self and the world around me. The Wooster Group's *Hamlet* provides an artistic example of what the sciences are telling us about the self: that it is not as stable or individual as we initially thought. It is not that the Wooster Group reflects the science, but that it may shape the science that comes next.

The Inmost Part

Looking down a microscope, like looking through a seventeenth-century telescope, took practice
—Lisa Jardine[53]

My ambition is, that I may serve to the great Philosophers of this Age, as the makers and grinders of my Glasses [lenses] did to me
—Robert Hooke's preface to *Micrographia*[54]

If as Lakoff and Johnson argue, the metaphors we use constrain what we can think of as "true," then the speaking and performing of a new metaphor can scaffold new conceptual structures. Playing in the spaces *between* what we think we know opens up new horizons of possibilities, such as Richard Schechner's work integrating research into rites and rituals into performance and theory. Schechner and Victor Turner expanded the category of performance by seeing it as ritual.[55] In his influential *Frame Analysis*, Erving Goffman suggests that spiritual things are similarly two things at once, "sacred relics, momentos, souvenirs, and locks of hair do sustain a physical continuity with what it is they commemorate."[56] Performance, then, uses play to transport the singular to a place of both/and: physical object (hair, cross, etc.) to spiritual or psychological other (one's love or god). Understood in this way, performance is less a category of deceit or "show" than it is a vehicle or transformative agent.

Before "The Mousetrap," but after about 50 lines of director's notes to the players, Hamlet tells Horatio to observe the play through his observations of the King:

> There is a play tonight before the King.
> One scene of it comes near the circumstance
> Which I have told thee of my father's death.
> I prithee, when thou seest that act afoot,
> Even with the very comment of thy soul
> Observe my uncle. If his occulted guilt
> Do not itself unkennel in one speech,
> It is a damned ghost that we have seen,
> And my imaginations are as foul
> As Vulcan's stithy. Give him heedful note;
> For I mine eyes will rivet to his face,
> And after we will both our judgments join
> In censure of his seeming. (3.2.75–87)

Hamlet assumes that the King will have a recognizable reaction to the performance of a scene that comes "near the circumstance" of an event he has experienced. If Claudius had not already performed the action to be imitated—Hamlet's logic seems to conclude—then he would not react to the player's actions. Hamlet needs both Claudius and Horatio to watch not just the scene, but the scene *and* its reflection in the key spectator's actions. After all of Hamlet's attempts to get the players to "suit the action to the word," the imitation most vital to his plan is Claudius's embodied simulation of the player's "near" imitation of his fratricide. When the scene onstage is seen, Horatio (with Hamlet) will observe Claudius; for Hamlet, "The Mousetrap" is the performance event *and* its reception—trap and mouse together.

We use fiction to find the truth. In *The Fate of Place*, Edward Casey argues that the discussions of space accustomed the Renaissance thinkers to think in terms of space without end (in counterdistinction to finite space, or: place). The understandings of Thomas Aquinas and Newton, for example, may differ, but

> both tendencies share one important thing in common: they were both conceived as ways in which infinite space can be *imagined*.... what the world and the universe would be like if God were to choose to alter things as they are radically.... When one begins to think this "otherwise," one is approaching things *secundum imaginationem*, "according to imagination"—not according to how things in fact are, have been, or will presumably be. Pondering the imagined situation in which God might destroy everything within the arch of the heavens or within the sphere of the moon'—thereby leaving "a great expanse and empty space"—Oresme remarks that "such a situation can surely be imagined and is definitely possible although it could not arise from pure natural causes..." By extension, infinite space is a matter of what can be imagined, of what *could be*; finite space is a matter of what *is* the case.[57]

The scholastics referred to the facilitation of thinking by exploring what is not *secundum imaginationem*. Explored in earlier chapters as a counterfactual space[58]—is, according to Bryan Reynolds, a subjunctive movement, defined as "the hypothetical dimension of 'what-ifs' and 'as-ifs' that unsettles certain authoritative processes in critical practice."[59] Reynolds and I argue that the comedy of Ben Jonson, for example, works to move spectators into an "as-if" space through its comedy, "Comedy can confuse and create doubt. It can reorder the existing logic and expose the possibility of alternate ways of thinking. These potential alternatives might not fit the simple, ordered world of the dominant paradigm and may allow us to imagine new worlds."[60] The inconceivable and the conceivable are mutually dependent; one is the *tool* with which to create the other.

When Lear enters in act five carrying Cordelia, he spends the majority of his dying breath trying to conceive of the death of his daughter. After proving himself to be tremendously articulate over the course of the play, he is practically tongue-tied, expressing his grief most poignantly in the repetition of "howl" upon entering and then later using five "never[s]" to understand that she will not return. He first declares that she is dead but then doubts his own perception; he asks for a mirror to make sure, "I know when one is dead, and when one lives. / She's dead as earth. Lend me a looking glass. / If that her breath will mist or stain the stone, / Why, then she lives" (5.3.261–64). When the mirror fails to bring the sign of life for which he is so desperate, Lear repeats his experiment with a feather hoping for different results, "This feather stirs, she lives! If it be so, / It is a chance which does redeem all sorrows / That ever I have felt" (5.3.266–68). Both explanations emphasize the cause and effect nature of an experiment: if x, then y. Moreover, these are experiments staged for the members of the court still living: they are his witnesses, his spectators. Though his words fail him, he turns to scientific observation and the performance of the experiment to understand what his mind cannot conceive.

In 1611, Galileo asked spectators to look at the heavens through his telescope and see the moons of Jupiter and the mountains on the moon. Despite the ocular "proof," the viewers were unconvinced; such visions were inconceivable. They were, however, impressed with the telescope's ability to render readable text on a far-away building.[61] Elizabeth Spiller argues that reading (made more common by the relatively new technology of the printing press) and the telescope were tools that "worked across distance and made it possible to see things that were otherwise inaccessible. Yet, in doing so, these were 'technologies' in which the means to new knowledge involved distorted and potentially dangerous forms of mediation."[62] As an example, Spiller points to the drawings in Galileo's *The Starry Messenger*, images created not to duplicate what he saw in his telescope but as "viewing aids" to give his readers an experience of observing that is more akin to reading.[63] The use of the telescope as a reading device, however, made it suspect, "In this historical context, the telescope became an image of doubtful knowledge because it was an instrument in which distortion became the means to truth."[64] Galileo's drawings make a distinction between the stars that are visible to the naked eye—with double outlines—and the ones that are only visible with a telescope. For Spiller, this itself is invention:

> What separates Galileo's work, however, is a new definition of the invisible. Where earlier illustrators had shown parts of the cosmos that were invisible to human sight, Galileo now depicts that which is invisible without a telescope. In doing so, Galileo adapts the familiar as a visual template within which new stars can be recognized. Such schematizations allow readers literally to "see" new formation inside an identifiable framework.[65]

It is not just the telescope that produces new knowledge, it is the relationship between the experiment of looking and the story told to make sense of what is seen.

Lear turns to a mirror and a feather to provide information that he may not be able to see with his naked eye. As Francis Bacon suggests in *The Advancement of Learning*, perception alone does not lead to knowledge:

> For the mind of man is far from the nature of a clear and equal glass, wherein the beams of things should reflect according to their true incidence; nay it is rather like an enchanted glass, full of superstition and imposture, if it be not delivered and reduced. (211)[66]

Bacon does not equate this delivery or reduction to fiction, however. In his *Novum Organon* Bacon posits three idols that cause distortion to perception: 1) Idols of the cave, 2) Idols of the market place 3) Idols of the theater. The first causes the individual to bias perception according to limited perspective and emotional valence. The second is a kind of group-think: we are biased by the "received wisdom" of our culture. The third reflects the power of the narrative—the story, the metaphor, the model—to bias perception. These Idols are important to acknowledge and work against because, as the quote above says, the mind does not take in information equally. What we see is what we get, but, unlike Gertrude's claim that "all there is I see" we do not see all that there is. For Bacon, and others of the scientific revolution, what is needed is rigorous observation, performance, and reception.

Steven Shapin argues that Robert Boyle's discoveries about the properties of air in the second half of the seventeenth century were due to more than his (admittedly important) invention of the air pump, but also to his use of "literary technologies...by means of which the phenomena produced by the pump were made known to those who were not direct witnesses; and a social technology which laid down the conventions natural philosophers should employ in dealing with each other and considering knowledge-claims."[67] For Boyle to be persuasive about the importance of his experiments he needed a clear and, seemingly, unmediated representation of nature and *also* a performance that mediated the observed to render it more legible and striking. Boyle's tool for seeing air, his air pump, allowed him to learn through a mediating device but, he argued, the processes by which the information gained through these experiments were shared had to be as unmediated as possible. He reported on his unsuccessful attempts to duplicate his experiments as well, as if to prove his reportorial objectivity and he warned against a florid style that "was, Boyle said, like painting 'the eye-glasses of a telescope.' "[68] According to Shapin, Boyle insisted that "Complex and circumstantial accounts were to be taken as *undistorted mirrors* of complex experimental performances, in which a wide range of contingencies might influence outcomes."[69] Not everyone could witness his experiment, but everyone could be told of the experiments and therefore how the experiment was conveyed would, he knew, impact the influence it had. The drawings he added to his published works aided the reader in translating the information into an experience that would change the powerfully held folk theories of air. According to Shapin, "visual representations, few as they necessarily were in Boyle's texts, were mimetic devices. By virtue of the density of circumstantial detail that could be conveyed through the engraver's laying of lines, the images imitated reality and gave the viewer a vivid impression of the experimental scene."[70]

Francis Bacon believed "Man, being the servant and interpreter of Nature, can do and understand so much and so much only as he has observed in fact or in thought of the course of nature: beyond this he neither knows anything nor can do anything." Man had to witness in order to conceive of the new. Despite Bacon's concern about the Idol of the Theater, the stories of important paradigm shifts in scientific understanding in the early modern period suggest that it was the staging and witnessing of the experiment that made them true, that changed how such things as matter, air, and the rotation of the spheres were conceived. Important as the tool is, it is the performance of the tool in action that creates and distributes knowledge. Lear uses the feather and the mirror to see that which he cannot see without a mediating device yet his final words are commands to the spectators, "Do you see this? Look on her! Look her lips, /Look there, look there!" (5.3.311). If they see it, it will be so. Similarly, Hamlet hopes to use the play, a representation of "something like" the murder of his father to assess the culpability of the King. Like Lear's mirror held to the lips of Cordelia to demonstrate life, Hamlet's "mirror held up to nature" will evoke a response from Claudius that will out his guilt. Hamlet and Lear hope to improve what they can see and imagine in order to enlarge what they know, but they—and through them Shakespeare—must perform the experiment for an audience. Seen in this way, performance is experimentation and experimentation is performance.

This does not mean that cause and effect are the same thing here or that the impact of one will be felt immediately. I am not arguing that *Hamlet* was performed one day and Bacon reconceived of intellectual investigation the next. But drama and performance offer a new staging of an old story that then begins a reconception of the questions and answers we are interested in. Laura Otis has shown that germ theory did not take hold until the mid-nineteenth century, even though the microscope technology had been around since 1670 and this is because what was seen under the microscope was culturally defined, "Cell theory relies on the ability to perceive borders, for to see a structure under a microscope means to visualize a membrane that distinguishes it from its surroundings"[71] and that the conception of the self as a semipermeable container was the result of the literature and art of the period as well as the cultural anxieties about the impact of imperialism. In contemporary philosophy of science, both Robert Crease and Stephen Hilgartner have explored the symbiotic relationship between theater and science, though from different perspectives. Crease argues that the metaphor of theater can be applied fruitfully to science, in particular the experiment, to illuminate areas of it for analysis. Hilgartner uses the theatrical analogy to foreground the role of the selective casting or staging of scientific research in the establishment of truth. Philosophers and historians of science reflect in their stories the importance of dramaturgic and performance analysis to reading and performing science.[72]

According to Crease, the experiment performs the science, rather than demonstrating it and is therefore open to performance analysis. Acknowledging that his application of the analogy is "a kind of experiment itself,"[73] Crease argues that the analogy provides a suitable language for understanding experimentation, as it highlights the practice, the adjustments, the rehearsal of the experiment: scientists must learn to "shape the performance of the instrument" prior to executing an experiment that may provide data to analyze.[74] Crease sees the witnessed experiment not as unproblematic, but rather that the performance of the experiment brought in to being that which could then be conceived. If experimentation is not understood as requiring practice, as being a performance, as having roles, then the results are taken as representations of what is true, rather than models of seeing. For Crease, such an approach is imperative to improving scientific investigation and also to seeing our role in enacting truth, "experimental activity amounts to the play of prudence and artistry in bringing forth natural phenomena, an activity that delights in the novel and surprising and can be accompanied by inspiration and the enchantment of creating."[75] A different way of performing creates a different way of knowing.

Hilgartner uses performance theories to look at how science is performed by advisors who are not passive presenters of research but rather "construct the personae they display, managing information and appearances in complex ways."[76] Hilgartner does not look at how the data is pulled together to form an experiment that is then performed, rather he analyzes "science advice as a form of drama."[77] Because science plays a huge role in the modern state—advising, making policy, and so on, "it is important to understand how science advisors work to achieve credibility and defend themselves against critics who challenge their objectivity, expertise, or integrity."[78] Just as Shakespeare's formulation that the purpose of playing is "to hold" masks the role of the holder in angling or pointing, Hilgartner argues that:

> Scientific texts conceal the history of their own production, but they do so neither automatically nor in a single, uniform way. The dramaturgical perspective calls attention to systems of stage management and the role of various modes of information control in creating authorized voices, authoritative knowledge, and credible science advice.[79]

Scientific experiment and performance can benefit from theatrical and performance analysis just as dramaturgic and performance analysis can benefit from scientific research.

The title page of Q1 *Hamlet*, the "bad Quarto," seeks legitimacy by including reference to its staging, "As it hath beene diverse times acted by his Highnesse servants in the Cittie of London: as also in the two Universities of Cambridge and Oxford, and else-where." This is *Hamlet* because it was performed and witnessed by audiences in several cities. The Q2 *Hamlet* tells the reader—in the same size font as it acknowledges the author—that the text therein is "Newly imprinted and enlarged to almost as much againe as it was, according to the true and perfect coppie." The first privileges the importance of performance in establishing authority, even if that authority is through the mediation provided by the players and playing. The second bestows authority on an unadulterated original reproduced in this version. The technology of the printing press allows for a reprinting as well as a reperforming of a once "true and perfect" copy. The author-ity comes from the space in between performance and reperformance, original and copy.

Conclusion

A Dying Voice

> *That are but mutes or audience to this act,*
> *Had I but time (as this fell sergeant, Death,*
> *Is strict in his arrest) O, I could tell you*
> *But let it be. Horatio, I am dead;*
> *Thou livest; Report me and my cause aright*
> *To the unsatisfied.*
> (5.2.335–40)

...

> *O god Horatio, what a wounded name,*
> *Things standing thus unknown, shall I leave behind me!*
> *If thou didst ever hold me in thy heart,*
> *Absent thee from felicity awhile,*
> *And in this harsh world draw thy breath in pain*
> *To tell my story.*
> (5.2.344–9)

...

> *I cannot live to hear the news from England,*
> *But I do prophesy th' election lights*
> *On Fortinbras, he has my dying voice.*
> (5.2.354–6)

Hamlet's dying voice is largely taken up with his concern for what will remain of his voice, his report, his name, his story. For five acts our protagonist has been trying to figure out (1) Whether or not he has a cause (2) What his name and story are, and (3) How to attach his voice to a strong arm (such as Fortinbras), i.e., combine intention, agent, cause, and effect. In his last few lines, Hamlet passes the buck to Horatio, in effect splitting off his story (Horatio) from his voice (Fortinbras), his strength (Fortinbras) from his authority (Horatio). Horatio, expected to report all this "aright" cannot possibly succeed. It is no wonder scholars have remained so unsatisfied. No wonder we continue to re-member *Hamlet* how we see fit. In our attempt to tell Hamlet's story, like Horatio, we tell our own. As Terence Hawkes suggests, for every age, there is a *Hamlet*.[1] Or, perhaps more accurately: a Horatio, the storyteller, charged to make whole. In *Hamlet*, Hamlet is dis-membered, pulled into parts by the demands of the play and court. At the end, forever unable to suit the action to the word, he asks to be re-membered. The theater is a place of remembering: the words of the author become the language of the character through the bodies of the actors and we are incarnated. Like virtue, *we* are personified in Hamlet's mirror.

A Rhapsody of Words

Language does something; it is not just a system of signs and signifiers that we use to narrate and describe events and actions in the real world. It is creative and banal and works to reveal and shape our thought; therefore, a study of language is a study of how we think. The categories we use to organize information are not created based on a transcendental truth. They can be changed, both linguistically and cognitively, and often have to be, when new information or ideas arrive, which prove them inadequate or inaccurate. It is through understanding the complexities of language—that the mirror held up to nature is not an obvious or literal phrase or idea—that we can imagine new ways of thinking and speaking, new metaphors, new stories. The powerful poetry of Shakespeare, the very "coinage" of his brain, gave us new words for new thoughts and new thoughts made possible by these new words.

Hamlet uses theater to assay the guilt of the king and the trustworthyness of the ghost. Hamlet assumed that a play could display an internal truth hidden by outward appearances and "enacting." While Hamlet's Mousetrap did not work exactly as he intended it to, his assumption that it would do something to its audience was correct. Language and performance works on an audience; we speak of being "moved" by a speech, of having our mind "changed" by an advertisement. Language is a cognitive therapeutic instrument because it is the means by which we tell the story. It is the story, rather than the truth, that generates thought, feeling, and action. It is the story, the "something like," that allows us to make sense of the senseless and to make a self out of an infinite and seemingly random series of neuron firings.

If Hamlet wants the play to catch the conscience of the king, Shakespeare's *Hamlet* seems more interested in the conscious-ness of the king; "Who's there?" In explaining why he believes the play might just be "the thing" needed to confirm Claudius' guilt, Hamlet says that in the theater, the past acts of "guilty creatures" will find the words to speak:

> I have heard
> That guilty creatures, sitting at a play
> Have by the very cunning of the scene
> Been struck so to the soul, that presently
> They have proclaim'd their malefactions:
> For murther, though it have no tongue, will speak
> With most miraculous organ. I'll have these Players
> Play something like the murther of my father
> Before mine uncle. (2.2.587–96)

Malef-actions may find words to expose the creatures guilty of initiating them. Of course, Hamlet then notices that conscience can make cowards, that resolution can be "sicklied o'er with the pale cast of thought" and that "enterprises of great pith and moment / With this regard their currents turn awry / And lose the name of action" (3.1.84–7). Action, under the spell of thought, can lose its very name. And yet, action can create consciousness, as he tells his mother she has been formed by what she has done:

> ...Such an act
> That blurs the grace and blush of modesty;
> Calls virtue hypocrite; takes off the rose
> From the fair forehead of an innocent love,
> And sets a blister there; makes marriage vows
> As false as dicers' oaths. O, such a deed
> As from the body of contraction plucks
> The very soul, and sweet religion makes
> A rhapsody of words! Heaven's face doth glow;
> Yea, this solidity and compound mass,
> With tristful visage, as against the doom,
> Is thought-sick at the act. (3.4.40–51)

This act takes the meaning from the words once used performatively in contracts and marriage vows. This act can make thought sick.

As Crane argues, Timothy Bright's *Treatise of Melancholy* (1586) can be seen as an early attempt to wrestle with the mind/body problem: if the mind (or, for Bright and others, the soul) is immaterial, how does it convey instructions to the material body? How is word suited to action? There are parts of our body that function without our being conscious of it—the ebb and flow of the lungs, the digestion of the intestine—and other vital actions that we must consciously instruct our body to take—eat, avoid predators. Breathing takes instructions from no one; eating takes instructions from someone. Hamlet's mirror does both too: it is didactically angled and invisibly held. Hamlet's mirror is a tool that can show, expose, and generate action; Shakespeare's *Hamlet* is a play that keeps forestalling action with words, words, words. Eventually, Hamlet's thoughts turn bloody and his "words"—wordswordswords—become two swords following the word.

Shakespeare assures us that Hamlet's story will be told, because the play ends with a promise of a performance to come. To tell Hamlet's story, Horatio must first stage it:

> give order that these bodies
> High on a stage be placed to the view,
> And let me speak to [th'] yet unknowing world
> How these things came about. So shall you hear
> Of carnal, bloody, and unnatural acts,
> Of accidental judgments, casual slaughters,
> Of deaths put on by cunning and [forc'd] cause,
> And in this upshot, purposes mistook
> Fall'n on th' inventors' heads: All this can I
> Truly deliver. (5.2.377–86)

The bodies onstage will enact "something like" the "carnal, bloody and unnatural acts" that we just saw for the "noblest" called to the "audience" (5.2.87) by Fortinbras. Theater stages what we can imagine is true, because it generates a fiction that is present and therefore possible. Meaning is made not conveyed. King Hamlet tells Hamlet his story (despite the soul-harrowing potential of the words entering Hamlet's ears) to insight revenge and right his end. Hamlet asks Horatio to tell his story (despite the fact that it will require Horatio to draw his "breath in pain") to right his name. The telling and hearing of the story is a physical act—it harrows and it pains. Mark Johnson, calling for an aesthetics of meaning making that does not privilege the science but insists on the centrality of the body, points out the role of art in creating the kind of "*corporeal encounter with our environment*" that is necessary for meaning:

> Art uses the very same syntactic, semantic, and pragmatic resources that underlie *all* meaning, but in art those resources are exploited in

remarkable ways that give us a sense of the meaning of things that is typically not available in our day-to-day affairs. [...] In art we seek intensification, harmonizing, and fulfillment of the possibilities for meaning and growth of meaning.[2]

Meaning comes from the transaction between storyteller and audience; the stage needs the bodies and the story needs the audience. The focus becomes what happens between performer and spectator: a neurological transaction, or neuroplay, that is both performed and received, staged and housed, you and me, at the same time.

Hamlet's eye, moving from Rosencrantz and Guildenstern to Claudius's face is always in this space of all spaces: where the audience and performers create the event of the performance, floating somewhere around where the fourth wall might be. The possibilities of the "infinite space" within Hamlet's brain and Shakespeare's Globe are endless in light of the work on the mirror neuron system. Cells firing in me if I do something or you do something suggest that the difference between us is one of parts, not wholes. An intention to lift a cup, thought to exist "inside the container" of the self, is registered by the witness and "external" show expresses "internal" intent. The mirror neurons, then, expose what Hamlet's mirror held up to nature does: we may want to believe that there is an internal self with agency that we can see and thus know, but it is our "blind spot," it is how we see and where we cannot see.

Although without reference to conceptual blending theory, many important scholars have written about debates concerning language and performance in the early modern period.[3] If the metaphors used by the poet to understand his world are different from our own, then the meaning he is attempting to communicate will also be different. To survey the work on *Hamlet* is to survey the history of Western thought over the last four hundred years. My findings in Hamlet's mirror are not necessarily radically new: other people have been interested in agency and epistemology in *Hamlet* and scholars have investigated the object and technology of the mirror for what it reveals about the period. Chapters 3 and 4 engage with the important historical and theoretical perspectives on the mirror and *Hamlet* that are aided, not upended, by an application of cognitive science to literary and historical scholarship. Without the language and methodology of cognitive linguistics, however, these ideas remain abstract and resist integration with other forms of inquiry. Conceptual blending theory exposes *how* Shakespeare means what he means, rather than *what* he means. It destabilizes previous conceptions of how meaning was made and provides a tool for watching the process of meaning making, from two often contrasting ideas into a third emergent idea. It allows for a reexamination of the role of performance in the epistemological shifts of the early modern period. I have applied conceptual blending theory to Hamlet's mirror held up to nature to exhume a network of associations scaffolding Shakespeare's *Hamlet* around the compression of cause and effect, agency and intention, seeing and knowing. Hamlet's mirror hides and creates agency, and this peep-show is reflected in the play's ambivalence about the link between action, cause, intention, and agency.

An Eye of View

Antonio Damasio begins *Descartes Error*, his influential book on the inseparability of emotion and reason, with the story of Phineas Gage who, in 1848, survived an accident where a railroad spike went straight through his frontal lobe. With a hole through his head, he was carted miles to a doctor, got out of the ox cart with minimal assistance, and recounted the details of the accident to bystanders as the doctor worked to dress and disinfect the one and a half inch "opening through the skull and integuments."[4] The miracle was reported in the local newspapers and the *Boston Medical and Surgical Journal*, and Gage's doctor pronounced him "cured" within two months. He lived without parts of his brain—speaking, seeing, touching, walking—but did not have the same personality, "After the accident, he no longer showed respect for social convention; ethics in the broad sense of the term, were violated; the decisions he made did not take into account his best interest, and he was given to invent tales 'without any foundation except in his fancy,' in Harlow's [the doctor's] words."[5] What was lost of his brain changed his mind. It was clear that the brain is for more than thinking and that it is not a whole discreet organ but an organism with parts. Since then, neuroscience has posed and answered and posed anew an amazing series of questions and invented tools to see with new eyes into the lights of the brain. A kind of "big bang" of neuroscience, Gage's accident marks, in many ways, the start of a period of intense interest in the brain and the mind: what was lost and what remained and how is it that a change of brain created a change of "Phineas Gage"? Who he was, not just how he processed and expressed information, could be traced to what was inside and how the parts worked to make up the whole. Here at the start of the twenty-first century, the integration of science and the humanities could provide the next century's big bang.

The separation between the "two cultures" is invented and unproductive. What happens in one building and what happens in the other differ in terms of method and evidence, perhaps, but the search for new answers and new questions is the same. Cognitive linguists want to know how "now is the winter of our discontent" constructs meaning and so do we. Neuroscientists want to know how a prosthetic alters the body map and so do we. Neurophilosophers want to know how the body creates the mind and how the mind creates the body and so do we. Cognitive scientists want to know how imitation forms cognition (and how this process can be interrupted and/or facilitated), how the environment operates within a cognitive system, and how memory is written down, reenacted, rewritten, and wiped away and so do we. We are uniquely positioned to interrogate the role of stories and metaphor in language and cognition. We are ideally situated to provide a meta-analysis of the language and translation issues in and between the fields of study. We know how the body moves in space, how empathy works between characters and between actors and audience, how actors learn lines, how dancers communicate grief, and how history has marked the arts and sciences ideologically.

This is not to say that the disciplinary walls should come crashing down or that all work is most fruitfully done at or on the wall. The research a theater scholar does in the neurosciences should then be applied to questions within theater studies. Neuroscientists should study art, but could benefit from the scholarship conducted over the last millennia on art, creativity, and aesthetics. Cognitive linguists broke away from the generative grammar theory because it failed to answer how meaning was made in poetry; they did not tell poets that their language made no sense according to their theory. Theory being wielded in the humanities should cohere with research conducted in the sciences on language, meaning, and cognition. I do not mean that we should cross check all of our answers, but if we are making claims about the use of language to circulate hegemony, for example, we should know whether our idea of how language works (cognitively as well as culturally) matches the evidence collected within cognitive linguistics that depicts a linguistic system based on profound creativity and instability. If we want to articulate the power of the body's wisdom on stage, we would be aided and supported by seeing the ways scientists have broken down divisions between the body and the mind, thinking and feeling, knowing and believing.

In Tom Stoppard's *Arcadia*, Thomasina searches for the equation of an apple leaf, because she wants math to explain all shapes, not just familiar geometric ones. Protesting the limitations of Euclidean geometry, Thomasina avers "armed thus, God could only make a cabinet."[6] Until recently, language theory worked to explain linguistic cabinets, not the kind of poetic cathedrals found in Shakespeare. Conceptual blending theory is an elegant explanation of language from the literal to the densely poetic. Because any three-year-old knows that the Runaway Bunny is a blend of information from different input spaces, it can be tempting to feel that blending theory lacks complexity or novelty; yet it is valuable precisely because it gives us a language to discuss what three-year-olds do every day and what Shakespeare did four hundred years ago.

Those that doubt the importance of the turn toward the cognitive in the humanities—or the turn toward the humanities of the cognitive sciences—have not been paying attention. Cognitive science has been influential in literature, music, and creativity for some time.[7] There are books recently published or forthcoming that use cognitive theory to rethink the medieval period for example, or that situate the early modern period within a material framework that includes the materiality of the brain.[8] Perhaps the greatest value of this interplay is in the avenues for research it opens up. Some of the avenues of research have already been called for: as discussed elsewhere in this book, F. Elizabeth Hart has called for a materialist linguistics; Bruce McConachie argues for the value of cognitive studies in historiography; Rhonda Blair has called upon cognitive science to inform acting theory. And more work remains. How can cognitive science be applied throughout the rehearsal process, from applying linguistics and narrative theory to table work to incorporating the science of vision and hearing to lighting and sound design? Consciously or unconsciously, artists operate on scientific understandings; sound designers I have spoken to, for example, are very aware of the neuroscience behind sound and its cognitive impact. As Joseph Roach has pointed out, the art of acting has also always been the science of acting, because the actor's method must reflect an understanding of the self and psychology.[9] As the science changes, so does the art.

Although it is still heresy to say so to many American trained actors, it seems to me that contemporary science offers a challenge to contemporary acting theory. Blair has argued that cognitive science can aid the actor, but aid the actor in producing performances of characters with an internal life.[10] What if we alter our conception of the self? What if cognition is embedded and dynamic, then should actors create characters or create a dynamic system amid and among themselves? If empathy is not elicited by conveying "real" emotions to an audience, how should actors learn to conduct or evoke emotions in the audience? If the way to my heart is through my motor cortex (via the mirror neurons) rather than my amygdala, what does that suggest about creating a "moving" performance? A different understanding of who we are necessitates not just new acting, but the new plays to reflect this growing shift in our categories. Some contemporary playwrights are already creating this kind of theater—and thus the actors necessary to make sense of this work—such as Richard Maxwell; and, of course, the work of Robert Wilson, Robert LaPage, and the Wooster Group (to name just a few) have looked away from psychological realism for awhile now.

There is a lot of play still to do. Scientists studying the mirror neuron system are publishing new research and designing new experiments every day and this work must be studied rigorously and then applied to theater and performance theoretically. How does research on distributed cognition impact how we understand the rehearsal room and process and the theater space and performance? The study of empathy and emotions, gaining tremendous popularity and importance, will continue to impact the questions and answers we have about what happens onstage, offstage, and in between.[11] There are opportunities for theater scholars to collaborate with scientists on empirical research. Most research involves one subject watching something on a screen; how can we help design and conduct experiments that examine what happens when a spectator becomes a member of an audience? When the unit of observation is the group? How do gestures operate to tell the whole story of a play? Is there a type of gesture that attracts audience attention more than others? Is there a moment or a discourse category that requires gestural accompaniment more than others? How does pacing impact comprehension? What, finally, is the live theatrical event? Do we actually react differently to live actors than we do to filmed actors, or is that just an assumption we use to protect stage from screen? If our bodies do not begin and end exactly where we think they do, might virtual theater offer the same benefits or experiences as live theater?

The more invested I become in this interplay, the more important it is that I understand the science to which I refer and that I deploy the sciences to ask and answer new questions within my own discipline. Although the sciences and the arts/humanities are coming closer and closer together, attention must be paid to the shorelines: where words and categories are reexamined for how they translate (what does "performance" mean in the sciences and what does "embodiment" mean for theater scholars?) and methods, goals, and evidence can be separate and equal. What the scientists want to know is what those of us in the humanities want to know: how did he/she/I/we *do* that? How did Shakespeare write a soliloquy that could and would be quoted by all English-speaking high school graduates? How do we remember it and why does it interest us? How does an actor weep for Hecuba and why is it that the audience weeps for the actor? What's Hecuba to him or him to Hecuba? As theater scholars and practitioners, we know the value of dialogue. We know that there is a difference between locus and platea. We go to the theater to see something we know made strange. We find community in the shared space of the dark theater. We are ideally situated in the academic web to comment on the network of ideas, research, and theories occurring across the disciplines. Integrating what scientists are learning about imitation, play, and language into performance and theater theory has the potential of proving what many of us experienced long ago watching *Annie, Long Day's Journey into Night, Arcadia,* or *Hamlet*: theater shapes and transforms our parts into our wholes.

Notes

1 Who's There?

1. Because "our" biology is basically the same (or as similar as it is different, if we view biology genetically) my investigation into the interplay of science and theater studies will omit a discussion of cultural, temporal, racial, political, gendered, historical, sexual, or any other important difference. The cognitive neurosciences are moving beyond an essentializing positivism and are embracing an embodied realism that neither denies the situated, raced, gendered, cultural, historical perspective nor does it deny a reality. It is my contention that we are enough the same to integrate scientific research that might provide information on what Louis Montrose has called the "cognitive and therapeutic instrument" of literature and performance.
2. George Lakoff, *Women, Fire, and Dangerous Things: What Categories Reveal about the Mind* (Chicago: University of Chicago Press, 1987), xv.
3. See Vittorio Gallese and Lakoff, "The Brain's Concepts: The Role of the Sensory-Motor System in Conceptual Knowledge," in *Cognitive Neuropsychology* 21 (2005).
4. See Seana Coulson and Cyma Van Petten "Conceptual Integration and Metaphor: An Event-Related Potential Study" *Memory & Cognition* 30, no. 6 (2002): 958–68.
5. It is, however, usually falsifiable. Even theories that remain contentious within cognitive science work on the assumption that a gathering of evidence and a growing body of work that finds the new interpretation capable of providing answers to previously unanswered questions will eventually gain consensus and the next set of research/questions will go from there. That it will be considered "true" until evidence arrives that suggests that it is "not true." F. Elizabeth Hart points out that literary theory should be evaluated for how they fit with research on language produced and studied within cognitive linguistics, since, "both deconstruction and materialist studies have internalized basic formalist assumptions about the operations of language that are indigenous to linguistic structuralism." She provides an

insightful "science based critique of Derridean language theory, focusing on the formalism latent in Jacques Derrida's narrative of différance." See Hart, "Matter, System, and Early Modern Studies: Outlines for a Materialist Linguistics," *Configurations* 6.3 (1998): 313–14. For a strong argument for the integration of the sciences into the humanities, see Bruce McConachie, "Falsifiable Theories for Theatre and Performance Studies," *Theatre Journal* 59, no. 4 (2007): 553–77.

6. There are, of course, areas of the brain responsible for different language skills, but most contemporary cognitive linguistics do not believe that these areas come "hardwired" with language facilities.
7. George Lakoff and Mark Johnson, *Metaphors We Live By* (Chicago and London: University of Chicago Press, 1980), 160.
8. Lakoff, *Women, Fire, and Dangerous Things*, 47–52.
9. Ibid., 67.
10. Ibid, 74.
11. Ibid., 205.
12. Ibid., 76.
13. There are still defenders of this view. See, for example, Steven Pinker, *The Language Instinct* (New York: W. Morrow, 1994) and *Words and Rules* (New York: Basic Books, 1999). Pinker follows the computational model of comprehension and construction and argues that there is a language center of the brain and that our "instinct" to use symbols to communicate is hard-wired.
14. Lakoff, *Women, Fire, and Dangerous Things*, 148.
15. Theodore Brown, *Making Truth: Metaphor in Science* (Urbana and Chicago: University of Illinois Press, 2003), 25.
16. Ibid., 9. Moreover, there is evidence that we use stories, religion, and myth to generate categorical variants to reinforce the category. Pascal Boyer finds that, across cultures and times, religious figures or stories tend to contain an element that "*contradicts information provided by the ontological category*"; "*religious concepts invariably include information that is counterintuitive* relative to the category activated," *Religion Explained: The Evolutionary Origins of Religious Thought* (New York: Basic Books: 2001), 64–65. This religious "other" helps clarify what we know as normal.
17. Lakoff, *Women, Fire, and Dangerous Things*, xvi.
18. This is meant to call attention to the inseparability of body and mind—I do not refer to brain here, as it is a part of the body but not equal to the mind. It is unfortunate that there is not a better term, since by writing them both, they remain separate, just yoked by a slash. I am often amazed at how intractable this separation is—especially in the arts, where there is talk of celebrating the body's wisdom as if there is wisdom that exists somewhere else. The sciences in this particular area are ahead of the arts. But the arts have not

come up with the term, the metaphor, to allow us to move past the conception of separation inculcated by Descartes.
19. In *More Than Cool Reason: A Field Guide to Poetic Metaphor* (Chicago: University of Chicago Press, 1989), Lakoff and Mark Turner argue that metaphoric thinking comes naturally and is not a specialized skill of the literary or poetic elite. We use metaphors to understand everything from "dead-end job" to "life is a tale told by an idiot." The metaphor LIFE IS A JOURNEY allows us to speak of "reaching goals" and "life in the fast lane." Because "knowing the structure of this metaphor [LIFE IS A JOURNEY] means knowing a number of correspondences between the two conceptual domains of life and journeys" (3).
20. In *Where Mathematics Comes From* (New York, Basic Books: 2000), Lakoff and Rafael Núñez argue that the history of mathematics is one of new metaphors generating new categories and thus new mathematic "realities." Zero was a metaphor before it was number; the only reason it became a number was because it provided enough value to justify the category extension of numbers. In "Telling New Stories: *Henry V*'s Blending and Reblending of Something and Nothing" in *Blending and the Study of Narrative*, eds. Ralf Schneider and Marcus Hartner (forthcoming 2010) I provide an analysis of the ideas of ones and zeros in *Henry V* based on Lakoff and Núñez's work, showing how Shakespeare stages and challenges the Chorus's idea of the "cipher" [zero] that can make a million in a "little place" (Prologue, 16).
21. Lakoff has written *Moral Politics: How Liberals and Conservatives Think* (Chicago: University of Chicago Press, 1996), *Don't Think of an Elephant!: Know Your Values and Frame the Debate* (White River Junction, VT: Chelsea Green, 2004) and *The Political Mind: Why You Can't Understand 21st-Century Politics with an 18th-Century Brain* (New York: Viking, 2008).
22. For more on the history of the shift in cognitive linguistics from generative or objectivist theories of language to compositional and experiential theories of language, see Lakoff, *Women, Fire, and Dangerous Things* (1987), Lakoff and Johnson, *Philosophy in the Flesh: The Embodied Mind and Its Challenge to Western Thought* (New York: Basic Books, 1999), and Gilles Fauconnier and Mark Turner. *The Way We Think: Conceptual Blending and the Mind's Hidden Complexities* (New York: Basic Books, 2002).
23. Lakoff and Johnson, *Philosophy in the Flesh*, 5.
24. Ibid., 271 and Lakoff and Turner, *More Than Cool Reason*, 19.
25. Lakoff, *Women, Fire, and Dangerous Things*, 267.
26. Mark Turner, *The Literary Mind: The Origins of Thought and Language* (Oxford: Oxford University Press, 1996), 16.
27. Lakoff, *Women, Fire, and Dangerous Things*, 271.

28. Mark Johnson, *The Body in the Mind: The Bodily Basis of Meaning, Imagination, and Reason* (Chicago: University of Chicago Press, 1987), 30–31.
29. Lakoff and Johnson, *Philosophy in the Flesh*, 26.
30. See, for example, Lakoff and Johnson, *Metaphors We Live By*.
31. Whereas I. A. Richards (*The Philosophy of Rhetoric*, The Mary Flexner Lectures on the Humanities. London: Oxford University Press, 1936) referred to the parts of a metaphor as tenor and vehicle, where the vehicle is that which is providing information about the tenor, Lakoff used "target" and "source." In Lakoff's early work, he denoted metaphor as "target IS source" but Turner and Johnson use the convention "TARGET IS SOURCE," which I find more useful as it gives more visual status to the terms. Fauconnier and Turner breaks this binary down by arguing that many things we assumed were metaphors cannot be understood with this simple binary equation.
32. Lakoff, *Women, Fire, and Dangerous Things*, 74.
33. Gilles Fauconnier, *Mental Spaces: Aspects of Meaning Construction in Natural Language* (Cambridge: Cambridge University Press, 1985), xvii.
34. Fauconnier and Turner, *The Way We Think*, 16.
35. Ibid., 17.
36. Ibid., 18.
37. The blend puts pressure on me to envision them as men, since female boxers are not yet common enough to challenge our prototype of the male boxer. Therefore, to talk about business in terms of boxing (or war) is to reinforce our conception of the boardroom as a place for men.
38. Fauconnier goes on to add: "We have also argued that the capacity for double-scope integration could well be the crucial distinctive feature of cognitively modern humans, and we have shown how such a singularity could have emerged through standard evolutionary processes" (8).
39. See Mark Turner, "Double-Scope Stories," in *Narrative Theory and the Cognitive Sciences*, CSLI (2003): 123–29 and 133.
40. Stephen Best and Sharon Marcus, "Surface Reading: An Introduction," *Representations* 108, (Fall 2009): 1.
41. Linda Charnes, *Hamlet's Heirs: Shakespeare and the Politics of a New Millennium* (New York: Routledge, 2006), 10.
42. I borrow this term from the subtitle of *Performance and Cognition* (New York: Routledge, 2006) edited by Bruce McConachie and F. Elizabeth Hart.
43. Mark Johnson, *The Meaning of the Body: Aesthetics of Human Understanding* (Chicago: University of Chicago Press, 2007), x.
44. Ibid., 117.
45. Ibid., 219.
46. See Freeman, "'Catch[Ing] the Nearest Way': *Macbeth* and Cognitive Metaphor," *Journal of Pragmatics* 24 (1995), 689–708. He uses

"image-schemata" from the work of Johnson, *The Body in the Mind*, Lakoff and Johnson, *Metaphors We Live By*, and Turner *The Literary Mind*, which are defined as skeletal structures that derive from an embodied understanding of abstract concepts such as life and meaning. "Container" is also an image-schema that drives the way we speak of the body, a room, a state, and others. These are similar to Idealized Cognitive Models, but where image-schema use an embodied image to structure understanding, an ICM is like a set of instructions used to match the image with the idea.

47. Freeman, "Catch[Ing] the Nearest Way," 693.
48. Barbara Dancygier and Eve Sweetser, *Mental Spaces in Grammar: Conditional Constructions*, Cambridge Studies in Linguistics 108 (Cambridge: Cambridge University Press, 2005). See also Sweetser, "'The suburbs of your good pleasure': Cognition, culture and the bases of metaphoric structure," in *The Shakespearean International Yearbook*, ed. G. Bradshaw, T. Bishop, and Mark Turner (Aldershot, England: Ashgate, 2004), 24–55 and "Whose rhyme is whose reason? Sound and sense in *Cyrano De Bergerac*," in *Language and Literature* (London: Sage, 2006), 29–54.
49. See Ellen Spolsky, *Satisfying Skepticism: Embodied Knowledge in the Early Modern World* (Aldershot, England: Ashgate, 2001), *Gaps in Nature: Literary Interpretation and the Modular Mind* (Albany: State University of New York Press, 1993) and, most recently, *Word vs Image: Cognitive Hunger in Shakespeare's England* (Basingstoke: Palgrave Macmillan, 2007).
50. Norman Holland, "The Willing Suspension of Disbelief: A Neuro-Psychoanalytic View" at PsyArt: A Hyperlink Journal for the Psychological Study of the Arts (article 020919): 4 &6. Accessed online February 4, 2005: http://www.clas.ufl.edu/ipsa/journal/2003_holland06.shtml. Holland's most recent book is *Literature and the Brain* (PsyArt Foundation, 2009). Though, as I have argued elsewhere, I do not share Holland's belief in the willing suspension of disbelief or in his suggestion that emotions and fictions are things that can be real or unreal.
51. John Tooby and Leda Cosmides, "Does Beauty Build Adapted Minds? Toward an Evolutionary Theory of Aesthetics, Fiction, and the Arts," *SubStance* 94/95 (2001): 7.
52. Bruce R. Smith, *The Acoustic World of Early Modern England: Attending to the O-Factor* (Chicago: University of Chicago Press, 1999), 21.
53. Ibid., 284.
54. For an excellent and early account of the history of cognitive science that led the way to the current interdisciplinarity and the possibilities such change suggests, see Mary Crane and Alan Richardson's "Literary Studies and Cognitive Science: Toward a New Interdisciplinarity" *Mosaic: A Journal for the Interdisciplinary Study of Literature* (June 1999).

55. Rhonda Blair has been an advocate of including cognitive science in studies of acting, using research on emotions and memory, for example, to enrich Stanislavsky-style actor training. In her essay, "Image and Action," Blair describes incorporating "image streams" into her work with actors in rehearsal, filling, as she argues, a "lacunae" in Stanislavsky's work. See also *The Actor, Image, and Action: Acting and Cognitive Neuroscience* (New York: Routledge, 2008). Her essay "Cognitive Neuroscience and Acting: Imagination, Conceptual Blending, and Empathy," *TDR* 53, no. 4 (2009): 92–103, includes studies in cognitive linguistics, mirror neurons, and memory. See John Lutterbie's "Neuroscience and Creativity in the Rehearsal Process," in *Performance and Cognition: Theatre Studies and the Cognitive Turn*, ed. Bruce McConachie and F. Elizabeth Hart (New York: Routledge, 2006): 149–66). See Hansen and Bruce Barton, "Research-Based Practice: Situating Vertical City between Artistic Development and Applied Cognitive Science," *TDR* 53, no. 4 (2009): 120–36.
56. See his latest book, *Engaging Audiences* (New York: Palgrave Macmillan, 2008). Before that, McConachie employed cognitive linguistics to reimagine historiography. In his book *American Theater in the Culture of the Cold War* (Iowa City: University of Iowa Press, 2003), McConachie shows how the image schema of containment structured the theater of the cold war period. McConachie illustrates how "containment was at the hub of a vast network of cold war conceptions that structured much of the dominant culture of the era" (12). This cognitive retelling of a historical period is important because it allows certain political and ideological entailments of the dominant image schema to become visible and thus questionable.
57. See Bryan Reynolds' introduction in his *Transversal Enterprises in the Drama of Shakespeare and His Contemporaries* (New York: Palgrave Macmillan, 2006), Blakey Vermeule, *Why Do We Care about Literary Characters?* (Johns Hopkins University Press, 2009), Naomi Rakotnitz, "Mirror Neurons and the Manipulation of Embodied Responses: Disgust in *The Libertine*," paper presented at Theatre and Cognitive Science Symposium (Pittsburgh, PA, 2009), and Pil Hansen, "A Perceptual Approach to Dramaturgical Practice," paper presented at the Theatre and Cognitive Science Symposium (Pittsburgh, PA, 2009).
58. Blair, ASTR plenary address, 2006.
59. Louis Montrose, *The Purpose of Playing: Shakespeare and the Cultural Politics of the Elizabethan Theatre* (Chicago: University of Chicago Press, 1996), 39.
60. Ibid., 40.
61. I am grateful to John Lutterbie for bringing this essay to the attention of the Performance and Cognition group and for encouraging active engagement with the criticisms of this kind of work.

62. See Amy Cook, "Staging Nothing: *Hamlet* and Cognitive Science," *SubStance* 35, No. 2.110 (2006): 83–99, "Interplay: The Method and Potential of a Cognitive Approach to Theatre," *Theatre Journal* 59, no.4 (2007): 579–94, and "Wrinkles, Wormholes, and *Hamlet*: The Wooster Group's *Hamlet* as a Challenge to Periodicity," *TDR* 53, no. 4 (2009): 92–103.
63. Mary Crane, "Surface, Depth, and the Spatial Imaginary: A Cognitive Reading of *the Political Unconscious*," *Representations* 108, (Fall 2009): 76.
64. This and all citations from Shakespeare are from the Riverside Shakespeare, second edition.

2 Linguistic Synaesthesia

1. Excerpted in *The Portable Enlightenment Reader*, ed. Isaac Kramnick, New York: Penguin Books, 1995), 207.
2. As Annabelle Patterson argues in *Shakespeare and the Popular Voice* (Cambridge, MA: Basil Blackwell, 1989) this definition of players and playing "admits that theatre was accountable to others. In its very brevity and abstraction the phrase mimics its own blunt suggestion, that dramatic fictions reproduce their own historical environment in condensed and densely signifying metaphors" (29).
3. Kathleen Irace, *The First Quarto of Hamlet*, ed. Brian Gibbons, *The New Cambridge Shakespeare: The Early Quartos* (Cambridge: Cambridge University Press, 1998), 9.
4. Harold Jenkins, *Hamlet* (London: Arden Shakespeare, 1982), 437–38.
5. See, for example, V. S. Ramachandran and E. M. Hubbard, "Synaesthesia—a Window into Perception, Thought and Language," *Journal of Consciousness Studies* 8, no. 12 (2001): 3–34 and D. L. Brang, Edwards, V. S. Ramachandran, and S. Coulson, "Is the Sky 2?: Contextual Priming in Grapheme-Color Synaesthesia," *Psychological Science* 19, no. 5 (2008): 421–28. There does seem to be some remaining disagreement on this; one study found that because a large percentage of synaesthetic linkages (e.g., R seen as red) are consistent across synaesthetes and nonsynaesthetes, such a condition is learned and simply stronger in synaesthetes. See A. N. Rich, J. L. Bradshaw, and J. B. Mattingley, "A Systematic, Large-Scale Study of Synaesthesia: Implications for the Role of Early Experience in Lexical-Colour Associations," *Cognition* 98, no. 1 (2005): 53–84.
6. Ramachandran and Hubbard, "Synaesthesia—a Window into Perception, Thought and Language," 9. For more on Ramachandran's research on phantom limbs, see *Phantoms in the Brain* (New York: Quill, William, Morris, 1998).
7. Ibid., 17.
8. Ramachandran and Hubbard, "Synaesthesia—a Window into Perception, Thought and Language," 3.

9. See Kenneth Burke, *A Grammar of Motives* (Berkeley: University of California Press, 1969), 503.
10. Ramachandran and Hubbard, "Synaesthesia—a Window into Perception, Thought and Language," 3.
11. Ibid.
12. Ibid.
13. Philip Davis, *Shakespeare Thinking* (London: Continuum, 2007), 93.
14. Davis suggests that Shakespeare's language is a kind of originary text: it makes us in its image. Further, he argues that Shakespeare's use of cross-sense language or word-class conversion (i.e., making a noun a verb) is cognitively constructive: "Shakespeare's lines are Renaissance brain scanners, where scanning is to do both with poetic rhythm and with neurological patterning. From eye to voice or ear to eye, from text to performance, in the interplay of line and sentence or metre and rhythm, between brain and mind: these are the great Shakespearean shifts of mentality, to and fro" (63).
15. Mark Johnson, *The Meaning of the Body: Aesthetics of Human Understanding* (Chicago: University of Chicago Press, 2007), 132.
16. Spurgeon, *Shakespeare's Imagery and What It Tells Us*, (Cambridge: Cambridge University Press, 1935).
17. Joel Altman, *The Tudor Play of Mind* (Berkeley: University of California Press, 1978), 45.
18. In "English Mettle," Mary Floyd-Wilson's essay in *Reading the Early Modern Passions* (Philadelphia: University of Pennsylvania Press, 2004) for example, Floyd-Wilson connects the importance of rhetoric in the period to ideas of emotional strength: "English valor is deemed unique, powerful, and sturdy because it requires the effort of such rhetoric" (145). Richard A Lanham goes further in *The Motives of Eloquence: Literary Rhetoric in the Renaissance* (New Haven, CT and London: Yale University Press, 1976) arguing that the self combines the rhetorical self and the serious self and that language plays a major role in identity. He attempts to reverse a discrediting of rhetoric as ancillary, viewing it as "half of man": "If truly free of rhetoric, we would be pure essence. We would retain no social dimension," 8.
19. As Reynolds and I argue in, "Comedic Law: Projective Transversality, Deceit Conceits, and the Conjuring of Macbeth and Doctor Faustus in Jonson's *The Devil Is an Ass*," in *Transversal Enterprises in the Drama of Shakespeare and His Contemporaries: Fugitive Explorations*, ed. Bryan Reynolds (London: Palgrave Macmillan, 2005).
20. Cited in Chris Hassel, Jr., "Military Oratory in *Richard III*" in *Modern Critical Interpretations: William Shakespeare's Richard III*, ed. Harold Bloom (New York: Chelsea House Publishers, 1988), 74.
21. Seana Coulson, *Semantic Leaps: Frame-Shifting and Conceptual Blending in Meaning Construction* (Cambridge, MA: MIT Press, 2001), 2.

22. For more on the womb/tomb in *Richard III*, see Linda Charnes, "The Monstrous Body in *King Richard III*," in *Critical Essays on Shakespeare's* Richard III (New York: Hall, 1999): 273–78 and Madonne Miner's "'Neither Mother, Wife, Nor England's Queen': The Roles of Women in *Richard III*," in *Modern Critical Interpretations: William Shakespeare's* Richard III, ed. Harold Bloom (New York: Chelsea House Publishers, 1988). For what CBT reveals about the dangers of the womb/tomb connection, see Amy Cook, "Interplay: The Method and Potential of a Cognitive Approach to Theatre," *Theatre Journal* 59, no. 4 (2007): 579–94.
23. Shakespeare does this in the St. Crispin's day speech in *Henry V*. Henry's extraordinary speech manages to transport his ragtag (and inadequate in numbers) group of soldiers into a unified force of determination by calling up the future pride and brotherhood their wounds will bring them. This obscures the fact that any wound would be more likely to lead to death than a reason to lift a pint of ale in the future. For Henry and his men, this day will be all that is remembered as they age, will enrich their manhood, give them a story for their sons, and gentle their condition (*Henry V*, 4.3.19–67). I provide a cognitive linguistic analysis of the ones and zeros in *Henry V* and how the mathematical scaffolding the Chorus sets up in the Prologue influences our understanding of the rousing "band of brothers" speech in act four in Cook, "Telling new stories: *Henry V*'s blending and reblending of something and nothing" in *Blending and the Study of Narrative*, eds., Ralf Schneider and Marcus Hartner, forthcoming.
24. Katy Butler, "Winning Words: George Lakoff Says Environmentalists Need to Watch Their Language," *Sierra*, July/August (2004): 65.
25. See Seana Coulson and Todd Oakley, "Purple Persuasion: Conceptual Blending and Deliberative Rhetoric," in *Cognitive Linguistics: Investigations across Languages, Fields, and Philosophical Boundaries*, ed. J. Luchenbroers, (Amsterdam and Philadelphia: John Benjamins Press, 2006): 47–65.
26. Gilles Fauconnier and Mark Turner, *The Way We Think: Conceptual Blending and the Mind's Hidden Complexities* (New York: Basic Books, 2002), 92.
27. Seana Coulson and Esther Pascual, "For the Sake of Argument: Mourning the Unborn and Reviving the Dead through Conceptual Blending," *Annual Review of Cognitive Linguistics* 4, (2006): 170.
28. Sanger, David E. "Bush Describes Kerry's Health Care Proposal as a CE Government Takeover." *Times*, September 14, 2004 and Wilgoren, Jodi. "Kerry Faults Bush for Failing to Press Weapons Ban." *New York Times*, September 14, 2004.
29. "Intensify vital relations" and "achieve human scale" are two of the governing principles of blending articulated by Fauconnier and Turner. The "governing principles" of an effective blend sound like

aesthetic principles that might describe any good piece of theater, rhetoric, or poetry. The tracts on the power of rhetoric during the early modern period said similar things, which can make Fauconnier and Turner sound derivative. It is not necessary, however, for them to be the first to say it; their aim is to say it such that it fits with research not on theater, rhetoric, or poetry, but on how we think and communicate. In this way, their methodology, aim, and evidence can inform the studies of those of us who are studying theater, rhetoric, and poetry. Not unlike Quintilian, Fauconnier and Turner can evaluate blends on "objective" principles; from this perspective, we could evaluate what makes a theatrical production "good" or "bad." See *The Way We Think*, 309–52.
30. Fauconnier and Turner, *The Way We Think*, 76 and 292.
31. Laura Bohannan, "Shakespeare in the Bush," in *Critical Essays on Shakespeare's* Hamlet, ed. David Scott Kastan (New York: Hall, 1995), 11.
32. Ibid., 16.
33. Harold Jenkins, ed. *Hamlet* (London: Arden Shakespeare, 1982), 547.
34. Ibid., 547. Jenkins is citing Plowden (*Reports*, 1816, i.253–64), 259.
35. Coulson, *Semantic Leaps*, 228.

3 Mirror | Mirror; Mirror | rorriM

1. Conceptual integration network is a semantic way of privileging the network that creates the blend. While much of the work on this subject insists on the primary importance of the network in understanding, and learning to decompress, the blend—and, indeed Fauconnier now insists that blending theory is a theory of the network, not just the result of the network, I use blending through most of this book because it has gained the most currency and the analysis of the network required to arrive at the blend, begins with perceiving that something is a blend.
2. Robert Weimann, *Author's Pen and Actor's Voice: Playing and Writing in Shakespeare's Theatre* (Cambridge, MA: Cambridge University Press, 2000), 165.
3. Kelly, Philippa. "Surpassing Glass: Shakespeare's Mirrors" *Early Modern Literary Studies* 8, no. 1 (2002): 3.
4. Stephen Orgel, *The Illusion of Power: Political Theatre in the English Renaissance* (Berkeley: University of California Press, 1975), 45.
5. Ronald Levao, *Renaissance Minds and Their Fictions: Cusanus, Sidney, Shakespeare* (Berkeley: University of California Press, 1985), 268.
6. Ibid., 272.
7. This claim comes from Richard Schechner's definition in *Between Theatre and Anthropology* (Philidelphia: University of Pennsylvania

Press, 1985) of theater as "twice-behaved behavior" a definition that launched a discipline and a thousand theoretical ships. See, for example, Rebecca Schneider "Archives: Performance Remains," in *Performance Research* 6, no. 2 (2000): 100–108 and José Esteban Muñoz on performance studies and the document in "Ephemera as Evidence: Introductory Notes to Queer Acts," *Women and Performance: A Journal of Feminist Theory* 8, no. 2 (1996): 5–16.

8. Bert States, "Performance as Metaphor," *Theatre Journal* 48 (1996): 5.
9. Bert States, *Great Reckonings in Little Rooms: On the Phenomenology of Theater* (Berkeley: University of California Press, 1985), 64. To be fair, as discussed earlier, a "mirror image" is a different blend, where the image in the mirror is blended with what is in front of the mirror and rather than compress the identities, they remain distinct such that "mirror image" highlights the differences between the two spaces while connecting them in a cause and effect chain, such that the mirror is seen as both the cause and the effect of the differences.
10. Hereward T. Price, "Mirror-Scenes in Shakespeare," in *Joseph Quincy Adams Memorial Studies*, ed. James G. McManaway, Giles E. Dawson, and Edwin E. Willoughby (Washington, DC: The Folger Library, 1948): 104.
11. Ibid., 106.
12. Rudolph Stamm, *The Shaping Powers at Work: 15 Essays on Poetic Transmutation* (Heidelberg: Carl Winter, 1967), 24.
13. And, of course, any magnifying glass Ophelia held up to Hamlet would simply enlarge the details of his epidermis; it would not look into him (it is not an anatomizing knife) nor is she interested in his insides. Stamm seems to express through this use of the magnifying glass metaphor the way in which Ophelia's poetry (or, more accurately, Shakespeare's poetry) improves our ability to see elements of Hamlet's state or character.
14. Herbert Grabes, *The Mutable Glass: Mirror-Imagery in Titles and Texts of the Middle Ages and English Renaissance*, trans. Gordon Collier (Cambridge: Cambridge University Press, 1982), 63.
15. Debora Shuger, "The 'I' of the Beholder: Renaissance Mirrors and the Reflexive Mind," in *Renaissance Culture and the Everyday*, ed. Patricia Fumerton and Simon Hunt (Philadelphia: Pennsylvania University Press, 1999), 26.
16. Two other useful articles on the mirror in the early modern period are Philippa Kelly's "Surpassing Glass: Shakespeare's Mirrors," *Early Modern Literary Studies* 8, no. 1 (2002): 21–32, and Rayna Kalas's essay on George Gascoigne's satiric verse *The Steele Glas*, "The Technology of Reflection: Renaissance Mirrors of Steel and Glass," *Journal of Medieval and Early Modern Studies* 32, no. 3 (2002): 519–42. Kelly argues that the reflection in the mirror is a "radically unstable trope of transition" (3). Through examining references to

the mirror in the essays of Montaigne and statements by the Earl of Essex, she shows a mirror that does not offer a reflection of the person in front of the mirror so much as a diversity of potential faces and angles from which to view the face. The mirror does not reflect an individual self, but the social faces of the self. By revealing the spot on your face, the mirror offers a glimpse at the current face as well as the ideal social face one uses the mirror to create. She finds a similar set of meanings in Shakespeare's plays. For Shakespeare, she argues, the mirror "is a trope of displacement that evokes the shifting shape of identity in modes of social exchange" (5). Hamlet's quest for a stable interiority is mocked by the multiplicity of Hamlets he finds reflected back to him throughout the play. If, as Kelly argues, the mirror presents not a stable self, not an inside but various outsides, then it cannot depict an inside. Yet, discussions with the self in the mirror suggest that there is nonvisible information being ascertained by the dialogue with the reflection. Rayna Kalas posits a connection between an economic system that is fixed and stable like the steel mirrors and one that is increasingly incontinent and temporal like the crystal glass mirrors that came to replace the older steel mirrors. Kalas finds that the shift in the trade and craft of the mirror's production reflects the shift in mirror technology. For Gascoigne, the new mirrors were a fanciful conceit from another country, providing a suspiciously easy reflection in a nonsubstance. "Whereas the steel glass is identified with the estates of the realm, with land and domestic resources, with social custom and degree, the crystal glass is identified with mercantile trade, with fluid and artificial value, with sudden social mobility" (528). For Kalas, the mirror reflects a changing social and economic structure. Again, the mirror is used as a symbol for something else with a questionable sense of what the object or its reflection is or means. Kalas points out that part of Gascoigne's critique of the glass mirror resides in the seamlessness of its object and reflection: "Gascoigne's punning language demonstrates how, in the all too perfect reflections of a glass mirror, the material composition of the instrument drops away, leaving the viewer to a mere impression of the image in the glass" (526). Without the need to polish the steel before use and with glass's materiality more mysterious and invisible, the reflection becomes divorced from the object that produced it. Kalas does not question how "the material composition of the instrument drop[ped] away" nor does she investigate what Gascoigne's impression was of that "image in the glass."

17. David Scott Kastan, "'His Semblable Is His Mirror': *Hamlet* and the Imitation of Revenge," in *Shakespeare Studies*, ed. J. Leeds Barrol (New York: Franklin, 1987), 113.

18. Jacob Burckhardt argued that the Renaissance was the birth of the individual from the group in *The Civilization of the Renaissance in Italy* (London: G. Allen, 1914). In *Renaissance Self-Fashioning: From*

More to Shakespeare (Chicago: University of Chicago Press, 1980), Stephen Greenblatt sees the self as a cultural artifact, fashioned from social forces. *Shakespeare's* Hamlet *and the Controversies of Self* by John Lee (Oxford: Clarendon Press, 2000) is devoted to looking at critical issue of whether Hamlet has a self-constituting sense of self. John Jeffries Martin argues against Burckhardt and Greenblatt in insisting that multiple models of identity circulated during the Renaissance in *Myths of Renaissance Individualism* (Hampshire, England: Palgrave Macmillan, 2004).

19. Katherine Eisaman Maus and John Jeffries Martin are two critics interested in troubling the backward-look on subjectivity in the early modern period. In *Inwardness and Theater in the English Renaissance* (Chicago: University of Chicago Press, 1995), Maus argues against those theorists who believe that inwardness and a subjective sense of self did not exist in the Renaissance and instead sees an anxiety about the difference between, the management of, and the political import of a hidden interior and a published or social exterior. The writings of the time exhibit a heightened interest in the possibility of hypocrisy, deception, and equivocation and a separation between the inner truth, which cannot be questioned or verified, and the outward show, which can never be trusted. Her interest here is in the epistemological question of how one person can know another and how this epistemology is articulated at the time. In *Myths of Renaissance Individualism*, Martin looks at how the Renaissance viewed the self, arguing against both Burckhardt, who saw the Renaissance as the birth of the individual from the group, and Greenblatt, who saw the self as a cultural artifact fashioned from social forces. Martin would like a more complicated view, one that sees multiple models of identity during the period. Like Hawkes, he calls attention to the perspective of the researcher: "when we think about the history of Renaissance identities, we tend to hold them up as mirrors to ourselves, and what we see depends almost entirely upon where we stand" (7). While he admits that his analysis is also situated from a perspective, he hopes to remove the teleological viewing of the Renaissance as the birth of who ever we think we are.

20. See Ferdinand de Saussure, [*Course in General Linguistics*, trans. Wade Baskin, ed. Charles Bally, Albert Sechehaye, and Albert Riedlinger (New York: Philosophical Library. Reprint, 1966); Noam Chomsky, *Aspects of the Theory of Syntax* (Cambridge, MA: MIT Press, 1969); Steven Pinker, *Words and Rules: The Ingredients of Language* (New York: Basic Books, 1999); and Althusser, "Ideology and Ideological State Apparatuses (Notes towards an Investigation)," in *Lenin and Philosophy and Other Essays* (New York: Monthly Review Press, 1971).

21. *Renaissance Clothing and the Materials of Memory* (Cambridge: Cambridge University Press, 2000) by Ann Rosalind Jones and Peter Stallybrass is an excellent example of the value of investigating the

period through the traces of its materiality. Andrew Sofer's *The Stage Life of Props* (Ann Arbor: University of Michigan Press, 2003) and Tiffany Stern's *Making Shakespeare: From Stage to Page* (London: Routledge, 2004) exhume relevant material in their analysis of Shakespeare. Janet Arnold's *Queen Elizabeth's Wardrobe Unlock'd* (Leeds: W. S. Maney & Son, 1988) and John E. Crowley's *The Invention of Comfort: Sensibilities & Design in Early Modern Britain & Early America* (Baltimore: Johns Hopkins University Press, 2001) help situate the mirror in this period.

22. Benjamin Goldberg, *The Mirror and Man* (Charlottesville: University Press of Virginia, 1985), 135. Goldberg traces a shift from religious mysticism to practical humanism on the surface of the mirror. From the Senecan and Augustine notions of the mirror as a method of moving closer to a divine ideal to the concern that mirrors were increasing pride and vanity, Goldberg looks at the connection between the science of the reflective surface and the symbolic use of the image. He argues that the breakdown in the purely theological association with mirrors occurred in part because of the improved technology of mirror creation.

23. Herbert Grabes borrows the term from Ernst Robert Curtius who promotes its integration into literary studies in *European Literature and the Latin Middle Ages* (Princeton, NJ: Princeton University Press, 1953, repr. 1973).

24. Quoted in Adam Max Cohen, *Shakespeare and Technology: Dramatizing Early Modern Technological Revolutions* (New York: Palgrave Macmillan, 2006), 169.

25. William N. West has produced exciting work examining the use of the word "confusion" on the early modern stage, suggesting that there is a shifting of the conceptualization of "confusion" in second half of the sixteenth century. He looks at the use of the word to describe the reaction of audiences to what they saw onstage and finds that this confusion was productive. In looking at The Spanish Tragedy in particular, West argues that, "The distance between revelation and action in *The Spanish Tragedy* thus suggests a theory of theatre as correctable or accidental confusion, and then critiques that theory through its own practices, which set confusion at the center of theatre's performative effectiveness" (225). See, West, "'But This Will Be a Mere Confusion': Real and Represented Confusions on the Elizabethan Stage," *Theatre Journal* 60, no. 2 (2008): 217–33

26. Goldberg, *The Mirror and Man*, 140.

27. Venice was notoriously proprietary about its mirror technology— moving the glass houses from Venice to the island of Murano for easier protection against espionage. This fear of espionage was well founded, as both England and France tried to import some of the artisans to start glass houses of their own.

28. Sabine Melchior-Bonnet, *The Mirror: A History*, trans. Katharine H. Jewett (New York: Routledge, 2002), 21.
29. Henry Peacham, *Minerva Britanna* (Menston, England: Scholar Press, 1973).
30. This painting is owned by the National Gallery; to see an image of it, go to http://www.nationalgallery.org.uk/paintings/jan-van-eyck-the-arnolfini-portrait
31. Lise Bek, *Reality in the Mirror of Art* (Denmark: Aarhus University Press, 2003), 236.
32. This painting is owned by Kunsthistorisches Museum, Vienna; to see an image of it, go to http://bilddatenbank.khm.at/viewArtefact?id=768
33. Goldberg, *The Mirror and Man*, 122.
34. This painting is owned by the Louvre; to see an image of it, go to the Flemish painting section of the Louvre's website: http://www.louvre.fr/llv/commun/home.jsp
35. Melchoir-Bonnet, *The Mirror: A History*, 17.
36. Cohen finds this an example of mirror scrying, the witches seeing the future in the mirror.
37. Foucault, *The Order of Things: An Archaeology of the Human Sciences*, New York: Pantheon Books, 1971; 3–18. Phelan, Peggy. *Mourning Sex: Performing Public Memories*. London: Routledge, 1997; 25.
38. This painting is owned by the National Gallery. To see an image of it, go to: http://www.nationalgallery.org.uk/paintings/hans-holbein-the-younger-the-ambassadors
39. David Castillo, "Introduction," in *(a)Wry Views: Anamorphosis, Cervantes, and the Early Picaresque* (West Lafayette, IN: Purdue University Press, 2001), 11.
40. These objects were not displayed when I was there in August 2001 and were only available for examination via their images and descriptions on file.
41. John Hungerford Pollen, *Ancient Furniture and Woodwork* (London: South Kensington Museum Art Handbooks, 1876). A copy of this book, cited in the records at the V&A, is held at the Harvard Library.
42. Malcolm Baker, Brenda Richardson, and Anthony Burton, *A Grand Design: The Art of the Victoria and Albert Museum* (New York: Harry N. Abrams, 1997), 203.
43. Accessed online: http://www.vam.ac.uk/vastatic/microsites/1159_grand_design/popup.php?img_id=175 June, 2009.
44. Erving Goffman, *Frame Analysis: An Essay on the Organization of Experience* (New York: Harper, 1974), 21.
45. Baker, Richardson, and Burton, *A Grand Design*, 177.
46. Ibid.
47. Ibid., 177–78.
48. Grabes, *The Mutable Glass*, 137.

49. Lily B. Campbell, ed., *The Mirror for Magistrates* (Cambridge: Cambridge University Press, 1960), 49.
50. Grabes, *The Mutable Glass*, 173.
51. Ibid., 10.
52. Ibid., 103.
53. Paul Vincent Budra, A Mirror for Magistrates *and de cassibus Tradition* (Toronto and London: University of Toronto Press, 2000), 29.
54. Johann P. Sommerville, ed., *King James VI and I. Political Writings: Cambridge Texts in the History of Political Thought* (Cambridge: Cambridge University Press, 1994), 179.
55. The writings of King James are filled with references to the mirror. For King James, the mirror was the exemplar to follow, the warning of bad behavior, the tool of seeing, and the embodiment of that knowledge. James exhorts his son to know the Bible, because "seeing in him [god], as in a mirrour, the course of all earthly things, whereof hee is the spring and onely moouer" (13). Here James's mirror shrinks and reflects salient features from all "earthly things" like the convex mirrors in the fifteenth-century paintings. King James hopes his son will see in God an image of ideal behavior, for "there shall yee see your selfe, as in a myrrour, in the catalogue either of the good or the evill kings" (15); looking at the self in the mirror, like reading the Bible, provides a way of assessing the self through mapping "good" qualities and "evil" qualities from the reflection of the self (or the scriptures) back to the king in front of the mirror. This mirror provides the king with corrective material by comparing himself to the image he sees in the Bible.
56. Cohen, *Shakespeare and Technology*, 160.
57. Mark Turner, *The Literary Mind: The Origins of Thought and Language* (Oxford: Oxford University Press, 1996), 84.
58. Cohen, *Shakespeare and Technology*, 169.
59. Fauconnier and Turner, *The Way We Think: Conceptual Blending and the Mind's Hidden Complexities* (New York: Basic Books, 2002), 291–92.
60. Mark Turner, "The Ghost of Anyone's Father," in *Shakespearean International Yearbook*, ed. Graham Bradshaw, Thomas Bishop, and Mark Turner (Hants, UK: Ashgate, 2004), 14.
61. For more on how talismans, sacred relics, and charms are blends, see Fauconnier and Turner, *The Way We Think*, 207. For more on how effigy works in the theater, see Roach, *Cities of the Dead: Circum-Atlantic Performance* (New York: Columbia University Press, 1996), 220.
62. It is precisely this coding and decoding that troubles so much of Shakespeare's plays. This has comic consequences in plays such as *Twelfth Night* and *Much Ado About Nothing*, and tragic consequences in plays such as *Hamlet*, *Macbeth*, and *Richard III*, where such a simple mapping and social contract is broken and characters must discover other methods of knowing.

63. Maurice Merleau-Ponty, *The Phenomenology of Perception*, trans. Colin Smith. (London: Routledge, 2002), xiii.
64. Goffman, *Frame Analysis*, 572.
65. See "Kerry's 36-Hr. Stump-athon" in *New York Post*, 26 June 2004.
66. George Lakoff, *Women, Fire, and Dangerous Things: What Categories Reveal about the Mind* (Chicago: University of Chicago Press, 1987), 128.
67. See, for example, the discussion on blindspots in chapter 6.
68. Harold Bloom, *Shakespeare: The Invention of the Human* (New York: Riverhead, 1998), 401.

4 Meaning Superflux—A Cognitive Linguistic Reading of *Hamlet*

1. Mary Thomas Crane, *Framing Authority: Sayings, Self, and Society in Sixteenth-Century England* (Princeton, NJ: Princeton University Press, 1993), 1.
2. Crane is not the only person to make this argument; in "Matter, System, and Early Modern Studies: Outlines for a Materialist Linguistics" *Configurations* 6.3 (1998): 311–43, F. Elizabeth Hart argues for a materialist linguistics that conforms to the following conditions: it includes the brain; it conceives of processes as being bottom-up, from being biological to abstract; it accounts for comprehension and creativity; understands that language includes history and changes through the human subject; it sees change as diachronic; and uses elements of poststructuralism, particularly the way it "elevates metaphor as the mechanism through which ideology circulates in cultural discourse" (328). Her example of materialist linguistics is an exciting start. She notes that between 1500 and 1700, approximately 31,000 words were added to the English-language vocabulary, a fact with both scientific and literary consequences.
3. Mary Thomas Crane, *Shakespeare's Brain: Reading with Cognitive Theory* (Princeton, NJ: Princeton University Press, 2001), 4.
4. Ibid., 10.
5. Ibid., 4.
6. Ibid., 24–25.
7. Ibid., 124.
8. Ibid., 141.
9. Ibid., 142.
10. Ibid., 120.
11. Ibid., 121.
12. Ibid., 78.
13. Ibid, 126.
14. Ibid., 130.
15. Ibid., 149.

16. For more on the body/mind problem, see Paul Churchland's *Matter and Consciousness* (Cambridge, MA: MIT Press, 1984); Daniel Dennett's *Consciousness Explained* (Boston, MA: Little, Brown, 1991); or Patricia Churchland's *Neurophilosophy* (Cambridge, MA: MIT Press, 1989).
17. Cited in Antonio Damasio, *Descartes' Error: Emotion, Reason, and the Human Brain* (New York: Avon, 1994), 249.
18. This is the "error," the "abyssal separation between body and mind" (249), to which Antonio Damasio refers in his influential *Descartes' Error*. The importance of this scientific understanding has been examined by scholars in theater and performance, in particular Rhonda Blair "Cognitive Neuroscience and Acting: Imagination, Conceptual Blending, and Empathy," *TDR* 53, no. 4 (2009): 92–103; Amy Cook, "Interplay: The Method and Potential of a Cognitive Approach to Theatre," *Theatre Journal* 59, no.4 (2007): 579–94; John Lutterbie, "Neuroscience and Creativity in the Rehearsal Process," in *Performance and Cognition: Theatre Studies and the Cognitive Turn*, ed. Bruce McConachie and F. Elizabeth Hart (New York: Routledge, 2006): 149–66); Bruce McConachie, *Engaging Audiences* (New York: Palgrave Macmillan, 2008), Naomi Rakotnitz, "Mirror Neurons and the Manipulation of Embodied Responses: Disgust in *The Libertine*," paper presented at Theatre and Cognitive Science Symposium (Pittsburgh, PA, 2009); and Ellen Spolsky, *Satisfying Skepticism: Embodied Knowledge in the Early Modern World* (Aldershot, England: Ashgate, 2001), and *Word Vs Image: Cognitive Hunger in Shakespeare's England* (Basingstoke: Palgrave Macmillan, 2007).
19. V. S. Ramachandran, personal communication, January 2001. Ramachandran has also written on this topic in *A Brief Tour of Human Consciousness* (New York: PI Press, 2004).
20. In Robert Weimann's *Author's Pen and Actor's Voice: Playing and Writing in Shakespeare's Theatre* (Cambridge: Cambridge University Press, 2000), he explains how in the first Quarto, Hamlet's advice to the players is very different from the "naturalism" traditionally understood by the "purpose of playing": "The Prince, 'thus' performing a clown's 'cinkapase of ieasts' and, with another 'thus,' so 'blabbering with his lips,' is telling the players what not to do, but he does so by doing it himself" (23). By saying one thing and doing the other, Hamlet is providing the "mirror image" of what he is saying.
21. We call it the "front" of the mirror because we picture it "facing" us, rather than, say, the wall. In *Women, Fire, and Dangerous Things: What Categories Reveal About the Mind* (Chicago: University of Chicago Press, 1987), George Lakoff argues that this common projection of front and back on to objects is a consequence of embodiment, though in the case of the mirror, we generally perceive it with our front, because that is what will be reflected if we are standing "in front" of it. Unless, of course, you are in a Magritte painting.

22. "To be, or not to be, that is the question: / Whether 'tis nobler in the mind to suffer / the slings and arrows of outrageous fortune, / Or to take arms against a sea of troubles, / And by opposing, end them" (3.1.55–59).
23. Debora Shuger, "The 'I' of the Beholder: Renaissance Mirrors and the Reflexive Mind," in *Renaissance Culture and the Everyday*, ed. Patricia Fumerton and Simon Hunt (Philadelphia: Pennsylvania University Press, 1999), 26.
24. Gilles Fauconnier also examines this example in *Mental Spaces: Aspects of Meaning Construction in Natural Language* (Cambridge: Cambridge University Press, 1985); it is originally from J. McCawley's *Everything that Linguists Have Always Wanted to Know about Logic* (Chicago: University of Chicago Press; 1981).
25. Themselves mirror images of each other, as Tom Stoppard theatricalized in *Rosencrantz and Guildenstern Are Dead*.
26. Stephen Greenblatt, *Hamlet in Purgatory* (Princeton, NJ: Princeton University Press, 2001), 211.
27. This remark has generated tremendous critical commentary. In *Shakespeare's Brain*, Crane notes the use of proxies in *Hamlet*: "Almost everyone in Denmark employs spies, messengers, or other proxies to act on their behalf" and argues that "political life in Denmark seems for most of the play to operate at one remove from sources of power" (129), extending the reach of power's arm through the use of others. Katharine Eisaman Maus argues that the idea of an inner self did exist during the English Renaissance. She focuses on the theater because its inwardness is one that is always performed and thus self-erasing as it is self-producing. See, Maus, *Inwardness and Theater in the English Renaissance* (Chicago: University of Chicago Press, 1995). However, as Crane argues, "most critics have been ready to assume that what Hamlet has within is some version of the modern subject, either fully formed or still in the process of formation" (116). My interest here is not Hamlet's subjectivity, but the experience of interiority the play gives its audience.
28. Janis Butler Holm, ed., "A Critical Edition of Thomas Salter's *The Mirrhor of Modestie*," in *The Renaissance Imagination*, Vol. 32 (New York and London: Garland, 1987), 69.
29. Moreover, Shakespeare's language here constructs a mirror in the chiasmatic phrase, since a mirror placed after the first "feeling" reflects "feeling" to "feeling." Such a mirror, of course, would also reflect "sight" back to "eyes"; like Horatio's two hands, the same and different.
30. I am grateful to Emily DiLaura for pointing out this connection to me.
31. In the first quarto of *Hamlet*, as Kathleen Irace points out, the clown in the gravedigger scene sings: "A pickaxe and a spade, a spade, / For and a winding sheet; / Most fit it is for to be made / For such a ghest most meet" (Q1.16.34) and though most modern editors spell it as

"guest" the spelling might be a way of evoking the ghost who is Denmark's spectral guest.
32. Fauconnier, *Mental Spaces*, xxiii.
33. As explored previously, Fauconnier and Turner define vital relations as the elements of an input space that connect it with another. See Gilles Fauconnier and Mark Turner, *The Way We Think: Conceptual Blending and the Mind's Hidden Complexities* (New York: Basic Books, 2002), 92.
34. Perhaps this is why Jacques Lacan assumed there is a time before such an association. In *Ecrits: A Selection*, trans. Alan Sheridan (New York: Norton, 1977), Lacan argued that babies recognize themselves in the mirror at about six months old. In "The Mirror Stage as formative of the function of the I," Lacan says that the infant identifies with the reflection (as "Ideal I" or Imago) and through this identification he assumes an image. Despite the fact that this Ideal I contrasts "with the turbulent movements that the subject feels are animating him" (2), he sees that the image is his. Research has shown that babies are able to imitate their mother shortly after birth and Lacan's theory does not hold up against what is known about mirror neurons and infant and child development now. However, it is interesting to note his need to create a beginning to the mind's ability to project information from referent to reflection: it is a similar line of study that anthropologists pursue in terms of the *homo sapien* ability to communicate and that biologists have studied in apes. The ability to recognize themselves in the mirror is well-developed in the ape and yet absent in almost all other animals.
35. See Sabine Melchior-Bonnet, *The Mirror: A History*, trans. Katharine H. Jewett (New York: Routledge, 2002) and Adam Max Cohen, *Shakespeare and Technology: Dramatizing Early Modern Technological Revolutions* (New York: Palgrave Macmillan, 2006).
36. The miniature portrait was similar to most mirror reflections of the time in that both provided a smaller version of the referent. Also, both mirrors and miniatures were worn as sartorial accessories. In "'Secret' Arts: Elizabethan Miniatures and Sonnets," in *Representing the English Renaissance*, ed. Stephen Greenblatt (Berkeley: University of California Press, 1988), Patricia Fumerton argues that the sonnet and the miniature functioned in Elizabethan Court society as a public display of the private. Miniatures were viewed in closets among intimates, held in the hand and showed only reluctantly. She describes a scene between Queen Elizabeth and a courtier whom Elizabeth was using to arrange a marriage between her sister Mary and Leicester where she brought him into her closet and opened a case within the closet to show him her miniatures. When he asked if he could take Elizabeth's miniature of Leicester to Mary, Elizabeth refused, preferring to send him with a diamond for her sister. Fumerton argues that these miniatures, worn to court, created a

sense of privacy or secrecy in the midst of the artifice of court. "The 'true' Elizabethan self expressed in publishing the miniature was always hidden, even from intimates, by the very nature of the artifice that published it" (100). Miniatures were often enclosed within an ornately decorated case—similar to the fancy, symbol-rich frames that held the mirrors—creating a layer of images and symbols to veil the image within.
37. Fauconnier and Turner, *The Way We Think*, 230.
38. Crane, *Shakespeare's Brain*, 132.
39. Ibid.
40. Ibid., 143.
41. Ibid., 142.
42. Ibid., 123.
43. Ibid., 78.
44. Ibid., 134.
45. Cognitive linguist Vera Tobin has investigated the degree to which compression operates to generate identity in works of art like *Hamlet*, such that we speak of the play as if it were a single entity. Similarly, we refer to the painting of ballerinas preparing to go onstage as "a Degas"—blending the painting with the artist. Tobin, " Grammatical and Rhetorical Consequences of Entrenchment in Conceptual Blending: Compressions Involving Change," in *Meaning, Form & Body*, ed. Fey Parrill, Vera Tobin and Mark Turner (CSLI Publications, 2010), 329–47.
46. Mark Turner, "Double-Scope Stories," in *Narrative Theory and the Cognitive Sciences,* ed. David Herman (CSLI, 2003), 130–31.
47. See Ellis, "Embodying Dislocation: *A Mirror for Magistrates* and Property Relations," *Renaissance Quarterly*, 53, no. 4, Winter (2000), 1032–53. Ellis finds in *A Mirror for Magistrates* an anxiety about social and property relations and an example of changing literary tastes.
48. Paul Vincent Budra, The Mirror for Magistrates *and de cassibus Tradition* (Toronto and London: University of Toronto Press, 2000), 58.
49. Ibid., 70.
50. Crane, *Shakespeare's Brain*, 118.
51. Kastan, " 'His Semblable Is His Mirror': *Hamlet* and the Imitation of Revenge." In *Shakespeare Studies*, edited by J. Leeds Barrol, (New York: Franklin, 1987), 111–24.
52. Fauconnier and Turner, *The Way We Think*, 261.
53. Crane, *Shakespeare's Brain*, 127.
54. Ibid., 149.
55. Ibid., 25
56. From *King Lear*: "Take physic, pomp, / Expose thyself to feel what wretches feel, / That thou mayst shake the superflux to them / And show the heavens more just" (3.4.33–36).

57. In *Hamlet in Purgatory*, Stephen Greenblatt argues that Catholics created the idea of purgatory through fictional accounts meant to shift the perspective of the listener. See also Chapter one of Reynolds's *Transversal Enterprises in the Drama of Shakespeare and his Contemporaries* (New York: Palgrave Macmillan, 2006) on the Jesuit's use of equivocation to escape detection without lying, and, in the same book, my article with Reynolds, "Comedic Law: Projective Transversality, Deceit Conceits, and the Conjuring of *Macbeth* and *Doctor Faustus* in Jonson's *The Devil is an Ass*," which argues that Jonson used comedy and ironic intertextuality to educate his audience to read through rhetoric and performance. As Joseph Roach argues in *The Player's Passion* (Ann Arbor: University of Michigan Press, 1993), the theater of the time was profoundly influenced by rhetorical studies. In *Renaissance Minds and Their Fictions: Cusanus, Sidney, Shakespeare* (Berkeley: University of California Press, 1985), Ronald Levao traces the interest in and anxiety over poetic fictions in the Renaissance period, particularly in the work of Sidney, Spencer, Shakespeare, and Nicholas of Cusa.
58. Jonah Barish, *The Antitheatrical Prejudice* (Berkeley: University of California Press, 1981); Joel Altman, *The Tudor Play of Mind* (Berkeley: University of California Press, 1978); Louis Montrose, *The Purpose of Playing: Shakespeare and the Cultural Politics of the Elizabethan Theatre* (Chicago: University of Chicago Press, 1996); and Bryan Reynolds, *Becoming Criminal: Transversal Performance and Cultural Dissidence in Early Modern England* (Baltimore: Johns Hopkins University Press, 2002).
59. Louis Montrose, *The Purpose of Playing: Shakespeare and the Cultural Politics of the Elizabethan Theatre* (Chicago: University of Chicago Press, 1996), 47.
60. Bryan Reynolds, *Transversal Enterprises in the Drama of Shakespeare and his Contemporaries* (New York: Palgrave Macmillan, 2006), 91.
61. Emily C Bartels, "Breaking the Illusion of Being: Shakespeare and the Performance of Self," *Theatre Journal* 46 (1994): 175.
62. Hitt, Jack, "Act V," *This American Life* (ed. Ira Glass, 1 hour: NPR, 2007).
63. Urbandictionary.com is a Web site that compiles definitions of slang words or phrases submitted by people who (ostensibly) use them. The order of definitions is decided upon by users who click the definition they find the most useful and accurate. I chose the first two, as the first one seems to convey what Hutch is saying about Hamlet and the second one conveys the disdain in the assessment. "Chump" is defined by *The American Heritage® Dictionary of the English Language, Fourth Edition* (2000) as "A stupid or foolish person; a dolt." I accessed both Web sites in August 2005.
64. The subtextual drama throughout this story is of the pondering journalist coming in to an ocean of dangerous fish who have acted, who

have abjured the moral debate Hamlet spends the play questioning in favor of the swift action that has put them in prison. Hitt also positions himself as Hamlet, asking "the question" to a group of prisoners. Hitt simultaneously glorifies their intelligence and acting skill and also associates Shakespeare, intelligence, and morality with the "minnows" of the sea, because Hutch goes from killer whale to minnow at moments of intellect or insight. I am reminded here of the idea of a "Shakespearean loser" postulated by D. J. Hopkins, Catherine Ingman, and Bryan Reynolds borrowing Richard Burt's appropriation of "loser" to evoke a culturally equivocal position of the academic "setting, even raising standards as well as ignoring them" (cited by Hopkins, Ingman, and Reynolds, 141). Their "Shakespearean Loser" revels in the contradictions, feeling aggrandized by the number of disparate elements, historical clues, in-jokes, and theories that may be introduced but can never be subsumed in any interpretation of Shakespeare or his plays. See Hopkins, Ingman, and Reynolds, "Nudge Nudge, Wink, Wink, Know What I Mean, Know What I Mean? A Theoretical Approach to Performance for a Post-Cinema Shakespeare," in *Performing Transversally: Reimagining Shakespeare and the Critical Future*, ed. Bryan Reynolds (New York: Palgrave Macmillan, 2003): 137–70.

5 Play's the Thing—A Cognitive Linguistic Performance Analysis

1. Gilles Fauconnier, "Compression and Emergent Structure," *Language and Linguistics* 6, no. 4 (2005): 7.
2. Mark Turner, *The Literary Mind: The Origins of Thought and Language* (Oxford: Oxford University Press, 1996), 76.
3. Tiffany Stern, *Making Shakespeare: From Stage to Page* (London: Routledge, 2004), 26.
4. Much the way contemporary audiences at a horror movie shout "don't go out there" at the screen when the young couple say they are going to "take a walk" after a few drinks in the old house near the lake, Stern's argument makes me think the groundlings at *Hamlet* would likely shout: "of course he is!" to Burbage when he wonders: "The spirit that I have seen / May be a devil" (2.2.1673).
5. Stern, *Making Shakespeare*, 74.
6. Harold Jenkins, ed., *Hamlet* (London: Arden Shakespeare, 1982) 294.
7. At the "Shakespeare and the Blending Mind" symposium organized by Michael Booth and sponsored by the John B. Haverford Humanities Center at Haverford College, Hart presented the possibility that, though the gravedigger would have been played by Robert Armin, Shakespeare might have used the skull to reference Will Kempe who had recently moved to the competing theater across town.
8. Stern, *Making Shakespeare*, 72.

9. Andrew Sofer, *The Stage Life of Props* (Ann Arbor: University of Michigan Press, 2003), ix.
10. Ibid., 63.
11. Bruce McConachie, *Engaging Audiences: A Cognitive Approach to Spectating in the Theatre* (New York: Palgrave Macmillan, 2008), 56–57.
12. Ibid., 63.
13. Barbara Dancygier has also been pursuing such a line of inquiry. A literary scholar who has been working with cognitive linguists such as Eve Sweetser, Dancygier's recent work looks at the compression inherent in the idea of stage time as well as how props become more and other than they are.
14. Gilles Fauconnier and Mark Turner, *The Way We Think: Conceptual Blending and the Mind's Hidden Complexities* (New York: Basic Books, 2002), 266–67.
15. Ibid., 266.
16. McConachie, *Engaging Audiences*, 48.
17. The two productions discussed here were chosen for several reasons. Perhaps most importantly, they are both archived at the Lincoln Center NYPL and available for further study.
18. By this point, the reader has probably tired of the actor/character notation convention. Unless I am referring to the textual character who can (debatably) be separated from the actor embodying him in a particular instance, I will continue to refer to the presence onstage as actor/character since it is pivotal to my point that, except in rare occasions (such as one to be discussed) onstage, there is no "Hamlet" totally separated from the actor embodying the words Shakespeare wrote. For a full discussion of the actor/character blend, see McConachie, *Engaging Audiences*, 44.
19. In Henry Peacham's *Minerva Britanna* (Menston, Eng: Scholar Press, 1973 [1612]), there are three representations of mirrors: one for self-love (Philantia), one in the hand of female beauty (signifying: "how we by fight are mooued to loue"), and one representing the power of pride to cause fires (the sun shines through it, like a magnifying glass). While its connection to Narcissus suggests the danger in vanity, its connection to the Bible conveys the self-knowledge gleaned from examination of the self in the "glass" of the Bible. For more on the early modern images and representations of the mirror, see chapter 3.
20. For more on the mirror in titles and the movement to anatomy, see Herbert Grabes, *The Mutable Glass: Mirror-Imagery in Titles and Texts of the Middle Ages and English Renaissance*, trans. Gordon Collier (Cambridge: Cambridge University Press, 1982).
21. Mel Gussow, "A 'Hamlet' Stamped with a Bergman Seal," *New York Times*, 10 June 1988, C5. This is interesting given the fluency with which I believe we all speak *Hamlet*: Gussow claims that we know *Hamlet* so well our fluency is transferred to Swedish. Knowing

Hamlet means speaking any tongue; as if the text of *Hamlet* was the Rosetta Stone of modern languages. Bergman himself said in an interview about English speakers understanding the Swedish production: "You know with 'Hamlet,' my God, there can't be any problems." Quoted in Cindy Babski, "Bergman Brings a Restive *Hamlet* to Brooklyn," *New York Times*, June 5, 1988.

22. Clifford Geertz, "Centers, Kings, and Charisma: Reflections on the Symbols of Power," *Culture and Its Creators*, ed. J. Ben-David and T. N. Clark (Chicago: University of Chicago Press, 1977), 153. Geertz explicates Weber's idea of "charisma" in terms of how three different rulers in three different cultures create charisma through a marking of center. Using analogy and allegory, these rulers perform power in moving from center to periphery and back, both physically and sociologically. Geertz's argument is predicated on the hope that understanding the construction of power might shake the "inherent sacredness of sovereign power" (151). The paradox of charisma being that it is rooted in the center but found most often in those at the periphery who would like to be closer.

23. Stephen Greenblatt, *Shakespearean Negotiations* (Berkeley: University of California Press, 1988). This leads him to the subversion/containment argument: "Thus the subversiveness that is genuine and radical...is at the same time contained by the power it would appear to threaten" (30).

24. Louis Montrose, *The Purpose of Playing: Shakespeare and the Cultural Politics of the Elizabethan Theatre* (Chicago: University of Chicago Press, 1996), 39.

25. Mel Gussow, "Theatre: Kevin Kline in 'Hamlet' at Public," *New York Times*, March 10, 1986, C13.

26. Gussow, "Theatre: Kevin Kline in 'Hamlet' at Public," *New York Times*, March 10, 1986.

27. Marvin Carlson, *The Haunted Stage: The Theatre as Memory Machine* (Ann Arbor: University of Michigan Press, 2001), 9.

28. Stern, *Making Shakespeare*, 73.

29. Michael Quinn, "Celebrity and the Semiotics of Acting," *New Theatre Quarterly* 22 (1990). Though not about casting per se, James Carmody's analysis of Robert Falls's production of *The Misanthrope* (which placed it in contemporary Hollywood) argues that the "semiotics of this transplantation, this translation" must be read against and through the meanings of both the classic text (and its "classic-ness") and the Hollywood signs the production points to. Indeed, he includes in his interpretation of the production the directors notes: "Even though these words [within the 'director's note'] were not spoken from the stage, contemporary theatre semiotics recognize them as an integral part of the Falls mise-en-scene in that they provide the spectator with information that conditions the spectator's ability to interpret the cultural and theatrical codes deployed on stage" (79–80). See Carmody,

"Alceste in Hollywood: A Semiotic Reading of *The Misanthrope*," *Critical Theory and Performance*, edited by Janelle Reinelt and Joseph Roach, (Ann Arbor: University of Michigan Press, 1992).
30. Bert O. States, "The Actor's Presence: Three Phenomenal Modes," in *Acting (Re)Considered: A Theoretical and Practical Guide*, ed. Phillip B. Zarrilli (London: Routledge, 2002). In addition, there are epistemological differences between a semiotic or phenomenological reading and a cognitive one. For clear arguments about the limitations of semiotics and phenomenology in light of cognitive science, see McConachie's *Engaging Audiences*, Hart's "Performance, phenomenology, and the cognitive turn," in *Performance and Cognition: Theatre Studies and the Cognitve Turn*, ed. F. Elizabeth Hart and Bruce McConachie (New York: Routledge, 2006) and "Matter, System, and Early Modern Studies: Outlines for a Materialist Linguistics," in *Configurations* 6, no.3 (1998): 311–43. For an analysis of what bodies bring with them onstage, see Petra Kuppers' "Fatties on Stage: Feminist Performances," in *Bodies out of Bounds: Fatness and Transgression*, ed. Jana Evans Braziel and Kathleen LeBesco (Berkeley: University of California Press, 2001), wherein she argues that fat women cannot play not fat women; since "the fat performer does not escape her physicality. Since her sign of difference is overpowering, she is in the same position as the woman of color—she cannot jump from discourse to discourse, from passing to being. Her 'essence' is always already embodied on stage" (281).
31. Joseph Roach, *Cities of the Dead: Circum-Atlantic Performance* (New York: Columbia University Press, 1996), 2.
32. Ibid., 80.
33. Joseph Roach, *It* (Ann Arbor: University of Michigan Press, 2007) 559.
34. Perhaps unconsciously referring back to his earlier writing on Betterton, Roach speaks of the "impossible contradictions" balanced by the celebrity with *It*. See Roach, *It*, 564.
35. Elinor Glyn's term in describing Clara Bow, the original "It Girl," cited in Roach, *It*.
36. Ibid., 568.
37. McConachie, *Engaging Audiences*, 43.
38. Karl Malden played Mitch in *A Streetcar Named Desire* on Broadway (1947) and then went on to win a Best Supporting Actor Oscar for his portrayal of Mitch in the film version (1951).
39. Since my aim is not to enter the crowded discourse surrounding Shakespeare on film generally and Almereyda's film in particular, I will isolate the depiction of the ghost. I have, however, benefited from the fine work in film studies on meaning making, actors, and so on. The edited collection *Remaking Shakespeare: Performances across Media, Genres and Cultures*, ed. Pascale Aebischer, Nigel Wheale, and Ed Esche (New York: Palgrave Macmillan, 2003) contains a number

of helpful essays, in particular Barbara Hodgdon's "Re-incarnations." Hodgdon's essay "Replicating Richard: Body Doubles, Body Politics," in *Theatre Journal* 50, no. 2 (1988) usefully examines the association between the actor's body (Ian McKellen's body coded "gay" and Al Pacino's coded as "anti-academic") and the character's body. See also, Lisa S. Starks, "The Displaced Body of Desire: Sexuality in Kenneth Branagh's *Hamlet*," in *Shakespeare and Appropriation*, ed. Christy Desmet and Robert Sawyer (London: Routledge, 1999); Courtney Lehman's *Shakespeare Remains* (Ithaca, NY: Cornell University Press, 2002) and Richard Burt and Lynda Boose's *Shakespeare, the Movie part I and II* (New York: Routledge, Second Edition, 2003), including Katherine Rowe's essay on Almereyda's *Hamlet* "'Remember Me': Technologies of memory in Michael Almereyda's *Hamlet*."

40. Mark Turner, "The Ghost of Anyone's Father," in *Shakespearean International Yearbook*, ed. Graham Bradshaw, Thomas Bishop, and Mark Turner (Hants, UK: Ashgate, 2004), 72.
41. Ibid., 91.
42. Ibid.
43. Although I find Turner's unearthing of the ghost blend helpful, as a reading of *Hamlet*, it falls short in that it fails to account for the performance conditions that required the ghost to be played by an actor who had to conform to real physics, not ghost physics. In other words, the actor playing the ghost (thought to be Shakespeare himself) needed the trap to get through the floor. Embodied by an actor, the network expands.
44. Turner, "The Ghost of Anyone's Father," 93.
45. Unattributed quote on Sam Shepard's Web site http://www.sam-shepard.com/presscowboys0406.html accessed January 17, 2010.
46. Another potential avenue of research is the casting of stars to be the voices of animated characters. When Cameron Diaz plays the "ugly" princess in *Shrek*, more than just her comic timing and vocal styling's are being referenced. Her physical appearance is an important part of the movie—since an ugly actor playing an ugly character who is perceived as beautiful would not have the kind of romantic impact Disney is looking for. Never present on film, Diaz's beauty is never absent from the spectator's thoughts.
47. Interview with Shepard on his Web site, excerpted from "Sam Shepard: Renaissance Cowboy," *Cowboys and Indians Magazine*, April 2006. http://www.sam-shepard.com/presscowboys0406.html Accessed January 17, 2010.
48. It is interesting to imagine whether Shakespeare had a similar effect as the ghost. Or if the story of his playing the ghost gained currency because it matched our idea of the great paternal figure we have all managed to disappoint. The casting also sets up irony and resonance: Shakespeare/playwright (as ghost) gives Burbage/actor (as Hamlet) direction (kill brother, leave mom alone) that Burbage/Hamlet then

ignores is not unlike Hamlet/playwright giving the player king directions to do only that which is set down for him and then having to witness the dumb show.
49. George Meredith's term, cited in Roach, *It*, 560.
50. Cited in Joseph Roach, *The Player's Passion: Studies in the Science of Acting* (Ann Arbor: University of Michigan Press, 1993), 34.
51. "Speak the speech, I pray you, as I pronounc'd it to you, trippingly on the tongue, but if you mouth it, as many of our players do, I had as live the town-crier spoke my lines. Nor do not saw the air too much with your hand, thus, but use all gently; for in the very torrent, tempest, and, as I may say, whirlwind of your passion, you must acquire and beget a temperance that may give it smoothness" (3.2.1–8). "Be not too tame neither, but let your own discretion be your tutor. Suit the action to the word, the word to the action" (3.2.16–18).
52. Maurice Merleau-Ponty, *The Phenomenology of Perception* (London: Routledge, 2002) and Giacomo Rizzolatti and Laila Craighero, "The Mirror-Neuron System," *Annual Review of Neuroscience* no. 27 (2004), 184–85.
53. David McNeill, *Hand and Mind: What Gestures Reveal about Thought* (Chicago: University of Chicago Press, 1992), 1. See also McNeill, *Gesture and Thought* (Chicago: University of Chicago Press, 2005).
54. McNeill, *Hand and Mind*, 1.
55. Ibid., 12.
56. Ibid., 13.
57. Ibid., 14.
58. Ibid.
59. Ibid., 14–15.
60. Ibid., 16.
61. Amy Franklin, "Interpersonal and Knowledge Coordination," (paper presented at the *The Ninth Conference on Conceptual Structure, Discourse, and Language*, Case Western Reserve University, Cleveland, Ohio, 2008).
62. The article reported on different studies that all pointed to the same conclusion about the role of imitation in persuasion. See Benedict Carey's "MIND: You Remind Me of Me," *New York Times*, February 12, 2008.
63. McConachie, *Engaging Audiences*, 87.
64. Tobin Nellhaus, "Performance Strategies, Image Schemas, and Communication Frameworks," in *Performance and Cognition: Theatre Studies and the Cognitve Turn*, ed. Bruce McConachie and F. Elizabeth Hart (New York: Routledge, 2006), 79.
65. Ibid., 87.
66. Ibid.
67. McNeill, *Hand and Mind*, 2. Italics in original.
68. McConachie, *Engaging Audiences*, 88.

69. Ibid.
70. Mudras are the specific and representational gestures used in classical Indian performance and ritual.
71. This work is starting to be done. Neal Utterback has begun empirical studies of the gestures actors and non-actors use to tell a story and connecting his empirical findings on gestures to conceptual blending theory. Utterback, "Affects of blending and perspective on the performance of gesture in narrative fiction" presented paper at the Fine and Performing Arts conference in Athens, Greece, 2010.
72. McNeill, *Hand and Mind*, 22. Italics in original.
73. Time, we imagine, exists in space, with either the self moving through space ("we're coming to the end of the year") or time moving past a stationary self ("the end of the year is approaching"). These are understood as two different special cases of the TIME PASSING IS MOTION metaphor; in one, time moves as an object moves, and in the other, the self (or "Ego") moves over space. Further studies have found that our conceptualization of time is inseparable from our physical experiences. While both ways of understanding time are usually equally comprehensible and equally given, "speakers who have just been moving (e.g., traveling on a plane or a train) or imagining self-motion are primed to give moving-Ego rather than moving-time interpretations of metaphorical time phrases in English." See Rafael Núñez and Eve Sweetser, "With the Future Behind Them: Convergent Evidence from Aymara Language and Gesture in the Crosslinguistic Comparison of Spatial Construals of Time," *Cognitive Science* 30 (2006), 405.
74. Ibid., 415–16.
75. When explaining how "nayra mara" is "tiempo antiguo" the speaker clarifies by gesturing more forcefully and further in front of him, suggesting that the schema of a path is the same, just that the past is in the opposite direction. In another example, the Aymara speaker says "aka marana" (this year) and gestures directly in front of him, between his legs.
76. Ibid., 438.
77. Ibid., 403.
78. One could argue that this is less interesting than the pointed hiding of Kenneth Branagh's hands in his poster of *Hamlet* that shows Hamlet from behind, his hands in front of him as if held in hand cuffs not visible to the camera.
79. When Hawke/Hamlet tells his mother to "Leave wringing of your hands" (3.4.34), she is picking up the phone (with both hands) to call someone to report the murder of Bill Murray/Polonius, creating a visual pun between the kind of hand wringing suggested in the text and the phone ringing Diane Venora/Gertrude hopes to produce.
80. The hands in this scene are far more prominent than they are in other scenes. The final scene, for example, masks the hands in the fencing

gloves, puts Venora/Gertrude's hands in gloves, and does not show them on the glass of poison. The events of the final scene, all those deaths, seem to happen without the hands to make them happen.

6 Past/Future, Microscope/Telescope, Performance/Science

1. Mary Thomas Crane, "The Physics of King Lear: Cognition in a Void," In *Shakespearean International Yearbook* (ed. Graham Bradshaw, Thomas Bishop and Mark Turner, Hants, UK: Ashgate, 2004), 3.
2. Ibid., 20.
3. Turner, *Shakespeare's Double Helix.* edited by Simon Palfrey and Ewan Fernie, Shakespeare Now! (London: Continuum, 2007), 7.
4. See Naomi Rakotnitz, "'It Is Required/You Do Awake Your Faith': Learning to Trust the Body through Performing *The Winter's Tale*," in *Performance and Cognition: Theatre Studies and the Cognitive Turn*, ed. F. Elizabeth Hart and Bruce McConachie (New York: Routledge, 2006). She argues that Shakespeare's *The Winter's Tale* displays the uncertainty of knowledge and the necessity of empathy and faith and through this reminds us of the interdependence of body and mind. Drama, according to Rakotnitz, provides "opportunities to *practice* and *refine* the complex and subtle ways through which we may better understand one another and reach for truth(s) in our lives" (125) and "(re)creates the trust of which philosophy deprives us" (128). Ellen Spolsky, *Satisfying Skepticism: Embodied Knowledge in the Early Modern World* (Aldershot, England: Ashgate, 2001) posits that skepticism in the early modern period was helpful, or—as evidenced in the many paintings of the Incredulity of Thomas and in Shakespeare's plays *Coriolanus* and *Othello*—not disbelief but rather a comfort with the ambiguity of knowledge. In "Why and How to Take the Fruit and Leave the Chaff," *SubStance* 94/95 (2001), she sees narrative as presenting a way of understanding fact and fiction as forever together and informing each other, "The usefulness of narrative, then, is not in its production of any one moral or another; it's in the constant possibility of drawing new inferences from the old texts" (195). F. Elizabeth Hart connects perspective to embodied realism in her essay "Performance, Phenomenology, and the Cognitive Turn," *Performance and Cognition: Theatre Studies and the Cognitive Turn*, ed. F. Elizabeth Hart and Bruce McConachie (New York: Routledge, 2006). See also: Lisa Zunshine, *Strange Concepts and the Stories They Make Possible* (Baltimore: Johns Hopkins University Press, 2008).
5. Mark Johnson, *The Meaning of the Body: Aesthetics of Human Understanding* (Chicago: University of Chicago Press, 2007), 283.
6. Harold Jenkins, ed., *Hamlet* (London: Arden Shakespeare, 1982), 252.
7. J. Payne Collier, ed., *The Works of William Shakespeare.* Vol. 7, 1843.

8. Boswell, James, ed., *Works*, 1821.
9. George Lakoff, *Women, Fire, and Dangerous Things: What Categories Reveal about the Mind* (Chicago: University of Chicago Press, 1987), 128.
10. See my discussion in Chapter five of Bruce McConachie's application of theories of vision in *Engaging Audiences: A Cognitive Approach to Spectating in the Theatre* (New York: Palgrave Macmillan, 2008).
11. For a series of optical illusions to find—and map the size and location of—your blindspot, you can go to Brynn Mawr's Serendipity Web site http://serendip.brynmawr.edu/bb/blindspot1.html. Or see *Eye and Brain* by Richard L. Gregory (London: Weidenfeld and Nicolson, 1966).
12. "Mind the Gap: The Brain, like Nature, Abhors a Vacuum," *Scientific American*, March 24, 2005. Accessed online October 3, 2007.
13. Anosognosia patients, who Ramachandran believes suffer from a kind of neglect syndrome, will insist that a paralyzed arm is moving or lifting a tray when it does not, and cannot, move.
14. V. S. Ramachandran and Sandra Blakeslee, *Phantoms in the Brain: Probing the Mysteries of the Human Mind* (New York: Quill, 1998), 127–57.
15. For V. S. Ramachandran and Diane Rogers-Ramachandran's accessible and provocative study of this research, see "How Blind Are We? We have eyes, yet We Do Not See" *Scientific American*, May 18, 2005. Accessed online October 3, 2007.
16. Ibid., 1.
17. Ramachandran and Blakeslee, *Phantoms in the Brain*, 123.
18. Ibid., 124.
19. Bruce Smith, "Hearing Green," in *Reading the Early Modern Passions*, ed. Gail Kern Paster, Katherine Rowe, and Mary Floyd-Wilson (Philadelphia: University of Pennsylvania Press, 2004), 166.
20. Ibid., 168.
21. Seeing the ghost in the shape of his father did not confirm that the ghost was his father, but did teach Hamlet that "one may smile and be a villain." Crane shows how despite Hamlet's decision to use the play to tent the king to the quick, once he sees what he thinks is an expression of guilt projected onto the king's external "show" in the prayer scene, he then is fooled by the king's external expression of piety.
22. In *Renaissance Minds and Their Fictions: Cusanus, Sidney, Shakespeare* (Berkeley: University of California Press, 1985), Ronald Levao sees in Shakespeare's work particular tension between the fictions onstage and the reality off stage. Levao argues that Hamlet's mousetrap is "Hamlet's reality played as fiction" (347) and that Hamlet is excited after the play because he has finally found a "vantage point" (347) from which to read what is going on.
23. Brian MacWhinney, "How Mental Models Encode Embodied Linguistic Perspectives," in *The Grounding of Cognition*, ed.

D. Pecher and R. Zwaan (Cambridge: Cambridge University Press, 2005), 3.
24. Ibid., 39.
25. See Brian MacWhinney, "The Emergence of Grammar from Perspective Taking," in D. Pecher and R. Zwaan, eds., *Grounding Cognition: The Role of Perception and Action in Memory, Language, and Thinking* (Cambridge: Cambridge University Press, 2005).
26. Francisco J. Varela, Evan Thompson, and Eleanor Rosch, *The Embodied Mind: Cognitive Science and Human Experience* (Cambridge, MA: MIT Press, 1993), 172.
27. Ibid., 149.
28. Ibid., 173.
29. Johnson, *The Meaning of the Body*, 117.
30. Ibid., 119.
31. Evelyn Tribble, "Distributing Cognition in the Globe," *Shakespeare Quarterly* 56, no. 2 (2005), 135.
32. Ibid., 155.
33. Turner, *Shakespeare's Double Helix*, Edited by Simon Palfrey and Ewan Fernie, Shakespeare Now! (London: Continuum, 2007), 73.
34. Paula M. Niedenthal, Lawrence W. Barsalou, Francois Ric, and Silvia Krauth-Gruber, "Embodiment in the Acquisition and Use of Emotion Knowledge," in *Emotion and Consciousness*, ed. Lisa Feldman Barrett, Paula M. Niedenthal and Piotr Winkielman (New York: Guilford Press, 2005), 26.
35. Ibid., 30
36. Jean Decety's work on empathy and nocioception has been tremendously influential. See Decety, "To What Extent Is the Experience of Empathy Mediated by Shared Neural Circuits?" *Emotion Review* (2010): 1–4; "Dissecting the Neural Mechanisms Mediating Empathy and Sympathy," *Emotion Review* (in press). Rhonda Blair incorporates his work into her cognitive interpretation of performance in "Cognitive Neuroscience and Acting: Imagination, Conceptual Blending, and Empathy," *TDR* 53, no. 4 (2009): 92–103; and Perrine Ruby and Decety, "How Whould *You* Feel Versus How Do You Think *She* Would Feel? A Neuroimaging Study of Perspective-Taking with Social Emotions," *Journal of Cognitive Neuroscience* 16, no. 6 (2004): 988–99.
37. Eve Sweetser, "Blended Spaces and Performativity," *Cognitive Linguistics* 11, no. 3/4 (2000): 312.
38. Ibid., 314.
39. For more on what mirror neurons are and the research suggesting the presence of a mirror neuron system in humans, see *Imitation, Human Development, and Culture*, vol. 2, ed. Susan Hurley and Nick Chater (Cambridge, MA: MIT Press, 2005); *Mirror Neurons and the Evolution of Brain and Language* ed. Maxim I. Stamenov and Vittorio Gallese (Amsterdam: John Benjamins, 2002). Jean Decety, among others, has

cautioned against conflating the mirror neuron system with the shared neural substrate. See Decety, "Dissecting the Neural Mechanisms Mediating Empathy and Sympathy," *Emotion Review* (in press).

40. I explored the implications of mirror neuron research previously in "Interplay: The Method and Potential of a Cognitive Approach to Theatre," *Theatre Journal* 59, no. 4 (2007) and "Wrinkles, Wormholes, and *Hamlet*: The Wooster Group's *Hamlet* as a Challenge to Periodicity," *TDR* 53, no. 4 (2009). Both Rhonda Blair and Bruce McConachie have also written about mirror neurons. See McConachie, *Engaging Audiences* and Blair, "Cognitive Neuroscience and Acting: Imagination, Conceptual Blending, and Empathy," *TDR* 53, no. 4 (2009).
41. Lakoff, *Women, Fire, and Dangerous Things*, 72.
42. Donald C. Freeman, "Othello and the 'Ocular Proof,'" in *The Shakespearean International Yearbook*, ed. Graham Bradshaw, Tom Bishop, and Mark Turner (Aldershot, England: Ashgate, 2004), 59.
43. Quoted in Cohen, *Shakespeare and Technology: Dramatizing Early Modern Technological Revolutions* (New York: Palgrave Macmillan, 2006), 13.
44. Pascal Boyer, *Religion Explained: The Evolutionary Origins of Religious Thought* (New York: Basic Books, 2001), 114.
45. Michael Feingold, "The Wooster Group Plays Someone Else's Hamlet...And Both Teams Lose," *The Village Voice*, 30 October 2007. A version of this section on The Wooster Group *Hamlet* was first published in *TDR*.
46. Robert Brustein, "More Masterpieces," *PAJ: A Journal of Performance and Art, PAJ 90* 30, no. 3 (2008): 5.
47. Ibid., 6.
48. For an exciting discussion of the application of "wormholes" to literary scholarship, see Linda Charnes, "Reading for the Wormholes: Micro-Periods from the Future," *Early Modern Culture, an Electronic Seminar; special Issue: Timely Meditations* (2007) and *Hamlet's Heirs: Shakespeare and the Politics of a New Millennium* (New York: Routledge, 2006).
49. Josh Abrams and Jennifer Parker-Starbuck, "Politics and the Classics," *PAJ: A Journal of Performance and Art 85* 29, no. 1 (2007): 97.
50. Steven Leigh Morris, "Wooster Group's *Hamlet*; Alex Lyras' *The Common Air*: All the World's a Remix," *LA Weekly*, February 4, 2008.
51. Michael Feingold, "The Wooster Group Plays Someone Else's Hamlet...And Both Teams Lose," *The Village Voice*, October 30, 2007.
52. Ben Brantley, "Looks It Not Like the King? Well, More Like Burton," *New York Times*, 2007.
53. Lisa Jardine, *Ingenious Pursuits: Building the Scientific Revolution* (New York: Anchor Books, 1999), 44.

54. Ibid., 44–45.
55. See Victor Turner, *The Ritual Process: Structure and Anti-Structure* (Chicago: Aldine, 1969) wherein he describes the liminal nature of ritual in that it transforms someone from one place or phase to the next. Liminal people, half way between one state or social status and another, are reduced to nothing, passive, humble, and near naked (95–96); they are between two states and yet share properties with neither.
56. See Erving Goffman, *Frame Analysis: An Essay on the Organization of Experience* (New York: Harper, 1974), 300. Following on Edwin Hutchins theory of Material Anchors (wherein a physical object contains information regarding its history, meaning, or use), Fauconnier and Turner understand a church or grave as a blend of location with an inaccessible entity such as the divine or the dead (207). See Edwin Hutchins, *Cognition in the Wild* (Cambridge, MA: MIT Press, 1995).
57. Edward S. Casey, *The Fate of Place: A Philosophical History* (Berkeley: University of California Press, 1997), 110.
58. See also Ellen Spolsky's cognitive historical study of early modern art and theater *Satisfying Skepticism: Embodied Knowledge in the Early Modern World* (Aldershot, England: Ashgate, 2001) or her earlier *Gaps in Nature: Literary Interpretation and the Modular Mind* (Albany: State University of New York Press, 1993).
59. Bryan Reynolds, *Transversal Enterprises in the Drama of Shakespeare and His Contemporaries* (New York: Palgrave Macmillan, 2006), 284.
60. Amy Cook and Bryan Reynolds, "Comedic Law: Projective Transversality, Deceit Conceits, and the Conjuring of Macbeth and Doctor Faustus in Jonson's *The Devil Is an Ass*," in *Transversal Enterprises in the Drama of Shakespeare and His Contemporaries: Fugitive Explorations*, ed. Bryan Reynolds (London: Palgrave Macmillan, 2005), 92.
61. For more on Galileo's experiments and his attempts to make better observers out of his contemporaries, see Elizabeth A. Spiller, "Reading through Galileo's Telescope: Margaret Cavendish and the Experience of Reading," *Renaissance Quarterly* 53 (2000): 192–221.
62. Ibid., 194.
63. Ibid., 200.
64. Ibid., 194.
65. Ibid., 202.
66. Bacon, Francis, *The Advancement of Learning*, (Rockville, MD: Serenity Publishers, 2008), 119.
67. Steven Shapin, "Pump and Circumstance: Robert Boyle's Literary Technology," *Social Studies of Science* 14, no. 4 (1984): 484.
68. Ibid., 495.

69. Ibid., 494, emphasis mine.
70. Ibid., 492.
71. Laura Otis, *Membranes: Metaphors of Invasion in Nineteenth-Century Literature, Science, and Politics* (Baltimore: Johns Hopkins University Press, 1999), 4.
72. I am grateful to Philip Auslander for recommending these texts to me. He used them as central texts in his "Science, Technology, and Performance" course he teaches at Georgia Tech in 2007.
73. Robert P. Crease, *The Play of Nature: Experimentation as Performance* (Bloomington: Indiana University Press, 1993). 15.
74. Ibid., 6.
75. Ibid., 14.
76. Stephen Hilgartner, *Science on Stage: Expert Advice as Public Drama* (Stanford, CA: Stanford University Press, 2000), 6.
77. Ibid., 19.
78. Ibid., 3.
79. Ibid., 19.

Conclusion: A Dying Voice

1. Hawkes, "Telmah," In *Shakespeare & the Question of Theory*, edited by Patricia Parker and Geoffrey Hartman, (New York: Methuen, 1985), 310–32.
2. Johnson, *The Meaning of the Body: Aesthetics of Human Understanding* (Chicago: University of Chicago Press, 2007), 25 and 261. Italics in original.
3. In *Renaissance Self-Fashioning*, Stephen Greenblatt argues that Marlowe's use of proverbs suggested that they held currency; in Marlowe's writing, a proverb can operate like the sound bite that positions Bush as a gun seller: as the "compressed ideological wealth of society" (207). Mary Crane has argued that the importance of commonplace books in sixteenth-century England suggests a similar sense of currency in sayings. Once gathered, these commonplaces could then be reassimilated or "framed" within a new context. Thus they created "a central mode of transaction with classical antiquity and provided an influential model for authorial practice and for authoritative self-fashioning" (1). The debates about the power of language, confession, and equivocation circulated widely during the Reformation, and Shakespeare may have read Robert Southwell and Henry Garnet's *A Treatise on Equivocation* when he wrote the Porter's drunken treatise on an equivocator "that could swear in both the scales against either scale; who committed treason enough for God's sake, yet could not equivocate to heaven" (2.3.8–11). F. Elizabeth Hart posits a connection between the unparalleled "lexical expansion" during the early modern period and a concomitant intellectual expansion. She calls for a materialist linguistics that would examine

the scientific and literary consequences of the addition of more than 30,000 new words to the English-language vocabulary between the sixteenth and eighteenth centuries. Hart argues that tracing the evolution of vocabulary can be linked to a concomitant shift in the minds/bodies/brains speaking and conceptualizing the new words. See Hart, "Matter, System, and Early Modern Studies: Outlines for a Materialist Linguistics," *Configurations* 6, no. 3 (1998): 311–43.
4. From the description of one of the doctors who arrived, cited in Damasio, *Descartes' Error: Emotion, Reason, and the Human Brain* (New York: Avon, 1994) 6.
5. Ibid., 11.
6. Tom Stoppard, *Arcadia* (London: Faber and Faber, 1993), 37.
7. I have referred to many of these works in earlier chapters. In addition to which, I would add the following: Alan Richardson and Ellen Spolsky's edited volume *The Work of Fiction: Cognition, Culture, and Complexity*, ed. Alan Richardson and Ellen Spolsky (Hampshire, England: Ashgate, 2004). In 2002, the journal *Poetics Today* had a special issue on "Literature and the Cognitive Revolution," including articles by Lisa Zunshine, Alan Richardson, Paul Hernadi, and Reuven Tsur, among others. See *Poetics Today* 23, no. 1 (2002). In 1999, neuroscientists V.S. Ramachandran and William Hirstein published "The Science of Art: A Neurological Theory of Aesthetic Experience," *Journal of Consciousness Studies* 6, no. 6–7 (1999): 15–51. The history of studying music and the brain is too long and wide to do justice to. For two of the recent and best-selling books, see Oliver Sacks, *Musicophilia: Tales of Music and the Brain* (New York: Knopf, 2007) and Daniel J. Levitin's *This Is Your Brain on Music: The Science of a Human Obsession* (New York: Penguin, 2006). Neuroscientist Ani Patel studied how the brain processes music by studying bird brains and his book *Music, Language and the Brain* (Oxford University Press, 2008) and won the 2009 Music Has Power award from the Institute for Music and Neurologic Function.
8. Paula Leverage, *Reception and Memory: A Cognitive Approach to the Chansons de Geste* is forthcoming in Rodopi's *Faux Titre* series (ed. Keith Busby and Michael Freeman) and Jill Stevenson's *Performance, Cognitive Theory, and Devotional Culture* (New York: Palgrave Macmillan, 2010). In addition to Mary Crane's *Shakespeare's Brain*, Bruce R. Smith's, *The Key of Green* (Chicago: University of Chicago Press, 2009) understands the history and art as always embodied and neurological.
9. Roach, *The Player's Passion: Studies in the Science of Acting*, (Ann Arbor: University of Michigan Press, 1993).
10. Blair, *The Actor, Image, and Action: Acting and Cognitive Neuroscience*, (New York: Routledge, 2008).

11. Fritz Breithaupt's *Cultures of Empathy* argues that empathy involves a relationship between three individuals, not the two individuals generally studied in lab situations. This triadic empathy relationship involves one witness to a conflict between the other two in conflict. For Breithaupt, it is the act of choosing a side, based on a reading of the narrative of the conflict, that generates empathy as an "emotional legitimization." His book relies both on readings of literature and cognitive scientific research on empathy. Breithaupt, *Kulteren der Empathie*: Suhrkamp Verlag (2009). I read a translation of sections by *Christopher Brendan Chiasson*.

Index

Abrams, Josh, 139
Almereyda, Michael, 92, 107–112, 119–121, 184–185
Althusser, Louis, 48, 171n.20
Altman, Joel, 28, 86
Ambassadors, The, see Holbein, Hans
anamorphosis, 52–53
anosognosia, 189n.12
Antitheatricalism, 23, 86, 180n.58
Arcadia, see Stoppard, Tom
Aristotle, 126, 135
Armin, Robert, 105, 181n.7
Arnold, Janet, 171n.21
author and authorship, *see* textual authority

Babski, Cindy, 182n.22
Bacon, Francis, 123, 145–146
Baker, Malcolm, 173n.42 173n.45
Barish, Jonah, 86
Barsalou, Lawrence, 134, 138
Bartels, Emily C., 86
Barton, Bruce, 164n.55
Bek, Lise, 51
Bergman, Ingmar, 97–101, 104
Best, Stephen, 13
Betterton, Thomas, 105
Bible, 75–76, 78, 174n.55
 see also blends, Jesus died for our sins
Blair, Rhonda, 17–18, 156
Blakeslee, Sandra, 189n.13

blending, *see* conceptual blending theory
blends
 abortion, 32, 36
 Bush as gun seller, 33–35
 character/actor, 87–90, 96–97, 102–107
 to drown, 38–41
 ghost of King Hamlet, 108
 Hamlet's mirror, 57, 101, 104
 Jesus died for our sins, 81
 killer cocktail, 31
 The Runaway Bunny, 12–13
 social lie, 10–12
 stem cell debate, 32–33
 Virtue, 48, 59–60, 62
 see also conceptual blending theory
blindspots, *see* vision
Bloom, Harold, 62–63
Body, *see* embodied cognition; mind/body problem
Bohannan, Laura, 37–41, 48
Boose, Lynda, 184n.40
Booth, Michael, 181n.7
Boswell, James, 126
Boyer, Pascal, 138, 160n.16
Boyle, Sir Robert, 123, 145–146
Branagh, Kenneth, 110, 187n.79
Brantley, Ben, 141
Breithaupt, Fritz, 194n.11
Bright, Timothy, 67–70, 79, 79–80, 103, 151

Brooklyn Academy of Music, 97
Brown, Theodore, 7
Brustein, Robert, 138
Budra, Paul Vincent, 56, 81–82, 173n.53
Bulwer, John, 112–113
Burbage, Richard, 94
Burckhardt, Jacob, 170n.18
Burke, Kenneth, 25
Burt, Richard, 181n.64, 184n.40
Burton, Anthony, 173n.42, 173n.45
Burton, Richard, 138–140
Bush, George W. *see* blends, Bush as gun seller
Butler, Judith, 135
Butler, Katy, 167n.24

Carlson, Martin, 105
Carmody, James, 183n.30
Casey, Benedict, 186n.63
Casey, Edward, 142–143
Castillo, David, 52–53
casting, 105–112, 181n.7, 183n.30
  cameo parts, 110, 185n.47
  intertextuality and, 94–97
  "It," 106–107
  Shakespeare as ghost, 185n.49
  see also blend, character/actor; Hawke, Ethan; Shepard, Sam
categories, 2, 150, 160n16, 161n20
  basic-level, 5
  prototype effects in, 5–6
  superordinate, 5
Chalmers, David, 132–133
Charnes, Linda, 13–14, 191n.47
Chomsky, Noam, 48
  see also generative grammar
Churchland, Patricia, 175n.16
Churchland, Paul, 175n.16
Ciulei, Livliu, 101–104
Clark, Andy, 132–133
cognitive efficiency of, 32, 35
  cause and effect, 35, 37, 59, 82–83
  identity to uniqueness, 33–35, 76–77, 80–81, 179n.45
  metonymy, 60, 71, 76
  see also conceptual blending theory
cognitive linguistics
  compositional grammar, 11, 48, 161n.22
  generative grammar, 4, 155, 161n.22
  objectivism, 2, 5, 6
  versus structuralism, 159n.5
  see also categories; conceptual blending theory; conceptual metaphor theory
cognitive science, 3–4
  acting theory and, 17, 156, 164n.55
  literature and, 14–19, 66, 156, 159n5, 163n.54, 194n.7
  music theory and, 194n.7
  theater/performance theory and, 17–18, 124
  see also body; categories; distributed cognition; embodied cognition; experiential realism; mind; mirror neurons; phantom limbs; synaesthesia; vision
Cohen, Adam Max, 49, 56–57
Collier, J. Payne, 126
comedy, theory, 179n.57
compositional grammar, 11, 48, 161n.22
compression: and information omission, 31, 35, 65, 79, 81
conceptual blending theory (CBT)
  agency and intention, 31, 38–41, 48, 73
  analogy and disanalogy, 7, 32–33, 73, 75, 78, 89, 108
  analysis of actors/characters, 96–97
  analysis of Bergman's *Hamlet*, 97–101

INDEX

analysis of Ciulei's *Hamlet*, 101–104
analysis of to drown, 38–41
analysis of *Hamlet*, 44, 57–63, 65, 153–154
causal tautology, 35, 59, 79, 83
counterfactuality, 36, 78, 81, 105, 143
definition of, 10–13, 18–20, 43
double-scope blends, 12, 162n.38
elaboration or "running the blend," 12, 31
emergent meaning/structure, 12, 91
governing principles of, 31, 167n.27
human scale story, 31–35, 73, 167n.27
integration; network, 27, 31, 65–66, 91, 168n.1
living in the blend, 97
mathematics, 91, 161n.20
political rhetoric, 27–37
revenge, 82–83
single scope blends, 12
vital relations, 33–34, 76–78, 80–81, 167n.27, 177n.33
see also blends; compression; mental spaces; personification
conceptual integration network, *see* conceptual blending theory
conceptual metaphor theory, 9, 11, 15, 118, 135
political application of, 18, 31, 161n.21
see also domains; idealized cognitive models; image schemas; metaphors
Cosmides, Leda, 16
Coulson, Seana, 3, 29, 31, 32, 32–33, 36
Craighero, Laila, 113
Crane, Mary Thomas
cognitive theory, discussion of, 16, 163n.54

early modern commonplace books, 66, 193n.3
Hamlet, analysis of, 66–68, 79–80, 83–86, 177n.27
King Lear, analysis of, 124
Crease, Robert P., 147
Crowley, John E., 171n.21
Crystal, Billy, 61–62

Damasio, Antonio, 138, 154
Dancygier, Barbara, 15, 182n.14
Davis, Philip, 25–26, 166n.14
Decety, Jean, 190n.35, 190n.38
Dennett, Daniel, 175n.16
Descartes, René, 69, 123
distributed cognition, 133
domains, 7, 9–12, 57, 135, 161n.19
see also mental spaces

Ellis, Jim, 81
embodied cognition, 8, 14–15, 76, 131–133, 137, 138, 152, 155
language, 20, 40, 104, 108, 131
separation of mind and body, 3–4, 6, 22, 39–40, 69, 155, 160n.18, 175n.18
simulation, 124, 133–135, 138, 142
see also gesture; mind/body problem
empathy, 134, 190n.35, 190n.38, 194n.11
equivocation, 171n.19, 179n.57, 193n.3
experiential realism, 2, 15, 161n.22
extended cognition, 132–133

Farquhar, George, 105
Fauconnier, Gilles
cognitive evolution, 162n.38
conceptual blending theory, 10–12, 31, 33, 35, 80, 131, 162, 167n.27, 177n.33
counterfactuality, as blend, 78
Death, personification of, 59

INDEX

Fauconnier, Gilles—*Continued*
  implications of conceptual blending theory, 5, 18–19, 93, 97, 104, 167n.27
  integration network, 76, 91, 168n.1
  revenge, as blend, 82
  see also conceptual blending theory; mental spaces
Feingold, Michael, 138, 140
first quarto, 23–24, 130, 148, 176n.20, 177n.31
  see also textual authority
Floyd-Wilson, Mary, 166n.18
Foucault, Michel, 52
Frame shifting, 29
Franklin, Amy, 115
Freeman, Donald, 15, 136
Fumerton, Patricia, 178n.36
Furtenagel, Lukas (*Hans Burgkmair and his Wife*), 51–52

Gage, Phineas, 154
Galilei, Galileo, 21, 144
Gallese, Vittorio, 3
Geertz, Clifford, 101–102, 183n.23
generative grammar, 4, 155, 160n.13, 161n.22, 171n.20
gesture, 112–122, 117–119, 186n.62
  see also McNeill, David
Glass, Ira, 86
  see also "This American Life"
Globe Theatre, the, 16, 94–95, 133
Goffman, Erving, 54, 61, 142, 192n.55
Goldberg, Benjamin, 49, 172n.22
Grabes, Herbert, 46–47, 49, 55
Greenblatt, Stephen, 73, 101, 170n.18, 179n.57, 193n.3
Grindal, Edmund, 86
Gumpp, Johannes (*Self Portrait*), 52
Gussow, Mel, 101–103, 182n.22

Hales v. Petit, 39–40
  see also Hamlet, gravedigger

Hamlet
  agency, and questions of, 41, 48, 58, 67–68, 79, 83–84
  epistemology, interest in, 21, 38, 44, 123, 153
  ghost as reflective surface in, 47, 70, 85
  gravedigger, 39–41, 48, 79–80, 110
  Hamlet's advice to players in, 58, 98, 113, 176n.20
  miniatures as reflective surface in, 47, 70, 78, 85
  the mirror held up to nature in, 19–20, 43–49, 57–59, 68, 84
  the Mousetrap, 47, 61, 84, 100, 101, 142, 150–151, 189n.21
  perspective, shifting in, 75–76, 125–126
  Reynaldo as reflective surface in, 71, 78, 129
  Rosencrantz and Guildenstern as reflective surface in, 72, 125–126, 130–131, 177n.25
  see also Almereyda, Michael; blends, mirror; Bergman, Ingmar; Ciulei, Livliu; first quarto; "This American Life"; Wooster Group, The
Hans Burgkmair and his Wife, see Furtenagel, Lukas
Hansen, Pil, 17, 164n.55, 164n.57
Hart, F. Elizabeth, 124, 156, 175n.2, 193n.3
Hassel, Jr., Chris, 29
Hawke, Ethan, 108, 110–111, 119–122
Hawkes, Terrence, 47, 150
Hayles, N. Katherine, 138
Heidegger, Martin, 5, 132
hemisphere neglect, 127
Hilgartner, Stephen, 147–148
Hirstein, William, 194n.7
Hitt, Jack
  see "This American Life"
Hodgdon, Barbara, 184n.40

Holbein, Hans (*The Ambassadors*), 52
Holland, Norman N., 16
Hopkins, D. J., 180n.64
Hubbard, E.M., 165n.5
Hutchins, Edwin, 192n.55

Idealized Cognitive Models (ICM), 6, 163n.46
 action and intention, 40
 cluster models, 6
 mother, 6
 ordinary communication, 136
 seeing, 6, 75, 126
 social feedback loop, 60–62, 76
image schemas, 8–9, 15, 163n.46
 BODY, 108, 176n.21
 CONTAINER, 9, 15, 48, 61, 72, 108
 FRONT-BACK, 176n.21
 FUTURE IS AHEAD, 117
 PATHS, 15
imitation, 134–136, 140–142, 155
in utramque partem, *see* Altman, Joel
Ingam, Catherine, 180n.64
input space, *see* conceptual blending theory; domains; mental spaces
integrations networks, *see* blends; conceptual blending theory
intention, 33, 39–41, 58–59, 66, 73, 79, 83, 153–154
intentional attunement, 136
intertextuality, 94–96, 179n.57
inwardness and interiority, 44, 47–48, 66–67, 72, 84, 139, 171n.19, 177n.27
 see also image schemas, container; self/subjectivity
Irace, Kathleen, 24, 177n.31

Jacob, Pierre, 96
Jardine, Lisa, 141
Jeannerod, Marc, 96
Jenkins, Harold, 24, 39, 76, 85, 95, 126

Johnson, Mark
 embodiment, 8–9, 14–15, 125, 133–134, 152–153
 image schemas, 9, 26, 62
 metaphors 5, 10, 141, 162n.31, 162n.46
Jones, Ann Rosalind, 171n.21

Kalas, Rayna, 169n.16
Kastan, David Scott, 47, 82
Kelly, Phillippa, 169n.16
Kempe, Will, 105, 181n.7
Kerry, John, 33–35, 61–62
King James, 56, 174n.55
Kline, Kevin, 97, 101–104
knowing is seeing, *see* metaphors, to see is to know
Krauth-Gruber, Silvia, 134
Kuppers, Petra, 184n.31

Lacan, Jacques, 178n.34
Lakoff, George
 categories, 6–8
 conceptual metaphor theory, 8–11, 15, 62, 161n.19, 162n.31
 conceptualization of the self, 72, 80
 experiential realism, 2, 5, 8–9, 161n.22
 Idealized Cognitive Models, 6, 62, 126, 136
 image schemas, 8, 62, 162n.46, 176n.21
 mathematics, 161n.20
 political implications of CMT, 8, 30, 141
 see also categories; conceptual metaphor theory; Idealized Cognitive Models
Lanham, Richard A., 166n.18
LaPage, Robert, 157
Las Meninas, *see* Velázquez, Diego
Lee, John, 170n.18
Lehman, Courtney, 184n.40
Levao, Ronald, 45, 179n.57, 189n.21
Leverage, Paula, 194n.8

INDEX

Levitin, Daniel J., 194n.7
Lutterbie, John, 17, 164n.55

MacWhinney, Brian, 131
Maltin, Leonard, 109
mapping, *see* projection
Marcus, Sharon, 13
Martin, John Jeffries, 170n.18, 171n.19
material anchors, 192n.55
materialist linguistics, 156, 175n.2, 193n.3
Maus, Katherine Eisaman, 171n.19, 177n.27
Maxwell, Richard, 157
McConachie, Bruce, 17, 96–97, 106, 115–117, 124, 156, 164n.56, 191n.39
McNeill, David, 113–117
Melchior-Bonnet, Sabine, 49–50
mental spaces, 11,18, 31, 34, 57, 62–63, 65, 76, 91, 111–112
  see also conceptual blending theory; domains; input space
Merleau-Ponty, Maurice, 61, 113, 132
metaphors
  dead metaphors, 7
  GAINING STATUS IS RISING, 135
  gestures as, 113–114
  TO HEAR IS TO HEED, 129
  LIFE IS A JOURNEY, 8, 161n19
  mirror as, 45–47, 55–56
  science, 7, 147
  TO SEE IS TO KNOW, 10, 31, 62, 65–66, 75–76, 85, 123, 129–130
  synaesthesia, as, 25
  thought as, 3, 5, 8–9, 15, 118, 141
  TIME IS MONEY, 10
  TIME PASSING IS MOTION, 118–119, 187n.74
  see also conceptual metaphor theory; domains
metonymy, 60, 71, 76

Metsys, Quentin (*The Moneychanger and His Wife*), 51–52, 77
mimesis, 47, 82
mind, *see* embodied cognition; mind/body problem
mind/body problem, 69, 151–152, 175n.16
Minerva Britanna, *see* Peacham, Henry
miniatures, 178n.36
Mirrhor of Modestie, *see* Salter, Thomas
mirror
  agnosia (or "looking glass syndrome"), 128–129
  art, representations in, 50–52
  Bible, representations in, 182n.20
  blend of, 19–21, 44, 56–59, 65, 68, 76–77
  book titles, 46, 55, 182n.20, 182n.21
  concave, 46
  convex, 46, 49–52, 57–58, 77–78
  critical uses of, 45–46
  frames, 53–55
  history of, 48–57
  image, 70, 128, 169n.9
  images of vanity, 50, 98
  Lucrezia Borgia's, 53–54
  magnifying glass, 46, 169n.13
  object onstage, 94, 98, 101–102
  scenes, 45–46
  scrying, 173n.36
  symmetry as, 70, 98–101
  technology of, 49–50, 172n.27
  visual tool for seeing, 51–53, 69–71, 74–75, 104, 145–46
  see also anamorphosis; mirror neurons
A Mirror for Magistrates, 55, 78, 81–83
mirror neurons, 113, 135–136, 153, 157, 190n.38
The Moneychanger and His Wife (1514), *see* Metsys, Quentin

Montrose, Louis, 18, 86, 101–102, 159n.1
Morris, Steven Leigh, 140
Muñoz, José Esteban, 168n.7

Narcissus, 50, 182n.20
Nellhaus, Tobin, 115–116, 121
New York Shakespeare Festival Public Theater, 101
Newton, Isaac, 73–74
Niedenthal, Paula, 34
Núñez, Rafael, 117–119, 161n.20, 187n.74

Oakley, Todd, 31
objectivism, 2, 5–6
Orgel, Stephen, 45
Otis, Laura, 147

Parker-Starbuck, Jennifer, 139
Pascual, Esther, 32–33
Patel, Ani, 194n.7
Patterson, Annabelle, 165n.2
Peacham, Henry, (*Minerva Britanna*), 50–51, 182n.20
performance analysis, 89, 91–93, 97–112, 116, 119–122, 147–148
performativity, 67, 101–102, 142, 151
personification, 59, 60, 62–63, 80
perspective
  acting, 85–90, 106–107
  Elsinore, 84–85, 130–131
  gesture, 113–115, 186n.72
  language 131, 188n.4
  rhetoric, 28–30, 136–137, 179n.57
  visual, 53
phantom limbs, 189n.13
Phelan, Peggy, 52
Pinker, Steven, 48, 171n.20
Pollen, John Hungerford, 53
polysemy, 4, 66
Price, Hereward, 45–46
Princess Bride, The, 137
projection (or mapping)
  between spaces, 7–13, 34–35, 37, 46, 57, 82, 89, 91, 107, 109
  identity, 60, 72, 76, 89, 110, 128, 178
  see also blends; compression; conceptual blending theory; conceptual metaphor theory
props, 94–96

Queen Elizabeth, 178n.36
Quinn, Michael, 105, 183n.30
Quintilian, 28, 113–114, 167n.27

Rakotnitz, Naomi, 17, 124, 164n.57, 188n.4
Ramachandran, V. S., 24–25, 69, 127–129, 165n.5, 189n.12
Reynolds, Bryan, 17, 86, 143, 164n.57, 179n.57, 180n.64
Rhetoric, 28–30, 32, 36, 86, 88, 93, 136–37, 166n.18, 167n.27
Ric, Francois, 134
Richards, I. A., 3, 161n.31
Richardson, Alan, 163n.54, 194n.7
Richardson, Brenda, 173n.42, 173n.45
Rizzolatti, Giacomo, 113
Roach, Joseph, 105–107, 110, 112, 156, 174n.61, 179n.57, 184n.34
Rogers-Ramachandran, Diane, 127–128
Rosch, Eleanor, 5, 131–132, 135
Rosencrantz and Guildenstern are Dead, see Stoppard, Tom
Rowe, Katherine, 184n.40

Sacks, Oliver, 194n.7
Salter, Thomas, 74–75
Saltz, David, 117
Saussure, Ferdinand de, 48, 171n.20
Schechner, Richard, 141–142, 168n.7
Schneider, Rebecca, 168n.7

science
    importance of metaphors to, 7
    integration with the humanities,
        18, 155–158
    performance as, 141, 147
    performance of, 147–148
    see also Brown, Theodore;
        cognitive science; Crease,
        Robert; Hilgartner, Stephen;
        vision; *individual scientists*
secundum imaginationem, see Casey,
    Edward
Self-Portrait (1646), *see* Gumpp,
    Johannes
self/subjectivity
    early modern period, ideas of, 16,
        47, 66–68, 86, 169n.16,
        170n.18, 171n.19, 177n.27,
        178n.36
    face as, 60–62, 75–77
    intentional agent, as an, 40, 59,
        79, 153
    linguistic construction of, 72–73,
        80, 147
    theatrical creation of, 88–90,
        106, 138, 141
semiotics, 96, 105, 183n.30
Shakespeare, William
    Cymbeline, 72
    ghost of King Hamlet, 185n.49
    Henry V, 77, 161n.20, 167n.23
    Henry VI, part 1, 77
    Henry VI, part 2, 84
    Julius Caesar, 69, 73, 94–95
    King John, 93
    King Lear, 124, 143–144,
        145–146, 179n.56
    Macbeth, 15, 51–52, 174n.62
    Much Ado About Nothing,
        174n.62
    Othello, 95, 136–137, 188n.4
    Richard II, 69
    Richard III, 28–30, 86, 174n.62
    Twelfth Night, 174n.62
    Winter's Tale, The, 70
    see also *Hamlet*

Shapin, Steven, 145–146
Shepard, Sam, 92, 107–108,
    109–112, 119–122
Shuger, Debora, 47, 72
simulation
    see embodiment, simulation
Smith, Bruce, 16, 129–130, 194n.8
Sofer, Andrew, 95–96, 171n.21
Spiller, Elizabeth A., 144
Spolsky, Ellen, 15–16, 124, 188n.4,
    192n.57, 194n.7
Spurgeon, Caroline, 26–27
Stallybrass, Peter, 171n.21
Stamm, Rudolph, 45–46
Starks, Lisa S., 184n.40
States, Bert, 45, 105
Stern, Tiffany, 94–95, 105, 171n.21
Stevenson, Jill, 194n.8
Stewart, Jon, 36
Stoppard, Tom, 155–156, 158,
    177n.25
Stormare, Peter, 97–101
surface reading, 13–14
Sweetser, Eve, 11, 117–119, 129,
    135, 163n.48, 182n.14,
    187n.74
symptomatic reading, 13–14
synaesthesia, 24–26, 165n.5

Tallis, Raymond, 18–19
Terry, Randall, 36
textual authority, 23–24, 134, 148
    see also first quarto
"This American Life," 86–90
Thompson, Evan, 131–132, 135
Tobin, Vera, 179n.45
Tooby, John, 16
Tribble, Evelyn, 133–134
Turner, Henry, 124, 134
Turner, Mark
    conceptual blending theory,
        10–12, 18–19, 31, 33, 35, 56,
        78, 80, 82–83, 97, 104,
        167n.27, 192n.55
    conceptual metaphor theory,
        161n.19, 162n.31

image schema, 9, 162n.46
King John, analysis of, 93
literature and performance, 5, 15, 97, 104
personification, 59
see also blends, ghost of King Hamlet; Jesus died for our sins, *The Runaway Bunny*; conceptual blending theory
Turner, Victor, 142, 192n.54

Utterback, Neal, 186n.72

Van Eyck, Jan (*The Arnolfini Portrait*), 50–53
Van Petten, Cyma, 3
Varela, Francisco J., 131–132, 135
Velázquez, Diego (*Las Meninas*), 52
Vermeule, Blakey, 17
Victoria & Albert Museum, 53

vision
  blindspots, 75–76, 126–127, 189n.10
  intromission/extromission, 126
  inattentional blindness, 127
  visual intentionalism, 96
  visuomotor perception vs. representation, 96, 135–136
  see also Idealized Cognitive Model, seeing; perspective

Wanselius, Bengt, 98, 99
Weimann, Robert, 45, 86, 176n.20
West, William N., 172n.25
Wilson, Robert, 157
Wooster Group, The, 21, 123, 138–141, 157

Zunshine, Lisa, 124, 188n.4, 194n.7

GPSR Compliance
The European Union's (EU) General Product Safety Regulation (GPSR) is a set of rules that requires consumer products to be safe and our obligations to ensure this.

If you have any concerns about our products, you can contact us on

ProductSafety@springernature.com

In case Publisher is established outside the EU, the EU authorized representative is:

Springer Nature Customer Service Center GmbH
Europaplatz 3
69115 Heidelberg, Germany

www.ingramcontent.com/pod-product-compliance
Lightning Source LLC
LaVergne TN
LVHW011819060526
838200LV00053B/3836